The Limits of Global G

Are we creating an ungovernable world? Can we be confident that our existing modes of global governance are sufficient, or sufficiently adaptable, to meet the challenges of rapid and pervasive globalisation? Are there sound reasons for supposing that humanity's actions and creations will stay within the bounds of our processes of deliberation and regulation?

The Limits of Global Governance addresses these questions and provides a provocative examination of the cognitive, practical and political limits on our ability to exercise systems of regulation and control on the same scale as the globalising forces already shaping the human condition. Issues that are addressed include:

- an examination of the many meanings of 'global governance'
- a contextualised view of global governance within the complex interaction of human and natural systems
- an analysis of global governance at a fundamental and conceptual level
- a case study of disseminative systems and global governance

This book is essential reading for those with research interests in Global Politics, International Relations and Globalisation.

Jim Whitman is Director of the MA programme in the Department of Peace Studies at the University of Bradford, Co-editor of the *Journal of Humanitarian Assistance* and General Editor of the *Palgrave Global Issues* series.

The Limits of
Global Governance

Jim Whitman

Routledge
Taylor & Francis Group

LONDON AND NEW YORK

First published 2005
by Routledge
2 Park Square, Milton Park, Abingdon, Oxon OX14 4RN

Simultaneously published in the USA and Canada
by Routledge
270 Madison Ave, New York, NY 10016

Routledge is an imprint of the Taylor & Francis Group

© 2005 Jim Whitman

Typeset in Garamond by
Keystroke, Jacaranda Lodge, Wolverhampton
Printed and bound in Great Britain by
TJ International Ltd, Padstow, Cornwall

British Library Cataloguing in Publication Data
A catalogue record for this book is available from the British Library

Library of Congress Cataloging in Publication Data
Whitman, Jim.
    The limits of global governance / Jim Whitman.
        p. cm.
    Includes bibliographical references and index.
    1. Globalization–Political aspects.   2. International organization.
    I. Title.
    JZ1318.W485 2005
    327.1–dc22   2004026539

ISBN 0–415–33902–2 (hbk)
ISBN 0–415–33903–0 (pbk)

For my parents
Harry R. Whitman
&
Lillian D. Whitman

Contents

Preface

The purpose of this book is to review the many meanings of 'global governance' and to contextualise them within an understanding of the complex interaction of human and natural systems. Instead of engaging in sectoral analyses or contending with various schools of thought, this study concentrates on the limits of global governance, both conceptual and practical, when set against the full range of human activity and its consequences. The objective is to inform thinking at the most fundamental, conceptual level, about the prospects for global governance.

The argument does not set one global governance theory against another to see which has the most theoretical purchase or practical utility, but addresses a limitation they all have in common. This can be expressed quite simply: the global governance literature does not directly address the question of whether a globalised and globalising world can actually be governed. It is assumed – taken as a 'given'. This can be expressed negatively: Are we making an ungovernable world? The question is not the same as asking whether world government is a practicable possibility. After all, the starting point for nearly all global governance perspectives is a recognition that power, authority and the capacity to affect significant outcomes is no longer the exclusive preserve of states; and the global governance literature has already provided useful insights into the many ways in which state and non-state actors are variously configured to ensure at least the partial governance of specific areas, geographic or thematic.

But a compartmentalised world is only a useful abstraction: it does not accord with the nature and complexity of the most pressing public policy issues, social tensions and environmental stresses, particularly as globalising forces continue to shape the fundamentals of our environments and our relations. Working from an understanding of global governance that applies to human security and not only high-level oversight of selected fields, this book examines how much of the world – both human and natural – requires the establishment and exercise of regulatory and control systems. The kind of metaphor common to a good deal of the green literature – such as 'blueprint for a green planet' – has charm but little validity. There are no blueprints, no pauses and no 'guide for the perplexed'. Indeed, *comprehending* the staggering complexity and dynamism of our world is itself one of the conceptual challenges examined here.

Recently, some of the most forward-looking and creative work in both IR and IPE has been concerned with global governance in one form or another. However, my concern is not with international peace and security as such – vital though this is – but with something more fundamental and on which international peace and security ultimately depend. The focus is on the human capacity to exercise control, or at least to set and maintain parameters, for a just, equitable, stable and sustainable way of life. This entails not only what has come to be known as human security, but also environmental sustainability. The phrase that best describes the full range of human action and consequence is 'the human condition'. As used here, this is not a passive state, but a depiction of human circumstance and capacity – and that capacity includes not only the ability to conceive and exercise governance, but also the capacity to undertake action which eludes, frustrates or complicates governance.

The portrayal of the field of global governance studies as they have developed to date is necessarily condensed. My intention is to highlight and then to question the assumptions implicit to most of the work in the field, but without the suggestion that these works lack either theoretical grounding or analytical purchase. I hope this book will be regarded as complementary to existing governance studies and a small contribution to the larger enterprise of understanding the nature and extent of governance challenges now opening up before us.

In presenting the themes in this book to various seminar groups over a few years, I have often been met with the question, 'Well, then, who or what can/should be exercising global governance on this scale, or to this degree?' Anyone who conducts research into governance and global governance – or international politics more generally – can think of ways in which our various governments and our institutions, both public and private, could be made to work more efficiently and/or with an orientation that favours human betterment to a greater degree than at present. However, my interest in this work is not to examine political and organisational limits that are failures to reach optimum levels of performance. Instead, the limits under examination are larger and more fundamental – those that appear as unbridgeable gaps between what we are able to do and what we perceive is necessary or important to accomplish – hence the question, 'Are we making an ungovernable world?'. As expressed by the late Sir Geoffrey Vickers, whose splendid series of books have so clearly influenced the writing of this one, 'I hope not for greater efficiency in our problem-solving, but for better understanding of our problem-setting . . .'.

The limits under consideration are cognitive and practical as well as political. None are easy to quantify and their description in thematic terms (albeit with numerous examples) means that some room for progress or manoeuvrability might be possible in certain cases. Nevertheless, these limits already demarcate the reach of global governance on any of its better-known conceptions. And beyond the limits of what we can comprehensively and effectively regulate and control, a globalising humanity is feverishly at work transforming the human condition, for better and for worse; by accident and design.

Admittedly, it is not an easy thing to confront the possibility that we are in the midst of constructing a runaway world, but in the words of Thomas Hardy, 'If a path to the better there be, it begins with a full look at the worst.'

Acknowledgements

It is my good fortune to work in the Department of Peace Studies, Bradford University. I am very grateful to my colleagues and to my students, past and present, for creating and sustaining such a positive and supportive ethos. In particular, Malcolm Dando's fine scholarship and intellectual curiosity have always been an inspiration and I remain grateful for everything he has taught me.

In the company of scores of other people around the world, I am indebted to Michael M^{cc}Gwire for his guidance and support – and most of all, for his generosity of spirit. Helen Yanacopulos has taught me more than she would probably admit to and certainly more than she realises. Amanda Rees has still not despaired of widening my intellectual horizons, or of teaching me things I was once tasked to teach her. Chris Alden and David Pocock have made the work of creating and maintaining the *Journal of Humanitarian Assistance* a very enjoyable as well as rewarding experience – and an integral part of our friendship.

My partner Maureen Loveland imparts meaning and delight to everything we share.

I am grateful to the following publishers for copyright consent to reproduce material that appeared earlier in article form: Sage Publications for permission to reproduce a slightly altered form of 'Global governance as the friendly face of unaccountable power', *Security Dialogue*, Vol. 33, No. 1 (March 2002), pp. 45–57; Carfax Publishing, for permission to reproduce a large part of 'Global dynamics and the limits of global governance', *Global Society*, Vol. 17, No. 3 (July 2003), pp. 253–72; the Royal Institute of Inter-Faith Studies for consent to reproduce in Chapter 1 a portion of 'Global governance and the mitigation of complex risk,' *Bulletin of the Royal Institute for Inter-Faith Studies*, Vol. 6, No. 1 (Spring/Summer 2004), pp. 11–27; Chapter 7 was originally published as 'Disseminative Systems and Global Governance', in *Global Governance: A Review of Multilateralism and International Organizations*, Vol. 11, No. 1 (Jan–March 2005), copyright © by Lynne Reinner Publishers. Used with permission.

Abbreviations

AIDS	acquired immune deficiency syndrome
BSE	bovine spongiform encephalopathy
CDC	Centers for Disease Control
CFC	chlorofluorocarbon
DDT	dichlorodiphenyltrichloroethane
DNA	deoxyribonucleic acid
DVD	digital versatile disk
EU	European Union
G7	Group of seven
GATT	General Agreement on Tariffs and Trade
GM	genetic modification/genetically modified
GMO	genetically modified organism
HIV	human immunodeficiency virus
IMF	International Monetary Fund
INGO	international non-governmental organisation
IPE	International Political Economy
IR	International Relations
IT	information technology
LTCM	Long-Term Capital Management
MBM	meat and bone meal
NAFTA	North American Free Trade Agreement
NASA	National Aeronautics and Space Administration
NGO	non-governmental organisation
NRA	National Rifle Association
OECD	Organization for Economic Co-operation and Development
PBDE	polychlorinated diphenyl ethers
PCB	polychlorinated biphenyl
SARS	severe acute respiratory syndrome
SIV	simian immunodeficiency virus
TRIPS	trade-related aspects of intellectual property rights
UN	United Nations
UNEP	United Nations Environment Programme
vJCD	variant Creutzfeldt-Jakob Disease
WTO	World Trade Organization

1 The human condition

All societies, whatever their level of development or degree of integration into national and international political and economic systems, have broadly similar requirements for their stable continuance. All must establish and maintain cultural relations which regulate impulses to individual freedom against the need for social order; all must adjust their cultural relations to the constraints and rhythms of the physical environment; and all must have systems of adaptation to changing circumstances – not so much in order to achieve goals as to avoid threats. The challenge, in other words, is to maintain stability through time and to try, as far as possible, to mediate change in accordance with prevailing values and established modes of social intercourse.

According to Geoffrey Vickers, 'This means that there are limits to the possible rate at which human history can change without disintegration, since coherent change involves change in the whole set of cultural standards by which a society interprets its situation; and these standards are related to the life experience and hence the life span of individuals.' This might at first seem overstated, or perhaps only applicable to those unfortunate human groups once subjected to the fastest and most brutal forms of colonialism, or more recently, rapid and ill-advised 'development'[1] which sacrifices the viability of human communities for an expansion of national gross domestic product.

Yet it is becoming increasingly difficult for all of us, including the relatively powerful and privileged, to conceive and maintain a world view which is coherent, inclusive and sufficiently robust to make sense of and to deal with the many issues and pressures which now impinge on our lives with ever greater frequency. Even at the everyday level, for individuals as well for social groups, there are more variables and fewer certainties; greater turbulence; remote lines of causation impacting on important aspects of our lives; and a vast increase in information which often seems further to complicate rather than clarify our milieu and our choices. Although the particulars vary considerably from case to case, we all feel this to some degree, whether we are charged with public service, managing a business or simply ordering priorities and tracking trajectories so that we can make a way in the world for ourselves and our families. The wider view – that is, the conditions under which most human beings live – adds considerably to our discomfort. One can witness in anti-globalisation and anti-free trade protests and in the rise of various fundamentalisms[2] the angry, leading edge of a deeper disquiet, not only that the world we have made for ourselves is not entirely tractable in its engineered complexity, but also that it is morally odious in some of its outcomes and implications.

Disconcertingly, the steady accretion of knowledge does not often seem to be advancing the cause of comprehension, confident prediction and rational control. If there is a 'frontier of knowledge' as that term was once understood, it is surely the great advances being made in the field of genetics. But everything we learn, every advancement of this knowledge comes with a host of problems: ethical dilemmas; legal questions of an unprecedented character; issues of ownership, control, and responsibility; and possibly, levels of risk which fall outside not only established controlling or prohibitive mechanisms, but also outside our ability to make definitive scientific inferences. Clearly, our science and technology are part of the human predicament, not free-standing techniques and tools, available to 'solve' our human problems. This can be seen in the controversy over whether the possible benefits of genetically modified crops outweigh the possible dangers.[3] For all that such cases entail scientific novelty, their form is familiar:

> Human life is a tissue of relationships with the physical world and with other people. The object of policy at every level is to preserve and increase the relations we value and to exclude or reduce the relations we hate. But these 'goods' cannot be simply accumulated, like packets on a supermarket's shelves. They are systematically related; some require each other; nearly all compete with each other for limited resources, especially time and attention which are, of all resources, the least expansible. We may want more abundance with more leisure, more freedom with more order, more interaction with less interference, and so on; but we know that if we pursue each independently of the others, we shall attain none of them. In trying to make life 'good', we are seeking not to accumulate 'goods' but to impose on the flux of affairs a form which will yield what seems the most acceptable combination of goods within our reach. Thus the good life we aspire to, at every level, is a work of art and like every work of art is achieved by selecting and therefore also by rejecting what is incompatible with the chosen form.[4]

However, the art of judgement so described is all the more difficult for the worst kinds of change – rapid, pervasive and largely outside the deliberative capacities of the societies affected. As globalisation quickens and spreads, it is small wonder that troubling developments and social ructions have become the stuff of daily news practically everywhere: the transference of established industries and secure employment to low-wage economies; the migration of peoples; the explosion in the number and density of megacities; pollution and environmental degradation with planetary implications – to list but a few.

The apparent divergence between information, knowledge and practical capacity on the one hand and comprehension, order and coherence on the other is further exacerbated because of the scale and intensity of human activity both distant and close to home. What now counts as the 'operating environment' for many of our responsibilities and activities has vastly expanded, without a corresponding increase in our ability to exercise control over it – and in some cases, even adequately to comprehend it.

One telling measure of the strain on the adaptive capacity of our cultural systems in the face of wide-ranging and rapid change is our understanding of and response to morally challenging developments at individual, organisational and societal levels. However difficult the number and kind of moral issues now confronting us, so long as they pose challenges *within* our established modes of moral deliberation and action rather than challenges *to* those systems, we have some hope of mediating morally significant change – much of it globally-driven, but often felt at the level of individual conscience. But what if the world we have made has brought us not only hard cases and a proliferation of global issues, but also an altered human condition; a world of expanding and deepening moral urgency which entails difficult problems of locating, assigning or fulfilling moral responsibility? It is becoming clear that some of the largest and most morally consequential determinants of human well-being for the coming decades are being shaped by default; and that the moral responsibilities of our institutions are likely to be at full stretch even in reactive mode.

A largely unremarked consequence of globalisation is the way in which it has extended the compass of morally significant action and omission – at least for those in the developed world.[5] Much of what once might have been mundane is now morally charged, so that it is difficult to ponder the question, 'How to live a good life?' while maintaining an awareness of the amount of suffering in the world to which we either contribute, or about which we do nothing, despite our means. How can we retain the coherence of an ostensibly blameless life against the pull of moral claims constantly made on us, directly and indirectly?

> Information technology . . . helps expose the emptiness of much that has passed for sound ethics. For instance, a bench test that most ethical theories pass with flying colours is the problem: what should you do if you are walking along, minding your own business, and you hear a cry for help from a drowning man? But almost no one faces predicaments with that logical form anymore; instead, we hear, every day, while desperately trying to mind our own business, a thousand cries for help, complete with volumes of information on how we might oblige. On this ubiquitous problem, traditional ethical systems are essentially reduced to silence or the most transparent handwaving.[6]

The many moral claims on us extend beyond emergency relief for humanitarian disasters to considerations of the conditions under which much of our food is produced and our clothing manufactured. Indeed, If we accept that climate change is morally as well as practically consequential, and if we know that the aggregate effect of car driving substantially contributes to it, does the relative *practical* insignificance of one's act also diminish its moral weight to vanishing point? Moral scrupulousness commensurate with our knowledge of the facts of human suffering and the state of the world hardly seems compatible with the way of life we in the developed world routinely enjoy.

Although moral significance now seems to have become a near-ambient accompaniment to our everyday conduct, we are not paralysed, either individually or collectively. The focus here, though, is not on the kinds of psychological blocking, compromises or contradictions that might well be necessary for individuals,[7] but on our still more difficult efforts to establish and/or maintain standards of ethical conduct and limits of moral acceptability in public arenas. These collective efforts are also becoming considerably more stressed as the nature and pace of social, political, economic, scientific and technological changes accelerate and combine. The felt necessity to incorporate broadly agreed moral standards into matters of public policy remains a striking feature of our appreciation of the requirements of a humane and sustainable social order;[8] however, the ways in which broadly shared moral values have shaped or conditioned the larger contours of public life in the past do not appear to be capable of dealing with the morally consequential possibilities of our globalised and globalising world. For example, consider the following – an overview of possible military applications of biotechnology – produced by the strategic assessment centre of a *Fortune 500* company:

> Perhaps the most troubling aspect of genetic technology, and at the same time arguably the one with the most powerful potential, has to do with altering the genetic code in order to 'engineer' human beings to specific, desired 'design specifications.' Through a combination of selective breeding, gene therapy, and genetic screening, it will be possible if we so choose to 'design' individuals with certain characteristics, such as greatly enhanced strength, enhanced hearing or sight, or even, taking the idea to an extreme, capabilities not normally present in human beings (i.e., individuals with gills who can serve as 'superSEALs,' or individuals who can nourish themselves photosynthetically and thus require a considerably reduced logistical tail). Recent and ongoing genetic research and experimentation has made strides toward identifying the genes that control complex mental and emotional function. As this work proceeds, it becomes conceivable that we could, for example, 'breed out' fear and other characteristics that may impede battlefield capability in the soldier. Alternatively, we could 'breed in' an unprecedented capability to process and understand the enormous amounts of data and information with which the soldier on the digitized battlefield will be faced – a sort of 'super auto pilot' function for battle command. The possibilities are as endless as they are discomforting.[9]

The 'endless' and morally consequential possibilities of biotechnology applications also include the release of genetically modified organisms into the environment, human cloning[10] and the patenting of genetic information ranging from human brain genes to basmati rice.[11] Nor is the biotechnology sector unique for the number and kinds of moral and practical challenges it presents.

Can our character as moral beings and the kinds of private and public moral deliberations we conduct ensure that we are able to control the applications and outcomes of our creations (including globalisation)? Even if we do not consider the very existence of biological and toxic weapons a moral failure, the recent collapse of the negotiations for a new Biological and Toxic Weapons Convention protocol[12] – organised along political and prudential lines as much as moral ones – hardly bodes well for our ability to cope with the number, variety and seriousness of the moral challenges we can already see taking shape.

In our present circumstances, it is no wonder that we now so routinely seek to assign duties to institutions. Some hope might be invested in the thought that moral considerations in the public sphere are often closely enmeshed with and sometimes difficult to separate from a range of more practical and legal issues – something that can be seen in the rapidly changing and increasingly allied fields of biotechnology, medicine and health care. Yet it is of note that explicitly moral and ethical matters are usually entrusted to the consideration of ethical committees and expert panels, while in the assignment of duty, the morally consequential aspects of issues are often the poor relation in any configuration of interests that also contains considerable political, legal and economic stakes.[13] In such cases,

> [P]hilosophers may find themselves involved in an exercise that is essentially technocratic. The complicated business of research, development, and application in modern life includes a moment when 'value issues' need to be studied and where the contributions of knowledgeable, degree-carrying experts can be enlisted. In the United States, for example, The National Science Foundation has for many years included a program on 'ethical and value studies' that supports university scholars who do research of this kind. The underlying assumption seems to be that this is an important area that the nation needs to cultivate. The sponsors may hope that officially designated 'values experts' will eventually be able to provide 'solutions' to the kinds of 'problems' whose features are ethical rather than solely technical. This can serve as the final tune-up for working technological models about to be rolled out of the showroom door. 'Everything else looks good. What are the results from the ethics lab?'[14]

In addition, the nature of already established institutions will broadly determine the moral content of newly assigned duties since, for example, the United Nations is not a humanitarian or developmental institution, but a political one.[15] While it can be galling to have moral issues treated as though they were epiphenomenal, the accountability, moral or otherwise, of what are sometimes rather tellingly called 'artificial persons' is often disappointing and frustrating.[16] In any event, the assignment of explicit moral responsibilities to institutions would not confer moral agency upon them; and even a positive answer to the question of whether institutions *can* have moral agency[17] does not, of itself, tell us anything of the practical prospects for making globalised configurations of public and private interests subject to moral review.

The original compass of a question posed by Thomas Aquinas now seems to have considerably wider practical and moral purchase than he intended: 'Whether all things that the human person wills, he wills on account of the final end?'[18] There is no shortage of morally reprehensible conditions which we produce by default or which we create and sustain through a confected ignorance or studied disregard. But even though aggregate human impacts upon the natural world and human well-being essentially comprise countless willed acts, establishing a direct causal link between individual agency and morally or politically significant outcomes in the global arena is problematic. Certain global dynamics obscure the distinction between remote and proximate causation; and there is difficulty in locating causative agency in situations where individual actions are highly dispersed or might be spread over years or decades.[19] And aspects of globalisation can act as 'force multipliers' on the significance of an act. Increasingly, for both individuals and institutions, the presence of all of the fundamental requirements for *any* genuine moral agency – autonomy, cognisance and predictable lines of causation within the sphere of action – are becoming difficult at best, as the globalisation of social relations continues apace. As these relations grow in number, complexity and intensity, we are likely to note growing dissonance between our professed values, our stated intentions and our willed actions. This is already an important, underlying element of various anti-globalisation movements, carried in charges of hypocrisy and double standards against governments and corporations.

The strained quality of moral deliberation and ethical conduct has its counterpart in many other aspects of contemporary life. When we act, we act upon as well as within our physical and human environments. Social and political life has never been different, but a more intricately connected human world (and a seriously debilitated physical surround) gives those actions new weight and meaning. In other words, the significance of individual actions and those of the communities to which we belong, whether they are political, social or commercial, extend well beyond our immediate milieu. This point is implicit in the pleas made to us to conserve energy; to shop, eat, invest and travel ethically; it is also obvious in global environmental pollution, to which the cumulative effects of privileged lives contribute disproportionately. An observation that has become a mainstay in studies of globalisation is that space is 'shrinking' and that a great deal of human interchange has become 'deterritorialised'. It might well prove that the proclaimed death of geography[20] is as premature as the 'end of history'; in any event, what needs to be stressed here is the relational rather than spatial character of our changing operating environment, because as the barriers between individuals and between communities continue to weaken, then relations (including, but not limited to, relations of moral obligation) multiply – many of them highly problematic, in line with aspects of our inequitable and unsustainable ways of life.

Of course, long before our world was routinely characterised as 'global', the sphere of significant action and consequence for many forms of human endeavour extended considerably beyond what could be apprehended locally and immediately.[21] Much as we might admire the directness of ancient Athenian democracy, we have had to develop alternatives to direct decision-making for polities in which citizens number in tens of millions. In the same vein, societies *have* adapted to sweeping changes in the past – with difficulty, but without dissolution. The Industrial Revolution in the UK is an obvious example. However, when the historical and geographical circumstances of the Industrial Revolution are taken into account, as well as modes of social accommodation worked out over generations, the breathtaking pace of the industrialisation of present-day China is clearly of a completely different order, as are its implications for other nations and peoples and for the global environment.[22]

As human numbers increase, as human activity expands and we transform our environments, the felt loss of familiar worlds – bounded, closely observed and subject largely to incremental change – is a common cry. 'The world is too much with us', lamented Wordsworth nearly 200 years ago. Doubtless, he would regard the contemporary world's easy availability of trans-continental flights as a 'sordid boon' – but boon it is, at least for some people and for some purposes. Not everyone is subject to the same degree of alienation, disen-franchisement and bewilderment by borders and boundaries made ever more porous, or as we become subject to decisions and events at a considerable remove from the world we thought we knew. The 'good life' is certainly not good for everyone – even for the majority; but on whichever side of numer-ous national or global divides we find ourselves, the divides themselves are becoming more visible, more charged with meaning and more difficult to reconcile in an equitable way. And there is no 'opt-out' for the privileged – not only because the prosperous and secure have the most to gain by maintaining the status quo (however difficult this might prove),[23] but also because the viability of the planetary environment is now directly subject to human choice – and default.

Regulating relationships and achieving goals

In our efforts to organise our individual and collective affairs, it soon becomes clear that the maintenance of satisfactory relationships is prior to, and very often, a necessary condition for the achievement of goals. This is the meaning behind the historically unprecedented attempt to regulate human relationships through the articulation and advancement of human rights. The idea and ideal of human rights can be expressed in terms of one or more goals – such as freedom, equality and justice, but the human rights enterprise requires us to find ways of making power accountable to law. In other words, human rights are essentially concerned with mediating the relationship between individuals and the holders of power. But power is not confined to states and its abuse not limited to tyrants. From the perspective of regulating relationships, the human rights regime as it applies to negative human rights ('freedom from') now shares the field with an expanding arena of human rights claims, paralleling the diffusion of power to a variety of non-state actors. Thus we now have human rights claims made in respect of environmental protection; natural resource development; biotechnology and many other areas of human endeavour. At the same time, controversies surrounding what distinguishes a human right from a political entitlement continue unabated, as do efforts to implement 'second generation' or positive human rights.[24] In addition, the practical compass of universal human rights has many blind spots:

> [T]he liberal construction of rights is repeatedly put forward as the definitive word on complex values such as freedom, justice and equality. There is little acknowledgement that this model of human rights, which claims so much, can produce systemic myopia as well as its own forms of abuse, or that the actual history of rights practices has been experienced in sharply different ways by people who at any given time were included or occluded by its terms. Stepping back from these architectures of rights, without negating them in blanket fashion, can allow us to weigh our purposes and our methods in pursuing rights enhancement.[25]

These deficiencies require acknowledgement and redress, but doing so will entail enlarging or at least reconfiguring the arenas within which we specify and pursue human rights. So it is that with every extension of human activity and its consequences comes a re-combination of human relationships, entailing new stresses, differences and claims – practical, political and moral – for which human rights controversies are perhaps the most sensitive barometer.

The goal of environmental sustainability is also essentially relational. After all, although world biodiversity loss can be characterised as a single issue, it is an outcome of remarkably numerous, diffuse and complex interactions between human communities and the natural world. The decrease in the world's aggregate biodiversity is not a problem that can be directly solved; instead, nets of relations must be understood and reconciled, by which we have some hope of framing less deleterious ways of life. So although many international negotiations are convened to address environmental problems, they are not essentially goal-seeking; rather, they are attempts to comprehend and to re-balance relations, within and between human and environmental realms. This is true of such diverse matters as fisheries quotas, negotiated carbon emission levels and the regulation of trade in endangered species.

Of course, power and interests are fully operational even in matters extensive and shared, such as the quality of the global commons – and all the more where disparities of wealth, power and potential benefit feature, as in the negotiation of intellectual property rights to date.[26] And in any field of human activity, with every increase in the number of interested parties, active players, affected communities and altered environments, the regulation of relations becomes more important, but also more difficult. Matters are further complicated by the globalisation of social relations, in three ways.

The first is the ease and speed with which advances in travel, communications, economic development and technological advance can generate problems both within and between communities. The spread of the SARS virus by means of the world's transport infrastructure is a case in point;[27] and the electronic communication of politically contentious or culturally offensive material is another.

The second is that costs and benefits, claims and grievances cut across socio-spatial boundaries and political communities, hugely complicating consensual, equitable settlements. International politics do not take place in a realm that is removed from the pressures, sensitivities, expectations and fears that comprise national and local politics. And not all domestic political dynamics are compatible with matters of environmental quality or sustainability. (And nor, plainly, do they routinely prioritise the human security of distant strangers.) Think of the way in which culture and ways of life, employment, access to food and water, the demands of a rapidly growing population or of rapidly expanding industry and many other fundamentals of life at local and national level can drive environmental degradation – or be affected by international environmental agreements. These and a host of other matters are an essential context for understanding why the politics of the environment at every level are so difficult.

Third, social and environmental impacts and considerations can be driven by the needs and interests of communities at a considerable remove from the communities and areas affected. This is plain enough in many instances of natural resource extraction, but the following example illustrates an environmental crisis which is in fact a manifestation of many other dynamics – environmental and socio-political; local and distant.

According to a report published by the Centre for International Forestry Research,[28] international demand for Brazilian beef is hastening Brazilian deforestation at an alarming rate – some 25,000 square kilometres in 2003 alone. In addition to the rapid globalisation of the beef industry, low land prices in the Amazon basin and the apparent inability of the Brazilian government to prevent illegal land clearance and ranching, 'the Brazilian cattle industry has also benefited from a recent devaluation of the Brazilian currency, a decrease in the nation's incidence of Foot-and-Mouth disease, and, possibly, fears of avian flu [in Asia], which may have led the public to choose beef over chicken'. The extent of the deforestation – the worst in any two-year period – was only revealed by satellite data.

The belated manifestation of the 'problem' – deforestation – is an unanticipated outcome of numerous other human dynamics (exploiting local economic opportunity; the globalisation of markets; currency devaluation, itself an outcome of other domestic and international forces; and East Asian consumer choice) and environmental factors, notably Foot-and-Mouth disease and avian flu. This tangle of relationships is a compelling example of the extent to which many elements of the maintenance of social stability and the mediation of change at local, regional and national levels have acquired a global aspect, but of which the affected communities often lack a clear understanding of the range and power of the dynamics involved, or do not possess concomitant political leverage over them.

External pressures and competing claims

Implicit in the notion of social adaptation are the existence of socio-political boundaries; social cohesion; capacity or resilience commensurate with the challenges being faced; sufficient time in which to deliberate and act; the ability to determine causal dynamics; and a goal or adapted state which is deemed acceptable by the majority and which is sustainable. These requisites are easily identified in small social groups outside of the main currents of development and globalisation, but such groups are increasingly uncommon and generally thought of as 'isolated'. It is all too easy for those accustomed to urban life to underestimate the adaptive strains involved for all people in the disappearance of village life throughout the world, particularly in view of the speed of this change. On the largest scale, consider that on Arnold Toynbee's estimate, some three quarters of humanity were still living as peasants as late as 1946.[29] And the rate at which minority languages throughout the world are disappearing under a variety of pressures[30] is a telling index of the extent to which many societies succumb to powerful demands and influences of a kind that are outside of lived experience and for which the ability to mediate them is absent – or impossible.

But within large, complex, highly urbanised polities, adaptation to change is no less difficult. The spatial and socio-political boundaries which give polities their shape and coherence have become semi-permeable in both directions: they allow the passage of sometimes powerful elements 'in' (ranging from pollutants generated in neighbouring states to cultural influences conveyed electronically) and they are insufficient to prevent the individuals and interest groups from looking and acting 'outside' for the satisfaction of their needs and interests. Entire classes of individuals can absent themselves from the local concerns of the area of which they are nominally a part, or act collectively on a calculation of private interests which run contrary to a broader conception of the public good. This is the meaning of what J. K. Galbraith termed 'the culture of contentment'; and of tax revolts.[31] To this should be added those who are variously excluded – minorities marginalised economically and/or politically, or otherwise disenfranchised or disengaged.

Transboundary dynamics of all kinds affect the perceptions, aspirations, identities, interests and preferences of men and women to the degree that the meaning of 'citizen' must now take its place within ever-changing configurations of identity and allegiance.[32] Although states have never been coextensive with societies, the ability of the former to satisfy growing and diversifying social needs and aspirations appears to be weakening in the face of the globalisation of social relations; and relative to the empowerment of individuals and groups. At the same time, as the most important areas of human activity and human relating continue to globalise, the interdependence of all peoples and societies is increasing. And every increase in interdependence requires an increase in regulation and control. We can witness this not only in international efforts to address threats to planetary ecology, but also in the tremendous growth in global business regulation.[33] But the adaptive strains that arise from globalisation, visited on political systems and experienced down to the individual level, should not be underestimated, not least because they will not decrease in number or diminish in strength.

> In a multiply interdependent world each of us is bound to be in fact dependent on more systems than we can include in the pattern of our commitments, that is our loyalties, the claims which we allow not merely as matters of fact, but as matters of self-expectation. [. . .] The traditional pattern for human social living is one in which the members of a society share both a culture and a territory and are dependent on wider or overlapping systems only to the extent that can be satisfied by accepting them as facts, without becoming involved in acute conflicts of loyalties.[34]

The fragmentation of social coherence is not a passive fact, but diminishes the adaptive capacity of societies in two mutually reinforcing ways: it weakens their ability to mount concerted responses to changing circumstances; and it makes them more open to challenge and claims from within. The second and larger difficulty is that an increase in the orientation of individuals and groups towards disembedded loyalties, special interests and private concerns is diminishing the adaptive capacity of their societies, even as it becomes more important.

Returning to the requisites for the adaptive capacity of societies, the complexity and speed of recent and continuing technological, economic, environmental and social change place considerable strain on our deliberative and ordering capacities. This is clear in the range of vexed questions that attend the revolution in the biological sciences and the technological innovations it has fuelled. We cannot simply 'accommodate' matters as diverse and challenging as the possibility of human cloning, the uses and abuses of genetic information, the implications of biomedicine, gene patenting and various kinds of genetic commerce.[35] (Already, the human rights claims over the ownership and use of human body parts has been joined by property rights claims.[36]) Yet there is little evidence that we will curtail scientific advance in these fields on a precautionary basis – and national restrictions are in many cases either inadequate[37] or perceived as competitively disadvantageous.

To varying degrees, individuals and societies are subject to the willed actions of distant others, both directly and indirectly. This does not necessarily imply passivity, but the consequences of interdependence are not always or easily within the sphere of competence of those affected. Purposeful action of every kind is now informed by, and in turn informs, the inter-relatedness of all individuals and societies. Although humanity is not a single actor, the inter-relatedness of all individuals and societies means that various combinations of activity have made of the human condition a human arena of practical dimensions. With that, the external pressures on, and competing claims within societies become more intertwined and more difficult to separate and prioritise, even as they become more acute.

> The environment of each society and of each individual in each society is becoming increasingly a human environment, created by other societies and other individuals. The interdependence of all of them mounts but the means of regulating their mutual relations, even including markets for commodities, products, currencies, skills, and 'labour' is breaking down. Even the relations between the human species and its habitat are becoming problematic, not through failure of technological inventiveness but through the failing responses of the patient earth.[38]

In short, the nature and rate of change that societies now face is unprecedented in human experience and it is by no means clear that our cultural and political systems, developed and modified to respond to very different ways of life, are themselves sufficiently adapted to maintaining the order and stability of the world we are busy creating for ourselves.

Human striving and the human condition

Nevertheless, it is possible to overstate the human predicament – and some of the sociological 'risk society' literature does just that. The premier theorist of risk society is Ulrich Beck, who defines it as follows: 'The concept [risk society] describes a phase of development of modern society in which the social, ecological and individual risks created by the momentum of innovation increasingly elude the control and protective institutions of industrial society.'[39] This point is now well-documented and is arguably the most important contribution of the literature to our understanding of the consequences of modernity. However, it is also argued that the scale of the unforeseen and unwilled risks generated by our industrialising processes undermine the very foundations of our cherished notions of progress, including our capacity for meaningful choice and the exercise of control. Beck continues: 'Risk society is *not an option* which could be chosen or rejected in the course of political debate. It arises through the automatic operation of autonomous modernisation processes which are blind and deaf to consequences and dangers. In total – and latently – these call into question and indeed abolish – the basis of industrial society.'[40] The conclusive sweep, bold assertiveness and thought-provoking implications in much of Beck's primary writing on this theme (and much that has followed in its wake) is impressive, but deserves close scrutiny for what it overlooks and conflates.

First, it greatly simplifies the nature and variety of risk (actual and perceived), by condensing and then elevating it as a – indeed, *the* – critical issue for social theory. In fact, though, individual, social and institutional responses to risk and its components are more extensive and nuanced than much of the risk society literature allows for. Indeed, outside the sociological literature, there is an extensive literature on risk measurement and risk management.[41] Matters as wide-ranging as the expansion of Tort Law from the start of the Industrial Revolution to the present;[42] the difficulty of making scientific inferences;[43] and the growth of 'decentred' regulation[44] indicate that grappling with risk has long featured as an important element in the social and political organisation of developed countries and continues to do so. In addition, risk society analyses also greatly reduce and simplify lived experience. Subsuming other characteristics of our time under a single, compelling theme (globalisation, post-modernity, 'the end of history' and neo-liberal hegemony all come to mind) holds a certain attraction, but they have little validity as all-encompassing depictions of the human condition. In the same way that the costs and benefits of globalisation are not homogeneous, neither is the perception of, or responses to 'world risk society'.[45] Human existence has always been subject to 'indeterminancy' – and even today, for the majority of people its quality is survivalist, not intellectual.

Second, much of the best-known risk society literature mistakes momentum for inevitability. What Ulrich Beck terms 'the inexorability and uncontrollability of industrialism'[46] gives the manufacture and distribution of risk a curiously agentless quality, similar to the stronger characterisations of 'unstoppable' globalisation. As a result, difficult problems are presented as ineluctable fate, thereby foreclosing the possibility of political engagement and reducing us to angst, cynicism or weary resignation:

> Cynicism about progress allows one to live comfortably once again. It lays down the burden of defending a now unstoppable naïve industrialism, or of taking up arms against it. One can recline at one's ease, or dance on the rim of the volcano. . . . On the other side, there are those who see enlightenment converted into its opposite, as a train heading in the wrong direction, driverless; they can neither get off, nor pull the emergency brake, nor make the train run backwards.[47]

The assertion that, for the majority 'the industrial dynamic . . . paralyses action and relieves one of the duty to act'[48] is remarkably corrosive; a point which leads to a kind of self-satisfied, jocular fatalism:

In these overpowering analyses one can read for oneself how the authors are spellbound by the automatic process they describe. Sometimes a helpful little chapter is tacked on at the end, which bears the same relationship to the general hopelessness as a sigh to the end of the world, and then the writer makes his exit and leaves the shattered readers behind in the vale of tears he has portrayed. (I can permit myself to banter like this, since I have already demonstrated my talent as an up and coming prophet of doom.)[49]

Clearly, there is little future or even room for academic manoeuvre in mesmeric doom. More recent work in this field evinces research agendas and a more outward-looking engagement with the question of whether 'social theory [can] play a meaningful public and political role'.[50] At the same time, though, individuals, communities and institutions must make their way through complexity, vulnerability and risk in ways which include but extend well beyond the techno-hazards and 'big science' which are the mainstays of risk society theorising – including the threat of terrorism in the aftermath of 9/11. It is one thing to seek to demonstrate that 'the return to the theoretical and political philosophy of industrial modernity in the age of global risk is doomed to failure';[51] but quite another then to return to the question, 'How might we live?' particularly when diagnosis is also so frequently presented as prognosis. Whatever the nature and degree of risk perception, individual and shared, few of us have the luxury of ignoring the imaginative and practical challenges of building viable social futures.[52] The depiction of modernity's daunting structural outcomes is the strength of risk society analyses; however, these insights might best be regarded as a *challenge* to purposeful action, not its refutation.

Contemplating the human condition, we can emphasise biological considerations (at the most fundamental, felt level, the blunt fact of human mortality), or we can stress the weight and meaning of human beings as social and political animals.[53] But a globalised and globalising range of interdependencies, both human and environmental, mean that the human condition is becoming ever more a matter of our own making. The reality of climate change demonstrates this, but there is a still larger point to be grasped: that outcomes of that magnitude, both undesirable and unwilled, can arise from the undirected activity of humanity, which is poorly understood in its aggregate, cumulative and systematic effects.

There are also the brute facts that some 800 million human beings remain malnourished; and that some 10 million children in the developing world die each year, many from preventable illnesses. These and the other scourges of gross inequality[54] are no less a part of the twenty-first century human condition than the direct benefits of globalisation enjoyed by comparatively few. So the globalisation of social relations has not made a 'global society', except in the most generic sense[55] because of the essentially passive or disempowered position of the poorest peoples and states; and also because increased human interaction and interdependence are every bit as likely to generate turbulence and tension as to deliver the kinds of coherence implicit in the term 'society'. All societies are confronted, as they have always been, with the problems of establishing and maintaining stability for themselves, but now they must do so in conditions of unprecedented scope and dynamism. The particular concerns of individual societies vary greatly, but the number and gravity of issues they face are increasingly linked to the condition and disposition of other societies. So for a global society – or more precisely, for societies bound to one another by nets of globalised relations – we must increasingly think of these stabilisation efforts as having global variables – and global implications. The familiar business of societal and institutional governance opens out on to the larger world: the world of global dynamics and global politics. Whether it also opens out on to global governance is a question as daunting as it is important. It is also a conceptual challenge of a high order.

2 The development of the 'governance' concept

Governance and government

When former Prime Minister of the UK Harold Wilson retired from office in 1976, he wrote a book entitled *The Governance of Britain*, the aim of which was to describe 'how the British system of parliamentary and cabinet government works'. Wilson stated flatly that the book 'is not concerned with theories'.[1] Now, little more than a generation later, the complexities of governance cannot be confined to the machinery of government; and certainly no one would think of giving such a study that title.

The business of government is governance – the exercise of steering and control mechanisms for the purpose of maintaining the stability and order of the society in which it operates. The qualities of the social order, the means adopted and how these matters are determined and made accountable make representational and procedural matters important because of the considerable degree of power necessary to ensure the successful governance of modern states. Certainly, it extends well beyond a monopoly over the means of violence, to include the maintenance of relations which exceed individual and small-group comprehension and power – whether this means the functioning of internal systems (national health, transport infrastructure, defence) or the society's interface with other societies in the larger world.

It has always been the case that there is a good deal more to the maintenance of social relations than matters that fall within the remit of governments. But the study of governance has become important and compelling as questions of public policy grow in complexity; as the number and power of actors and interested parties within states – including unsanctioned or non-authoritative agents – increase; as states find themselves pinched between increasing public expectation and constrained or shrinking resources; and as various kinds of transnational relations proliferate, unmediated by government authority. The definitions of governance (below) are representative of the general consensus on the applicability of the term.

- Governance is a social function centered on the making of collective choices regarding matters of common concern to the members of human groups.[2]

- Governance . . . encompasses the activities of governments, but it also includes the many other channels through which 'commands' flow in the form of goals framed, directives issued, and policies pursued.[3]
- 'governance' [comprises] patterns that emerge from governing activities of social, political and administrative actors . . . [Thus], modes of social-political governance are always an outcome of public and private deliberation.[4]

A variation on these definitions is Jan Kooiman's use of the term 'governing' to include the activities of both governments and non-governmental actors; and 'governance' as a comprehensive, albeit theoretical term:

> *Governing* can be considered as the totality of interactions, in which public as well as private actors participate, aimed at solving societal problems or creating societal opportunities; attending to the institutions as context for these governing interactions; and establishing a normative foundation for all those activities. *Governance* can be seen as the totality of theoretical conceptions on governing.[5]

Nevertheless, both the actor realm and the activities under consideration in his definitions are compatible with the definitions of 'governance' which are now common currency.

The definitional clarity carries a certain open-endedness: who is capable of exercising governance over whom – or what – for what purposes, determined by what means? The governance conducted by democratic governments is purported to make the answers to these questions transparent, or discernible – or at least, accountable to electorates. But the above definitions of governance also encompass power relations that extend not only beyond governments, but which in some cases are actually antagonistic to their declared policies. Such generic definitions would not be necessary if our social and political worlds were hierarchically structured in every important regard; if arenas were discrete and a good deal less permeable than they are today; and if the exercise of varieties of power produced ordered and coherent outcomes. Indeed, were it only governments that exercised governance, we could say that the state is the actor; that the arena is public and that the level of governance is 'high' – largely, system-level considerations. But power in large, plural societies is both varied and diffuse; and even where governments establish legal requirements and boundaries for private organisations – corporate; religious; voluntary – these and other non-state and/or sub-state groups are capable of pursuing goals of considerable import, for themselves, for their wider social and physical environments and for governments. There is also a range of criminal activity of a complexity and sophistication which clearly requires governance, as is implied in the term 'organised crime'.[6] In addition, a good deal of what was once mistakenly regarded as chaotic lawlessness in some war-torn countries is now seen as 'warlordism'[7] – loathsome, but clearly a form of governance as defined above and elsewhere in the governance literature. Since governance is not merely the preserve of governments, the necessarily generous scope of these definitions embraces the observable but often informal, deep and intricate patterns of power relations in societies.

As the affective power of non-state groups has grown, the profile of what has come to be known as 'governance without government'[8] has had a considerable impact on thinking about public policy; on the developing relationships between public and private actors; and on the limits of governmental power. The latter point has been a particularly important and prominent source of debate about governance – some theorists adopting the position that governments have lost or are losing their power to govern; or – a related point – that they have lost their pre-eminence and are assuming a place within various self-organising networks. These perspectives are set out clearly in the following assertion by W. Kickert:

> The control capacity of government is limited for a number of reasons: lack of legitimacy, complexity of the policy processes, complexity and multitude of institutions concerned, etc. Government is only one of many actors that influence the course of events in a societal system. Government does not have enough power to exert its will on other actors. Other social institutions are, to a great extent, autonomous. They are not controlled by any single superordinated actor, not even the government. They largely control themselves. Autonomy not only implies freedom, it also implies self-responsibility. Autonomous systems have a much higher degree of freedom of self-governance. Deregulation, government withdrawal and steering at a distance . . . are all notions of less direct government regulation and control, which lead to more autonomy and self-governance for social institutions.[9]

What is unclear from such characterisations is how any social system in which private actors increase their power and autonomy at the expense of centralised, public actors can secure public goods – and, more profoundly, how a social system operating under these conditions can maintain its coherence. Recent corporate scandals and financial risk on a breathtaking scale[10] certainly cast a shadow over hopes one might entertain of the 'self-responsibility' of the autonomously powerful. Not surprisingly, a good deal of the most advanced study of the relationship between government and governance has been devoted to the nascent transition from 'unitary state to differentiated polity' and to the confrontation between 'Government [and] self-steering organizational networks'.[11]

The interest here is not in the kinds of inter-organisational policy networks that pose a number of challenges for centralised governmental structures, but in actors who are able to exploit gaps in the government–governance nexus – those who practise forms of governance not aligned to the machinery and/or purposes of government, formally or informally. So although governance can

reasonably be defined as '[a]ll those activities of social, political and administrative actors that can be seen as purposeful efforts to guide, steer, control or
manage societies', it is also manifestly more – and sometimes outside of – that
descriptive compass:

> [S]ystems of rule can be maintained and their controls successfully and
> consistently exerted even in the absence of established legal or political
> authority. The evolution of intersubjective consensuses based on shared
> fates and common histories, the possession of information and knowledge,
> the pressure of active or mobilizeable publics, and/or the use of careful
> planning, good timing, clever manipulation and hard bargaining can –
> either separately or in combination – foster control mechanisms that
> sustain governance without government.[12]

The full range of meanings carried in the phrase 'governance without
government' clearly extends well beyond the publicly determined and publicly
accountable business of government and, to varying degrees, larger public
policy networks. So in the absence of legal and political authority, who or what
is likely to engage in steering and controlling, with what ends in view?

What follows from this is that a society with a proliferating number of
autonomous actors makes governance more problematic for them, too, in line
with the number of variables impacting on a secure, stable and predictable
working environment; and because the 'governance without government'
phenomenon is also at work in other, interdependent societies. This highlights
the extent to which all forms of bounded (intra-societal) management are
themselves subject to 'outside' pressures and influences, to a degree that makes
the governance of these external relations a necessary counterpart to more
familiar managerial tasks. 'Governance' is therefore not merely a synonym for
'management', but also denotes the strategic context in which management
takes place. So, for example, the management of universities has familiar
parameters (recruitment of both staff and students; setting and collecting fees;
determining academic rules and procedures and the like), but all of these are
impacted by an expanding operating environment, in which other universities
– and the kinds of public and private support they receive – condition
and limit management decisions in any particular institution. University
recruitment is now global; international, private and charitable donors are
important sources of funding; faraway trends in teaching and learning and in
the relationship of academic degrees to employment prospects inform the
standing and even the viability of departments and disciplines; and corporate
funding of scientific research is yet another of the important, 'outside' factors
that feature as part of the contemporary governance of universities.

By the same token, some modern industrial and commercial enterprises
are now so large and diverse – and their operating environments so extensive
and dynamic – that 'corporate governance' has not only become a business
watchword: in some cases, where the term describes devolved leadership and

strategic direction, it is regarded as a practical necessity. To varying degrees, much the same applies to the maintenance of desired states and the achievement of self-determined goals for social groups and organisations, both large and small. Thus in recent years, we have seen studies of the governance not only of corporations and universities, but also of the civil service, churches, schools and even neighbourhoods.[13] This has also been reflected in some of the theoretical effort devoted to defining governance:

> [T]he term governance [is used] to denote the command mechanism of a social system and its actions that endeavour to provide security, prosperity, coherence, order and continuity to the system . . . Taken broadly, the concept of governance should not be restricted to the national and international systems but should be used in relation to regional, provincial and local governments as well as to other social systems such as education and the military, to private enterprises and even to the microcosm of the family.[14]

However, a growing number of governance actors in any field does not automatically carry the promise of greater coherence, order and continuity. There is a good deal of evidence to suggest that as governance by government weakens relative to governance exercised by private actors, the business of governance has become more difficult for all parties. In the depiction below, written in 1983, read 'governance' for 'governments':

> The peculiar difficulty of governments, whether political or industrial, in Western democracies at present is clearly due to the rise in power of organized sectoral minorities, each with an effective power to veto the others and thus to curtail the area within which the system which they constitute can in fact act as a whole, despite the fact that it has the authority and resources to do so.[15]

In the subsequent two decades, several trends have reinforced this difficulty. The first is what has come to be known as the 'hollowing out of the state'[16] and includes matters such as privatisation, devolution and erosion of state functions to private providers and contractors; and the loss of functions to international and (in the case of the EU) supranational institutions.[17] Second, the deregulation of financial markets and the globalisation of capital has greatly diminished the capacity of states to control some important economic variables. Third, there is also a more general fragmentation of established social and political orders and a concomitant (though not necessarily symmetrical) empowering of various sectoral interests, some consolidated and some short-term strategic and shifting.[18]

Moreover, unlimited economic growth – once assumed but now taken to be a necessity in some quarters – coincides with political enfranchisement (including the impetus to the distribution of wealth and the provision of social services) to give us two systems which are 'self-exciting' and mutually reinforcing.[19] Individuals and groups expect and demand more of their governments, partly as an outgrowth of the freedom and mobility available to individuals, both politically and economically. At the same time, economic expansion places increasing strains on regulatory authority, without an uncontested increase in the means to fund it – and perhaps more importantly, while suffering a steady erosion in its authoritative command. With every decrease in perceived competence comes a further distancing of individuals and interest groups from the commonweal. As 'sovereign individuals' assign their allegiance and pursue their security and interests outside their immediate societies and outside the aegis of their governments, the governments concerned come under the shadow of output-oriented legitimacy. The satisfaction of needs is an important criterion of legitimacy, particularly in modern democracies, but when those needs and wants are conceived on an exclusive basis, important strains develop and become evident.[20] The ideal of government of 'by and for the people' clearly implies a degree of self-identification and of social coherence which makes the governance practised by governments possible – and democratic ones especially. Is 'governance without government' compatible with this ideal – and if so, to what extent?

It is easier to identify the trends than to say what their outcome might be (in general or for specific states), but the trajectory is worrying enough:

> [T]he overarching question is what significance or meaning remains of the liberal-democratic notion of the state as the undisputed centre of political power and its self-evident monopoly of articulating and pursuing the collective interest in an era of economic globalization, a 'hollowing out' of the state, decreasing legitimacy for collective solutions, and a marketization of the state itself. Is it the decline of the state we are witnessing, or is it the transformation of the state to the new types of challenges it is facing at the turn of the millennium?[21]

The central difficulty is not so much the robustness of the state as an organisation of political community, but that the ability of societies to secure public goods is becoming a very difficult calculus with every increase in the number of significant actors, interested parties, affected communities and linked concerns or issues. The extent to which power, authority and legitimacy are being acquired, transferred or lost to non-state actors does not in itself guarantee state 'transformation' – at least of the sort which will be configured to meet twenty-first century challenges. It must be borne in mind that the nature and range of these challenges will not be confined to problems essentially external to the distribution of power and authority, such as managing transport systems or addressing localised pollution issues. Matters implicitly entailed in governance agents acting outside the compass of legal and political authority include questions of legitimacy, accountability and determinations of the public good at the most fundamental levels. And there is no reason to suppose that actors so empowered will prioritise public good over their private interests.

A polity can be 'differentiated' in many ways and it can ensure a good deal of freedom for autonomous actors of various kinds, but plurality and freedom are conditioned and limited by the demands of systemic order – those qualities of social life that meaningful and sustainable plurality and freedom require, in satisfactory if sometimes tensioned balance. In the same way that the utility of powerful cars is highly conditioned by the number of other cars within a driver's span, by the extent, quality and maintenance of the roads and by the appropriateness and effectiveness of traffic systems, there are limits to what the capacity of any autonomous actor can achieve in a system weakened and made more complicated by the simultaneous pursuit of the self-determined goals of others. The result is that common, shared requisites become more stressed, even as they become more important, since with every increase in autonomy or individual and group freedom, a greater degree of interdependence is created. The aims of governance actors, both governmental and non-governmental, typically include efforts to secure the order, stability and coherence of their own operating environments. The paradox is that governance *requires* these things, too.

This peculiarity need not lead us to the perennial Realist conundrum. Co-operative endeavour between states in an anarchic world is only difficult to credit or account for if states and the state system are abstracted from the non-survivalist aspects of societal governance and inter-societal exchange. If the disposition and behaviour of states is an aggregate expression of a selfish and fearful human nature, as 'classical' Realist theorising contends, it is small wonder that depictions of international politics can be reduced to stark self-help and zero-sum competition.[22] Whether varieties of international co-operation and the existence of functioning international organisations and regimes support Liberalist optimism or the more cautious and tentative take of the Structural Realists, both recognise the importance and worth of states acting in this way. It is the 'self-help' that arises from already consid-erable interdependence, made ever more imperative with every advance in globalisation. The Realist 'security dilemma' of individual states in the face of the proliferation of weapons of mass destruction persists, but it has now taken its place beside the survivalist requirements of international co-operation to secure the planetary ecology.

At the same time, however, there exists an argument that much of what has come to be known as governance – and global governance especially – is a form of power politics which Realists would be quick to recognise. What gives the following depiction a governance character is the combination of state and non-state actors pursuing a broadly shared ordering agenda:

> [A] radical agenda of social transformation is embodied within Northern strategic networks and complexes that are bringing together governments, NGOs [non-governmental organisations], military establishments and

private companies in new ways. Such complexes are themselves part of an emerging system of global liberal governance.[23]

This and related arguments are noteworthy for two insights they afford our broader understanding of the governance phenomenon. The first is their suggestion that the governance practised by configurations of state and non-state actors need not be motivated by broadly shared norms (at least socially benign or egalitarian ones), or be oriented towards the provision of public goods. Whatever the merits of particular arguments of the sort above, there is nothing about governance *per se* which confines it to a determination and delivery of public policy as the term is generally understood. Governance is no less subject to the opportunism, the self-interested accrual of power or the fulfilment of ideological impulses than is globalisation.[24]

The second insight is that the governance phenomenon is multifaceted, at work throughout the world, in many sectors and at all levels. A great deal of theoretical and empirical work on governance has been devoted to intra-state governance which is essentially concerned with the co-ordination of state and non-state actors – and not least, the articulation of a common set of priorities for society, through formal and informal public policy networks.[25] This accords with the commonest definitions of governance which refer to such purposes as 'co-ordination', 'coherence', 'order' and 'continuity' which easily convey the sense of broad consensus and the general good. But the suggestion that a 'global liberal governance' has begun to take shape through wider and certainly less disinterested governance mechanisms indicates that the exercise of governance carries possibilities that include but extend beyond the familiar compass of domestic politics. These accommodate the full range of human purposes, global arenas and a proliferation of actors, state and non-state; public and private, operating both within and outside of political and legal authority.

The denationalisation of hitherto national domains[26] has an active sense (the privatisation of state assets or functions), but also passive ones, not least the emergence of private, particularly market-oriented actors and various 'spheres of authority', both practical and normative.[27] But the consequences of an increase in 'governance without government' cannot be wholly contained within states themselves, since the governance exercised by governments has applicability to the now-familiar range of transnational and global interactions that are directly pertinent to the internal governance of all states. It is nothing new that many of the most difficult issues facing governments entail inter-national and/or global dimensions: various economic variables, human welfare and environmental sustainability, all subject to global exchanges,[28] are now frequently dominant. This has been the stuff of international politics (and international organisations in particular) since the emergence of the modern state system. So as governance becomes the most readily identifiable expression of the diffusion of power and/or authority within states, it is hardly surprising to find it appearing as a feature of inter-state relations, too.

In common with governance in intra-state settings, the shared purposes of state/non-state governance can also be directed 'outward', into the wider international system – such as in worldwide efforts to combat the piracy of software and other electronically-available consumer goods.[29] At the same time, however, these internationally-oriented state/non-state endeavours can exhibit 'steering and controlling' initiatives which are a source of considerable friction, between states as well as within them. Aspects of the intellectual property rights regime as they apply to patents on goods, notably pharmaceuticals, are a case in point. Likewise, the links between state-sanctioned arms exports and the 'illegitimate' trade in arms world-wide are probably more instructive about networks of governance than about national and international regulatory failures. And in addition to combinations of state and non-state actors pursuing common or compatible aims internationally, it is also the case that some of the more powerful non-state actors, alone or in combination, can shape control, steer and direct – (the operative words commonly applied to the activity of governance) – for ends that are both self-determined and exclusive. This is the nature of profit-making enterprises and includes the more contentious aspects of the considerable power of some transnational companies.[30] Various forms of the corruption of governments and government officials by outside actors[31] are also clearly instances of governance as it has been widely defined and understood.

Global governance as a research field

Global governance as state adaptation to global arenas and processes

The idea and ideal of world governance has a long history, with roots in religion, philosophy, law and political theory.[32] The majority of theories and proposals which comprise this tradition addressed the problem of peace and trust between political communities – concerns mirrored in the growth of treaty-based interstate relations and the larger development of international law.[33] As an intellectual enterprise, the search for ultimate authority has gradually been displaced[34] by more practical questions of power, authority and accountability, with the most considerable body of theorising following the contours of the development of nation states and the state system. With the establishment of the United Nations and the end of slavery and colonialism, the second half of the twentieth century saw the consolidation of a single, inclusive international system.

States and the system they comprise have both generated and responded to the combined dynamics of widening industrialisation, increased world trade, population growth and advances in technology. Taken together, these developments have given us globalisation of a character now so widely and deeply entrenched that we can readily employ the term to describe a generalised condition as well as one or more processes. Now that states routinely find themselves on both sides of the cause/effect and cost/benefit calculus of globalisation, one of the more profound outcomes for states and peoples alike is the emergence of a global politics – less hierarchically ordered than international relations, more turbulent and less coherent.[35]

Yet although states can no longer be regarded as occupying an exclusive domain at the pinnacle of a hierarchically ordered world, their power, authority and legitimacy remain unique – and important. It is not conceivable that any combination of NGOs could have agreed, enacted and where necessary, enforced the provisions that halted the worsening erosion of the earth's ozone layer.[36] This particular case not only illustrates the power still deployable by states, but also the extent to which the well-worked mechanisms of the international system can enable and harness that power.

State adaptations to internal and external pressures pertain partly to changes in organisational form and function, but they are principally about power and about efforts variously to extend, maintain, defend, devolve and share it. They are also about maintaining satisfactory conditions for the key parameters of state security. Some of these pressures and some of the threats to security and stability are incontrovertibly global – most plainly when planetary limitations manifest themselves as crises, but also with respect to exchanges which are largely deterritorialised and highly dynamic, such as the world-wide, electronic movement of capital. With governance-capacity adaptations induced by the spread and acceleration of globalisation, the term 'global governance' made a gradual, rather unpronounced entry into the lexicon over the past decade. Whatever the extent or focus of cases with some claim to be instances of global governance, the state or some aspects of state capacity are nearly always present, either actively, as an agent of change, or passively – that is, on the receiving end of, or respondent to, the actions of non-state actors or environmental constraints.

The state was never a 'fixed' concept in any event, but established debates are now faced with a plethora of developments that return us to fundamental considerations such as sovereignty, kinds and degrees of power, and relational power *vis-à-vis* non-state actors, markets and global capitalism more generally and their susceptibility to, or accommodation of, networked politics and changing, globalising norms.

The 'central but no longer predominant' view of states and state power – (by no means universal, even among global governance theorists) – does not undermine the disciplines of International Relations (IR) and International Political Economy (IPE), but enlivens debate about key concepts, the scope of enquiry appropriate to them and what constitutes a challenge to prevailing tenets.[37] In theoretical terms, the primacy of the state system as an abstraction has shrunk before the spectre of a fragile and threatened global environment, which can no longer be regarded as a static backdrop to the drama of inter-state contention; and in the face of the acquisition of power by a variety of non-state actors.[38] For this reason, it is now difficult to maintain 'anarchy' (the absence of an effective supranational authority) as an arena rather than merely as a condition of state interaction.[39] Yet states and the state system remain the starting point if not the centre of intellectual efforts to understand the fundamentals of large-scale political and social change. States remain the largest and most powerful concentrations of power and authority; and much of the freedom of action enjoyed by independent, non-state actors is secured by the integrity and coherence of states and by their co-operative endeavours, through international law, international organisations and the maintenance of regimes.

But the emergence of so many powerful actors and issues, many of them on both sides of the cause/effect momentum of globalisation, has not left states unaltered, in practical or in relative terms. The broad governance literature has made worthwhile contributions to our understanding of these structural and relational aspects of power as they have been affected by globalisation and other currents of contemporary life. Perhaps the most important is an opening out of the discipline of International Relations to the larger political environment in which states and the state system exist. A result of this is that a good many more scholars can now accept that the 'hard shell' of states is more like a semi-permeable membrane through which pass all manner of political, social, cultural and economic matters, some of them of considerable moment and a good many of them not mediated by the state. It is now more widely and readily acknowledged, if only in outline, that states operate in a dynamic environment rather than in a free-standing arena at some remove from the sustaining facts and mechanisms of wider human interaction and the natural world.

As IR and IPE adjust their disciplinary parameters to wider and more turbulent world politics, the challenge of understanding states and the international system as organisational forms is made more difficult by the necessary inclusion of considerations which in many cases have hitherto been overlooked. These challenges cannot be met without grappling with questions of governance, in respect of both state capacity and state interaction with novel actors and dynamics. The reverse – accounting for aspects of global order not determined by states – is also important:

> [T]he concept of governance without government is especially conducive to the study of world politics inasmuch as centralized authority is conspicuously absent from this domain of human affairs even though it is equally obvious that a modicum of order, or routinized arrangements, is normally present in the conduct of global life. Given an order that lacks a centralized authority with the capacity to enforce decisions on a global scale, it follows that a prime task of inquiry is that of probing the extent to which the functions normally associated with governance are performed in world politics without the institutions of government.[40]

Order in world politics in not merely the order of the international system by another name, particularly in an age of globalisation. But although there is an order to the sum of human interactions which cannot be reduced to international relations, this reinforces rather than diminishes the importance of understanding states, which remain the world's most important organisations of political community.

Another, related aspect of global governance as state adaptation is less about the implications of change for states than about opportunity for non-state actors and for practical and normative developments which are generally considered to fall outside of state purview. NGOs are the most obvious class of actors under this heading and there is now a considerable literature on NGOs in world politics,[41] sufficiently developed to include the kinds of novel organisational forms and operational modes some have assumed in order to operate at the highest and most influential levels. Although the work of NGOs does not always adopt an oppositional stance to prevailing orders, they have become important sources for formulating, articulating and promulgating norms – work that extends to corporations as well as to states and international organisations.[42] International NGOs (INGOs) Amnesty International and Transparency International have achieved such standing that their information is regarded as authoritative even by states, but it is their normative orientation – their desire to 'steer' states and other bodies towards operational and behavioural standards – that gives their work its governance character.[43]

These and other organisations and networks[44] have become an important source of the kinds of trans-national and/or extra-territorial allegiance for people whose interests, concerns and ideals are engaged by matters beyond their immediate circumstances. The shared endeavour of working to bring about normative and other social shifts which now takes so many forms seems remarkably untroubled by borders, boundaries or socio-cultural differences; and in many respects, global social movements seem to thrive on plurality, which is often a foundation for their claims to legitimacy. The activities of these groups and networks range from protest (the world-wide demonstrations against the 2003 war against Iraq were particularly striking) to formal lobbying (the work of Oxfam International at the World Bank and IMF, for example). Taken together with other deterritorialised initiatives, considerable interest has been raised over the concept of a nascent global civil society.[45] Some of this interest is itself more normatively than empirically driven: democratic and egalitarian ideals are prominent.[46] It might be attractive but it is also problematic to infer from disparate and wide-ranging activities something with the continuity, coherence and durability that the phrase 'society' would ordinarily require. So work in this field ranges from assertions as to the practical possibilities open to a global civil society that is admittedly 'emergent'[47] to rather more sceptical analyses.[48] But whatever the sum of the parts, the networking modes of operation that feature prominently in the civil society literature have attracted a still broader interest. This is because networked forms of organisation are hardly confined to NGOs, nor again, to socially benign purposes, as became clear when the nature of the threat posed by Al Qaeda came to public attention. Less dramatically, there is evidence that states too have also adopted networked modes of operation across a very wide range of functions and for a variety of purposes.

> Understood as a form of global governance, government networks meet [various] needs. As commercial and civic organizations have already discovered, their networked form is ideal for providing the speed and flexibility necessary to function effectively in an information age. [. . .] [T]hese are networks composed of national government officials, either appointed by elected officials or directly elected themselves. Best of all, they can perform many of the functions of a world government – legislation, administration and adjudication – without the form.[49]

Whether or not states' networked activities are sufficient to sustain the argument that they are now 'disaggregating into [their] component institutions, which are increasingly interacting with their foreign counterparts across borders',[50] it is plain that these activities are nevertheless of considerable import, and all the more when considered together with non-state activities of a similar kind, albeit with contrasting and sometimes conflicting purposes. Again, some analysts see in these developments an emergent form of political organisation – in this case, a 'global polity':

> [A]n understanding of the global polity [is one] in which the existence of norms and principles that guide states are also joined by an ever-thickening web of institutions and regulatory activities at the global level that approximate to some extent the developments that have occurred throughout the nineteenth and twentieth centuries within the borders of the sovereign state.[51]

These constructs keep us alert to the kinds of developments which in combination or over time might have serious consequences for world order. However, discerning form on such a large scale in the midst of an increasing number of significant actors, relational shifts and operational novelties means that conclusions have to be provisional or highly qualified.

In addition to states' direct adjustment to change and change-as-opportunity, there is also what might succinctly be called necessity – the routine maintenance of systems essential to the stability and prosperity of individual states and/or the international system. The alacrity with which states address financial crises that threaten loss and turbulence on a global scale points to systemic order as fundamental for the pursuit of their self-interest. A combination of dedicated international regulatory bodies and well-practised forms of multilateral co-operation also serve to make more routine adjustments to relations in finance, trade, the environment and other matters. These organisations and modes of co-operation are judged by some to comprise 'the building blocks of a global governance architecture'.[52]

Global governance incorporated into established theoretical schools

Given the importance of the state in the on-going processes of globalisation and the content and general orientation of the disciplines of IR and IPE, it is unsurprising that ideas about global governance have been incorporated into and to some extent, shaped by established schools within those traditions.[53] This takes two distinct if overlapping forms. In the first, it entails adopting 'global governance' as an alternative or additional expression of an already-developed perspective, or reinforces an established view of states, the international system or the nature of and prospects for inter-state co-operation. In some of the academic literature, the 'global governance' of certain spheres of activity is essentially a synonym for the 'international politics' of those activities. To some extent an outgrowth of international organisation, perspectives of this sort do not explicitly exclude non-state and non-international considerations, but the stance is perhaps best captured in the global governance 'architecture' metaphor.

In the second, 'global governance' has been applied as the summative expression of powerful normative drive or policy disposition, both positive and negative. In its strongest form, this is global governance as a form of goal-seeking hegemony and extends from assertions of ethical imperialism to the Comprehensive Development Framework of the World Bank.[54] Similarly, the term has also been used in critiques of neo-liberal capitalism and forms of elite control or domination to argue that there is an underlying logic if not pre-determined goal in such drives.

Global governance as a manifestation of longer/deeper trends, or as consolidation of socio-political, socio-economic and normative developments

Some analysts employ the growing interest in global governance to emphasise the size, shape, direction or momentum of a variety of forces poised between continuity and change in historical processes. Global governance as historical materialism is one example.[55] Likewise, the pressures exerted by globalisation and by powerful states and international organisations can be seen as top-down and largely directed or goal-oriented. These can be characterised as an emergent global governance. At the same time, the opportunities being opened up by globalising dynamics can be understood as bottom-up, with no single purpose or logic – hence the interest in the growth and consolidation of a putative global civil society and in a possible, nascent global polity.

But discerning patterns in the matrix of globalising forces and forms of political organisation is not confined to practical outcomes – and for many, the normative implications of one or another form of global governance are no less important. Long-standing concerns with structural injustice and, more recently, the interests of cosmopolitan theorists, find engagement in what global governance comprises, or should comprise – with direct bearing on the span of cosmopolitan theorising itself.[56]

A primary focus on normative outcomes alerts global governance theorists to the pitfall of a too-restrictive perspective, including liberal pluralist forms that preclude social purpose to global order(s); and top-down, directed forms of global governance that will not necessarily be egalitarian.

Globalisation, governance and global governance

This array of global governance perspectives is not unexpected; nor is it unwelcome, for all that some might worry over 'global governance' becoming a buzzword. 'Globalisation' has been subjected to very similar trials of categorisation.[57] But how is global governance distinct from the governance practised by states and other actors in international or other 'high' arenas, such as the global capital market? A precise understanding of global governance as a distinct form or level of governance carries all of the usual problems of definitional clarity.[58] It is of note that there are remarkably few definitions of global governance, given the proficiency with which social science disciplines usually generate them (one academic study listed 32 definitions of 'food security'[59]), and the relative size and breadth of the global governance literature. In many studies, 'governance' is sometimes applied to the steering and controlling of systems that are reasonably described as global, but without entering the more theoretical consideration of what global governance might comprise.[60]

Part of the difficulty as outlined above is the extent to which the concept of global governance is deeply rooted in IR. The adjective 'global' is now frequently used in international/world politics contexts to denote situations of considerable gravity and/or extent, distinguishing them from the historically more familiar themes of international relations, without the suggestion that there is a global *political* arena. So for international relations theorists, the political challenge of, for example, planetary environmental crises, conceptually as well as practically, is how to engage the international system in the global environment.[61] The globalisation literature has usefully added considerable emphasis to networked human systems such as currency transaction and communications links – characterised as 'transnational' within the context of the international system; and 'global' in terms of their extent and/or comprehensiveness. But as an ever greater portion of the human condition becomes subject to global exchanges, the alignment between national/international orders and global orders becomes more difficult to calibrate and organise, while relationships grow more complex and the governance issues they generate become more urgent. The sphere of human activity and consequence is global, but comprehension, coherence, consensus and command are sited in smaller, less comprehensive constituencies, subject to conflicting or competing interests and priorities.

Clearly, thinking about the globalised human condition requires us to consider the largest forms of human interaction and organisation – states and the state system – and other actors and organisational forms relative to them. The consideration of these forms are central, but they have also been predominant. As a result, a great deal of attention has been given to governance as an explanatory framework; and much less to governance as an activity.[62] Organisational adaptations, both reactive and opportunistic, are important for gauging the human capacity to exercise governance as well as for understanding the power and interests that inform it. Also important, however, are the combinational and cumulative outcomes of an ever-active, growing, modernising and technologically assisted humanity. Undirected human activity, abundant and largely mundane, comprises much of the substance and the burden of global order rather than its form, so its importance is sometimes overlooked; and the problem of regulating it is easy to disregard or underestimate.

Terminological precision will probably remain elusive, not only because the term 'global governance' is easy to appropriate but also because, like 'globalisation', it is locked into unending disputes about what constitutes the 'global' quality of so many developments and actions or the arenas in which they take place. What is clear is that vexed human and environmental relations of unprecedented scope and complexity, world-wide in their inclusiveness or implications, will require commensurate governance initiatives. Whether these initiatives are regarded as global, either individually or summatively, is perhaps a less compelling matter than the span of what we shall have to include.

3 Is governance global or just all over the map?

Although the focus in this chapter is on governance as purposive activity rather than as organisational adaptation, in world politics relative power is an inescapable feature of effectiveness. This is clear in the state/non-state dichotomy which features prominently in the global governance literature and in studies which examine the degree to which global governance is a site of contestation across that divide.[1] As outlined below, if social movements can be said to have influenced or indeed practised global governance, it is partly by dint of how they have positioned themselves relative to, and communicated with or about, other established actors.[2] In turn, as global governance exercised by states and established international organisations meets serious challenges, it is not merely organisational momentum and working assumptions that are brought into question: so too is the operating environment for all of the pertinent actors.

As we have seen, the best known texts on global governance describe the ways in which globalising forces facilitate the creation or consolidation of new centres of power, authority and competence outside the exclusive domain of nation states. These works analyse the outcomes of the proliferation of transnational dynamics of many kinds – from the generation and consequences of pollution to the electronic transfer of money and the growth of social movements. Governance studies are also a theoretical response to a distinct if nascent world politics, based on the accumulating evidence that international politics is no longer an impermeable actor realm.[3] Much of the pioneering work on governance and global governance has therefore focused on ' . . . the growth of institutions unique to transnational rather than territorial political spaces';[4] and on the tensions and deficits opening up between governments and new or newly empowered sites of governance.[5]

The question remains, 'what then is "global" about global governance?' James Rosenau makes an important distinction, to which the global governance literature largely conforms:

> There is a difference between governance of the world and governance in the world. The term 'global governance' does not necessarily refer to a central authority. Rather, global governance is a lot of governmental and

nongovernmental activities that occur in local places, the results of which contribute to the overall order of world affairs.[6]

Even so, as Martin Hewson and Timothy J. Sinclair point out, even James Rosenau's introduction to the seminal work, *Governance Without Government* ' . . . refer[s] almost interchangeably, to the "governance of world politics", "governance on a worldwide scale", the "governance of international orders", or "governance in a global order"'.[7] Although there has been a good deal of investigation into new forms and new sites of governance, what makes governances meaningfully global has received scant attention; indeed, the phrase has been applied variously to convey geographic scope, sectoral inclusiveness and authoritative reach.[8] An obvious counter to this and other critiques of the way in which 'global governance' is used is that although 'global governance' is a meaningful term it invites rather than precludes a differentiation of kinds and degrees of governance at the highest levels of human organisation and consequence. But it is curious that the generous scope of the global governance literature has not directly addressed the question, What would an adequate global governance be the governance *of*? If global governance 'is a site, one of many sites, in which struggles over wealth, power and knowledge are taking place',[9] then a typology of global governance as purposive activity can generate a great deal of material for the further analysis of world politics, but it cannot tell us whether the global governance now in place or any of its more plausible configurations will be adequate to securing a humane and sustainable global order.

Since much of the global governance literature is issue-specific or thematic, what counts as adequate in any of these cases might be considerable, but is framed separately from other sectoral concerns and is sometimes rather technocratic – remote from larger questions of human security and planetary sustainability. This point does not dispute the necessary abstractions of the social sciences or the importance of managing the human systems on which we depend, but highlights the need for a fully considered context for global governance case studies. By analogy: ethologists can make a detailed study of competition within or between species, and although the ecology that supports them might not make a significant difference to any of their particular encounters, their relationships are nevertheless bounded and to some degree conditioned by their larger physical environment, animate and inanimate. This is why ecologists argue that if a species is added or removed from an ecosystem, what results is not the same ecosystem plus or minus a species – but a different ecosystem.[10] Our abstractions are meaningful, but they remain just that: abstractions. If we take as our subject the human condition – which here includes the necessity to exercise governance of unprecedented range and complexity – then the cases on their own will not tell us everything we need to know.

The assumption clearly conveyed in the global governance literature is that through some combination of state/non-state endeavour, institutional buttressing and civil society mobilisation, we – humanity – will be able to meet the challenges of the twenty-first century. In the global governance literature to date, this takes four distinct if overlapping forms. The first is a focus on a greatly enlarged and empowered actor realm. The second concentrates on an advanced and strengthened multilateralism. The third is concerned with high-level sectoral governances. The fourth depicts global governance as a summative phenomenon – the assumption being that various kinds and levels of governance will find expression as a global aggregate.

Global governance as the activity of an extended and empowered actor realm

Much of the impetus behind this form of global governance derives from innumerable instances of individual and small-group empowerment; the possibilities opened up by electronic communications and the availability of international travel; the opportunities to pursue political and normative agendas across borders and around the world; and the considerable strength and reach conferred by networking and other forms of formal and informal association. And although civil society groups often oppose national and international agendas, there is also some hope invested in the momentum that can be generated by state and non-state coalitions – the best-known recent instance of which was the campaign to ban landmines, which led to the Ottawa Treaty in 1999.[11]

Theoretical positions have incorporated or coalesced around the broad phenomenon of transnational social activism, with particularly strong interest shown in the prospects for greater democratisation and more direct accountability of existing organisations and processes.[12] Issue-specific advocacy and single-issue campaigns have also attracted a great deal of attention, not only as matters important in themselves but also as harbingers of a more plural and possibly, 'bottom-up' global governance.[13] There has also been considerable interest generated by the emergence and activities of advocacy networks and their various organisational forms, including task-specific allegiances and more general networking modes of operation.[14]

The normative element of these efforts is particularly striking: extending scrutiny of human rights standards, particularly with respect to non-state actors; exposing tacit support for unacceptable practices; and, through an emphasis on democratic values, bringing power-as-legitimacy into the light of day, moving governance away from an infrastuctural background activity towards governance as a matter of public policy and choice. The heat generated by anti-globalisation and anti-WTO protests in recent years is an indicator of the extent to which the values and purposes of established mechanisms of global governance have not been subject to wide public deliberation (which includes less normative, more immediately self-interested concerns such as worsening employment prospects). The emergence of transnational social movements and INGOs is not only significant for what can potentially come within their sphere of influence, but also for the scrutiny they bring to the activities, power, reach, integrity and accountability of a range of powerful actors: states, international organisations and corporations.[15] Perhaps the most significant accomplishment of these various social movements is the degree to which they have expanded the political arena, so that the questions, 'Who should have voice and standing?' and 'Who should set the agenda?' are now an unexceptional accompaniment to the exercise of what is generally regarded as global governance.

However, it would be easy to overstate the importance and influence of this extended actor realm because disparities in power remain considerable; because 'activism beyond borders' might be too diverse in orientation, priorities and methods to have a substantial and lasting effect on existing power structures; and arguably, '[T]here are no structures above countries, in which mass political participation and genuine influence can be felt.'[16] Also, there has been a predictable backlash, especially from frequently targeted organisations like the Bretton Woods institutions – and although the following could be read as a strain of defensiveness indicating effectiveness, some of the criticisms carry weight:

> Mats Karrisson, the Vice President of External Affairs at the World Bank, recently attacked NGOs based in Washington 'for their weak accountability,' 'shallow democracy' and 'precarious legitimacy' as actors in the global debate.[17]

While it might be argued that the World Bank is itself singularly ill-placed to make such charges, transnational coalitions of various kinds are now being subjected to closer scrutiny as socio-political actors as much as for their sociological meaning and organisational novelty. As one study notes, 'The potential for conflict is particularly high in circumstances characterised by cultural differences, diverse ideologies, discrepancies in wealth, and power inequalities. These differences may be further complicated when international NGOs seek to work with grassroots movements.[18] It is also instructive to note the ease with which powerful but non-accountable bodies can use many of the same organisational and communicative devices to counter socially progressive initiatives. For example, in 1999, 2,000 delegates gathered in Geneva for the World Congress of Families II, its purpose to 'discuss ways to counter 85 anti-family initiatives advanced by the UN and other world bodies'. The coalition of fundamentalist Christians and Muslims was, according to one of the sponsoring bodies, 'the contemporary coming together . . . [of] only . . . the most orthodox of each group, people that are least likely to compromise'.[19]

Finally, although transnational corporations are frequently the target of various INGOs and activist coalitions,[20] they are private sector organisations – very much part of global civil society, however much the activism of social movements might make them appear to inhabit a free-standing realm of their own. Transnational companies can and do further their interests, sometimes entering NGO 'space' by creating their own NGOs, or funding sympathetic think-tanks – techniques probably made necessary by attacks on their credibility, integrity and legitimacy and worth of their operations.

Global governance as strengthened multilateralism

The commanding heights of global governance are held by multilateral organisations, institutions and other forms of inter-state co-operation, including the informal though significant meetings of G8 leaders. Together, these comprise extensive, powerful, interlocking interests, international laws, regimes and regulatory bodies and agreements. The existence of such developed multilateralism clearly illustrates how much of what even the most powerful states require for their routine functioning, security and prosperity cannot be secured by unilateral means; and that managed interdependence is preferable to wholesale competition. It is also clear that the globalisation of rules often facilitates other, more visible forms of globalisation, including a good deal of its infrastructure, such as air transport, telecommunications and trade.[21] In turn, globalisation and its effects, not all of them either anticipated or welcome, require further kinds and degrees of multilateral co-operation, in particular for regulatory purposes.

The apparent solidity and enduring importance of some of the largest institutional forms of multilateralism (not least the Bretton Woods organisations) might appear to give them special standing with respect to the orientation and interests of states, but although the WTO, for example, is able to apply retaliatory trade sanctions against a member state that contravenes the agreed rules of trade,[22] states' larger interests in expanding and maintaining a free trade regime are considerably more important. The negotiated dispute resolution mechanisms maintain a balance between state manoeuvrability and systemic order that meets with general agreement – and compliance. Beneath the formal structures of multilateralism, an extensive network of interests, influential actors, shared understandings and an overarching concern with systemic stability as it impacts on many fields is also operative, evident in the informal meetings at Davos and here expressed by a Bundesbank official regarding global financial regulation: 'There's the OECD, the European Commission, the BIS [Bank for International Settlements], the G-7, the IMF – networks at different levels. It's the whole network that matters, not the forum. You've got several hundred people in the Western world in constant dialogue. The IMF is particularly important, but they all are. And it's not just the top people.'[23]

Although inter-state co-operation remains the foundation of multilateralism, as inter-state concerns take on global characteristics and as an increasing degree of multilateralist endeavour becomes geared towards the globalisation of regulation, the way is open for the participation of a wider range of actors, notably international and national business organisations. To some extent, this development links global governance as strengthened multilateralim to global governance through the empowerment of non-state groups, although power differentials are still a limiting and conditioning factor for the participation and influence of the latter.[24] The tensions generated by multilateralism are not confined to differences in the outlook and interests between high and low: states themselves must balance the necessary degree of surrendering areas of sovereign control against the ability to satisfy domestic constituents who can and often do resent the costs involved in complying with the rules agreed by their governments. But this cuts both ways, as states, ever mindful of power realities, experience the need to expand, co-ordinate and harmonise rules and regulatory mechanisms:

> [O]ne reason why nations gave up their sovereignty over intellectual property law by signing the Trade Related Intellectual Property Rights Agreement (TRIPS) of the GATT Final Act was that they thought that the prospect of a national sovereignty subject to the bilateral domination of US trade sanctions might be a worse form of US domination for their citizens than a multilateral agreement (still dominated by US interests) that was open to some influence by their parliament and incorporated some protection against bilateral trade retaliation. In some cases they may have been wrong, in other cases right. But the principle is clear: if a nation's objective is to secure its citizens against domination, it can sometimes be better to give up national sovereignty in favour of a global regime with superior assurances of impartial dispute resolution.[25]

The options are not always so clear – and the resolution of an internationally recognised need for the global ordering or regulation of certain activities on the one hand, with individual states' perception of their own more immediate interests on the other, can greatly inhibit the creation and implementation of multilateral global governance initiatives. This is abundantly clear in the US repudiation of the Kyoto Protocol and more recent Russian fears that its provisions could stifle the development of Russia's economy.[26]

The agenda-setting and framing aspects of multilateral governance are keenly observed by states – nowhere more visible than in the structure of and shifting power currents within the United Nations. The history of the UN, its specialised agencies, funds and programmes are replete with the controlling behaviours of the its more powerful member states and those over whom they have considerable leverage. Despite the inhibiting, distorting effects of state interests on the development and performance of the UN, it is not difficult to substantiate the argument that it is still more than the sum of its parts: it was in the forefront of dismantling colonialism and advancing human rights; and it has provided the normative leadership and legitimacy-through-inclusiveness for world conferences on matters central to contemporary global governance – especially on the global environment. Small wonder that those who invest hope in the global governance work of non-state actors find the United Nations, its efforts and the arenas it creates are both congenial and efficient.[27] Likewise, the progressive, developmental and distributive ethos of much of the UN's practical work inclines it to be the most forward-looking about the worth and importance of global social movements and INGOs, most recently producing a commissioned report on the relationship between the United Nations and civil society. The report describes the developments that led to the study:

> The formation of global constituencies – networked governance, as it is sometimes called – enhances the authority and international stature of the actors. Often the global policy networks are multisectoral – including like-minded Governments, civil society and others – and focus on specific issues. These global policy networks have significantly influenced policy, shaped public opinion and helped to resolve disputes on such issues as debt, landmines, small arms, conflict diamonds, big dams and crimes against humanity, and involve Southern as well as Northern actors. They came together mostly outside the formal organs of the United Nations, later entering the United Nations fold once they had momentum.[28]

Both inside and outside the aegis of the UN, a good deal of global governance scholarship sees in the work of non-state actors the possibility of a re-oreintation of the flows of power that inform the larger multilateral structures of global governance:

> [T]he source of an evolving global governance structure . . . includes the simultaneous existence of 'top-down' and 'bottom-up' multilateralism . . . [There is] no doubt that the two forms of multilateralism not only co-exist but are also intersecting: but what is more interesting is the nature of the intersection. [. . .] Can the 'top-down' multilateral process become more democratic as it tries to accommodate the demands of civil society? What sort of accommodation will be needed in order to bring this about?[29]

Global governance as high-level sectoral governances

Multilateral global governance is dedicated to sector-specific activity, such as financial regulation, environmental redress and standard-setting and global health. There is no generalised, non-specific global governance. But it is worth noting sectoral governances as distinct from multilateralist endeavour more generally because they will inevitably comprise an essential part of the under-standing of global governance as a summative phenomenon (below); and, because they are goal-oriented, they provide important tests of coherence and effectiveness.

The sectors are easy to identify, but difficult to circumscribe, even at sub-thematic levels. So what the 'global governance of the environment' amounts to are specific instances of environmental global governance – of matters which are often vast in scope and hugely complex, practically and politically. (Witness efforts merely to reduce greenhouse gas emissions to an average of 5.2 per cent below 1990 levels by 2012 – the goal of the Kyoto Protocol.) And the same globalising forces that make the establishment, extension or refinement of governance mechanisms necessary also blur boundaries because they introduce a host of 'outside' conditions, actors and variables.

We can see this most clearly in the way that the natural world does not conform to our abstractions and boundaries; and in the way that electronic communication has greatly complicated the regulation of global finance. Following the financial crisis in Mexico in 1994 and 1995 (addressed by a $50 billion IMF-led programme), the Halifax Summit was convened in order to consider appropriate reforms to the IMF and World Bank. There, French President Jacques Chirac 'denounced international speculators as the AIDS virus of the world economy'.[30]

Because of the number, kind and speed of variables that can affect the global governance of a particular sphere of activity, a great deal of the largest sectoral global governance is belated – a form of crisis response. This is not wholly unexpected; and the IMF/World Bank stabilisation programmes in the wake of the Mexican and Asian financial crises and the World Health Organization's success in preventing SARS from developing into a pandemic can be reviewed with some satisfaction as well as relief. However, since much of the largest sectoral governance entails making running adjustments to systems growing in size, inter-connectedness and/or dynamism, the prospect of a larger crisis in managing the stability and sustainability of the world is not a fanciful one.

Many of the more worrying trends are visible in the governance of global health. Global health governance has a long history[31] and in recent decades it has witnessed an impressive growth in the breadth, extent and co-ordination of multilateral effort,[32] most recently in identifying and limiting the spread of SARS in 2003.[33] But there are innumerable matters which, though they fall outside of the governance of health in a strict sense, nevertheless directly impact on it, especially environmental change.[34] The objective of global health governance is not a disease-free world, but the elimination of preventable disease outbreaks (the eradication of smallpox in 1979 now stands as something of a rebuke in the age of HIV/AIDS), routine surveillance and co-ordinated response mechanisms. But although there have been commendable efforts to address particular large-scale health deficiencies and disease outbreaks, these examples of the governance of global health are overshadowed by a measurable decline in global public health systems around the world,[35] the result of conflicting priorities, complacency and most worryingly, a failure to grasp the implications for the spread of infectious diseases in a highly globalised world. The infrastructure of public health governance has shrunk, even in the developed world; and even more serious than the decline in the number of government public health departments and fully-funded and staffed laboratories is their diminished ability to co-ordinate their efforts in a timely fashion. 'All over the map' is a disturbing but apt description.

As in the establishment and maintenance of multilateral forums, power, interests and conflicting priorities are fully operative in sectoral global governance, even in matters as fundamental as threats to the global commons (climate change), or ones as morally consequential as allowing the manufacture of generic drugs to treat the world's poorest people. A single instance, here concerning the governance of health *within* a single state, is indicative of the kinds of pressures that bear on sectoral governances between them:

> Not even the CDC [Centers for Disease Control, in the United States] is immune from the virus of partisan politics; despite an overwhelming medical consensus, the agency has refused to take a position on the use of condoms to prevent AIDS and has curtailed the printing and distribution of any data on the control or treatment of sexually transmitted diseases that might offend the most conservative Christians. In response to political pressure from the NRA [National Rifle Association] and threats from Congress to withhold funding, the CDC has also discontinued its definitive research documenting the public health costs of handguns.[36]

Conflicts of interest are not confined to agenda-setting and behind-the scenes lobbying: at the global level, the health-related aspects of intellectual property rights are a compelling example of the importance of reconciling quite different but intersecting global governance arrangements.[37]

Global governance as a summative phenomenon

The human condition is regulated formally and informally by numerous mechanisms of varying degrees of legitimacy, effectiveness and connectivity. These can fairly be taken as a sum, however patchy and contested that sum is. The totality of all forms of governance is in an important sense, therefore, 'global' and this characterisation of global governance sees what has emerged – and will continue to expand and strengthen – as a summative global governance, state and non-state; public and private; high and low – and that this will suffice to secure the human future. Many characterisations of global governance, notably the report of the Commission on Global Governance, depict it as summative:

> Governance is the sum of the many ways individuals and institutions, public and private, manage their common affairs. . . . At the global level, governance has been viewed primarily as intergovernmental relationships, but it must now be understood as also involving non-governmental organizations, citizens' movements, multinational corporations, and the global capital market.[38]

If global governance is to be understood as a summative phenomenon, then it is already an established fact of world politics, however inadequate. But is 'governance on a global scale' global governance? This question is not semantic, but conceptual. The global arena is not co-extensive with the state system, or any combination of state and non-state bodies. Actor realms such as the state system and global governance as described above are human systems,[39] not free-standing entities. Because they operate in environments which they do not generate, encompass or control, they can be acted upon as well as act. However, an implicit assumption in much of the global governance literature is that the growth and intensification of human activity and its consequences has not brought about any structural change to the prospects for human security; and that the natural and human dynamics set off or amplified by globalising processes will remain within familiar or manageable organisational bounds. But the possible inclusion of a range of hitherto unempowered civil society actors does not alter the parameters of a global governance oriented towards meeting challenges *within* our established systems of regulation and control rather than challenges *to* those systems. The point is simple, but profound: all forms of human co-operation, however extensive and however efficient, are themselves dependent on, as well as responsive to, relatively stable and predictable natural and political orders. What we are beginning to witness, however, is not merely the emergence of a range of new problems or issues, but also disruption of the systems within which we perceive the necessity and summon the means to act.

Although smarter, more inclusive, better equipped governance(s) might suffice to deal with some of the immediate and politically contentious consequences of globalisation, the determining, conditioning and limiting dynamics generated by the interaction of human activity and environmental supports are of another, more truly global order. Our systems of regulation and control – 'global governance' as the term is now employed – are configured to a world which we are transforming – rapidly, radically and sometimes irreversibly. With those formations come alterations to the conditions on which our regulatory systems depend. More than thirty years ago, Geoffrey Vickers argued that ' . . . the natural order can no longer be regarded as an unchanging datum, but increasingly depends on, as well as dictating, the shape of every order which men seek to impose on their lives'.[40] It is perhaps all too easy to misread this, even now, as an early recognition of the human potential to create complex and intractable problems as formidable as climate change and ozone layer depletion. But Vickers' point went much deeper: ' . . . [W]e have created an ungovernable world, in which the natural order and a man-made order are blended as never before into a system which can neither be interpreted by natural or governed by man-made laws'.[41] This view does not challenge the validity or utility of 'governance in the world', but contextualises it. 'Global governance' as the term is now employed is not an activity, but an aggregate of sectoral ones: the global governance of matters such as the environment and international finance. The difficulty is that globalisation is not only altering social relations and the organisation of political community; it is also intensifying the pace and scale of the interaction of human and natural systems, with the result that, increasingly, the human condition is not only bounded by natural dynamics, but also shaped by anthropogenic ones – many of which fall outside the intellectual and practical compass of global governance.

The world beyond global governance

The first three of the preceding kinds of purposive global governance – as civil society empowerment, as enhanced multilateralism and as sector-specific governance – are important, but they do not inform our understanding of the necessary compass of global governance. The link between them can be seen in one of James Rosenau's clarifications, which clearly links governance as an actor realm with governance as a summative managerial phenomenon:

> [G]overnance occurs on a global scale through the coordination of states and a vast array of rule systems that exercise authority in the pursuit of goals that function outside national jurisdictions. Some of these systems are formalized, many consist essentially of informal structures, and some are still largely inchoate, but taken together they cumulate to governance on a global scale.[42]

On these and similar conceptions of global governance, it would appear that the main political challenge facing humanity in a rapidly globalising world is to make existing systems of governance more inclusive and more effective. This is certainly the perspective offered by the UN Vision Project on Global Public Policy Networks (an initiative devoted to the future of global governance), which identified two thematic 'governance gaps' that globalising forces have left in their wake. The first, an operational gap, opens up 'whenever policymakers and public institutions have simply found themselves lacking the information, knowledge and tools they need to respond to the daunting complexity of policy issues in a liberalizing, technologizing, globalizing world'. Second, a 'participatory gap has manifested itself as this same increasing complexity thwarts common understanding of, and therefore agreement on, critical policy issues. This has sometime led policymakers, intentionally or not, to exclude the general public or particular stakeholders from their deliberations'.[43] The world view on offer here and elsewhere is that an effective (if not comprehensive) global governance – enlarged, informed, networked and strengthened – will extend to accommodate the common affairs of humanity, even when they manifest themselves in matters as considerable – and global – as climate change. Conceived in this way, the work before us, then, is 'the coordination of formal and informal relations between states and other entities that operate on the international stage, i.e., a global governance framework'.[44]

Yet what might and indeed what needs to comprise global governance is not self-evident; and it is by no means clear that the sum of many governances – 'global' in different ways and to varying degrees – will deliver us something sufficient to ensure a stable and sustainable human future. For example, the World Trade Organization can fairly be characterised as an institutional mechanism for the global governance of world trade, but the environmental and human security impacts of its strictures are a source of considerable misgiving.[45] So it is open to question whether numerous global governances, including the global governance of world trade, are sufficiently compatible to deliver a global governance overall – that is, one that is politically viable, environmentally sustainable and inclusive of human well-being. There is a danger that the superficially attractive idea of a summative global governance masks the kinds of differences and antagonisms that are a mainstay of practically every other approach to politics. So if like the *New York Times* proclaiming its contents to be 'all the news that's fit to print', global governance is all that we see fit to govern, we are still left with the question of adequacy. Are our social and political orders – and the physical systems on which they are dependent and with which they interact – so discrete that the adequacy of a summative global governance can safely be taken for granted?

The argument of the chapters that follow is that we will shortly enter an era of crisis in global public policy, brought about only in part by our rigid, unintegrated and variously inadequate institutions of regulation and control.[46]

It is already plain that many configurations of human activity – political, industrial, consumerist – are capable of producing planetary impacts directly, cumulatively and (in unforeseen ways) synergistically – and many of the most considerable (radioactive contamination; species extinction; genetic manipulation; climate change) are not discrete events, but enter our natural and political environments as active constituents. So arguments about whether government can be demonstrated as sharing some part of the regulatory field with less familiar modes of governance, and whether a change in the number and relative power of the players will result in any significant change to the game, while significant, is less important than what might be afoot outside of that field. Metaphorically, how serious does a crowd disturbance have to become before it overwhelms the game? In both sectoral and aggregate terms, it is not self-evident that a more inter-connected political arena can address the conditions, determinants and limits of a sustainable human future. Whether these can be identified, agreed upon and brought within the bounds of governance mechanisms is not something that can be addressed by considerations of the relative power and effectiveness of various actors alone.

Although the recognition of a global arena to human affairs is implicit in the politics of climate change and the negotiations to address ozone layer depletion, there is a distinct reluctance to engage the notion of 'global governance' except as a greatly augmented multilateralism.[47] Because global governance studies are closely allied to International Relations theorising and because there is no supranational authority – and in terms of political organisation, no forms more authoritatively extensive than international bodies – there is an understandable reluctance to consider 'global governance' beyond the bounds of sectoral concerns and actor-specific issues of power, authority and accountability. Perhaps the most direct way of considering the necessary scope of global governance in a global, as distinct from an international, arena is to ask what an adequate global governance would be the governance *of*? What portion of the human condition requires active management – our governance – in order to ensure a stable and sustainable human future? Are there anthropogenic dynamics which, once set in train, will fall outside the reach of present and, perhaps, any conceivable governance system? Do we, or could we have global governance *of* the world *through* global governance 'in' the world? If not – and in the absence of any prospect of world government – will the ad hoc, sectoral governances which are said to comprise global governance suffice?

The contention here is that a global governance which is abstracted from the human capacity and propensity to generate systemic change differs little from Realist International Relations theorising in making two key assumptions. The first is that change will occur within and between rather than to systems – essentially, that the natural and political orders that make governance possible can largely be taken as given. The second assumption follows from this: that challenges can be met by adaptations to existing governance systems and by technological innovation. In other words, despite the complexity and dynamism of human–natural interactions, that our governance mechanisms will be adequate as reactive systems; and that we can afford to adopt a problem-solving disposition in the face of a changed and changing, acting and acted-upon global environment.

4 The interaction of human and natural systems

It is instructive to consider the sources of what can incontrovertibly be regarded as global issues or crises on a global scale, such as ozone layer depletion, climate change, biodiversity loss, the depletion of fish stocks in the world's oceans and the destruction of its remaining rainforests. All have manifested themselves as a consequence of countless, mostly mundane acts. It is now clear, for example, that the effects of driving a private motor vehicle are not merely local in a world in which there are now some 671 million others, together with a host of other carbon-emitting sites. More poignantly but no less meaningful is the spectacle of landless families clearing rainforest – or being paid to do so – as a means of securing a bare subsistence. These kinds of situations are not confined to the environmental realm, as a number of serious, unexpected financial crises in recent years have demonstrated. The underlying meaning of financial crises is not readily grasped in part because 'The typical economic model rules out the possibility that simple mistakes can take on a momentum of their own. Instead, they presume that mistakes will cancel themselves out or that self-regulating market forces will correct the mistakes. Unfortunately, these models rest on assumptions that are both severe and unrealistic.'[1]

There is a second notable feature to these alarming developments. It is that they are not discrete problems, contained or containable. To take but one, climate change is itself a complex and highly dynamic phenomenon which threatens a host of other widespread, highly intractable environmental and human crises. These are no longer confined to such matters as declining bird populations and thawing Arctic tundra, serious though they are: In February 2004, *New Scientist* reported the first human diaspora occasioned by climate change:

> The tiny South Pacific nation of Tuvalu was braced this week for high tides that could flood parts of its nine small coral-island atolls. The low-lying nation, halfway between Australia and Hawaii, is one of the most threatened by rising sea levels. One small island, Te Pukasavilivili, has already gone.[2]

Likewise in the financial world, 'What looked like a manageable problem in Thailand [in 1997] flared up into a continents-spanning emerging markets crisis that soon threaten[ed] broader deflationary damage. Even seasoned observers [were] stunned by the speed and multiple channels of the contagion – capital flight, declining commodity prices, portfolio readjustments away from emerging markets, highly leveraged hedge funds reversing gears.'[3]

It is not difficult to catalogue currents of change that are not merely linear and predictable, but that can spread within and between the human and environmental realms; that can arise suddenly and outside of our calculus of planning and risk assessment; and that can reconfigure important environments (both natural environments and operational ones) and relations of interdependence and causation. To understand these phenomena and to grasp the difficulties they present for global governance, we need to understand complex systems.

Systems

The world is not atomistic. There are few purposes for which the reduction of living creatures and observable phenomena to the sum of their parts would be productive because organisation and exchange are fundamental to all life and activity. The properties of the constituent chemicals of a corpse offer no account of a living creature, nor can we predict the behaviour of water from our knowledge of hydrogen and oxygen molecules. An understanding of life and life processes does not rest on whether a whole is more or less than the sum of its parts – it is both: the individual parts are constrained in some particulars while in an organised state, but at the same time, greatly enabled as elements of an ordered configuration.[4] These aggregates are systems.

> A system is a set of interrelated elements which interacts dynamically with its environment. For any given system, an environment is the set of all elements outside the system whose attributes affect the system, and also whose attributes are changed by the behaviour of the system. What is considered to be a system as distinct from its environment depends upon the level of analysis and the problem at hand.[5]

The human body is a system, but we can also speak meaningfully of (and treat) its several sub-systems – cardio-vascular, endocrine, immune. In each case, matters of nutrition, infection and other exchanges within the body itself (the 'interrelated elements,' above) impact upon the functioning of each subsystem; and the integrity and co-ordination of the subsystems determines the health of the body as a whole – and the health of the human person. In the same way, a given geographic region can contain many ecosystems, each with its interrelated elements and each affecting and being affected by the larger ecosystems of which they are a part. The internal workings of economies and their relationship to larger economic structures and forces can be viewed in much the same way.

Table 4.1 Categories of systems

Type	Chief characteristic	Example
Static systems	existence	chair
Metabolic systems	subsistence	river; fire
Self-sustaining systems	effectiveness; freedom of action	simple organisms
Self-organising systems	adaptability	ecosystems; human organisations
Non-isolated systems	coexistence	predators; firms
Self-replicating systems	reproduction	organisms; human organisations; culture
Sentient systems	psychological needs	humans; animals
Conscious systems	ethical reference	individual and collective human actors

Adapted from Hartmut Bossel, *Earth at a Crossroads: Paths to a Sustainable Future* (Cambridge: Cambridge University Press, 1998), pp. 38–40.

Systems are vulnerable to environmental stress: organisms die from sudden and/or excessive changes in their conditions; entire ecosystems can degrade; and human organisations, from families to empires, are subject to collapse from external pressures. So the parameters within which the dynamic interaction between systems and their environment take place are not limitless, nor in many cases highly elastic.

> Systems are nets of *relations* which are sustained through time. The processes by which they are sustained are the process of *regulation*. The limits within which they can be sustained are the conditions of their *stability*.[6]

Unlike homeostasis in biological systems, regulation in many human systems is a deliberative process. And although human freedom is conditioned by our place in natural systems and constrained by our participation in human ones, another range of capabilities, both individual and collective, are also uniquely enabled by the latter. The consequences are not always benign. The meaning of the literature on sustainability and 'sustainable growth' is in a recognition that humanity is fast approaching and in some cases has actually breached environmental limits. These radical, disruptive adjustments are dependent on an inter-relatedness between human systems and their environments which is not simple and linear, because the systems on both sides of these exchanges are complex systems.

Complexity and complex systems

The dynamics of change and stability, and of adaptation and continuity have never ceased to be a source of fascination, for intellectual as well as for practical reasons. There are endless matters which prompt speculative enquiry and scientific research under these themes: the evolution of life; how best to establish and run human organisations for set purposes; why stock markets fluctuate in the way that they do – and sometimes crash; how ecosystems cope with stresses and variables. There is an everyday recognition that some systems exhibit behaviours – that they are responsive and adaptive, generally robust in the face of challenges and capable of change while retaining their own integrity and continuity. These qualities characterise organisms and organic systems – hives, ecosystems, human organisations, the brain; but also human language and aggregates such as markets. These are all *complex* systems. We also recognise that other systems, however many parts they comprise, are not capable of direct interaction with their environments. These are said to be complicated. Cars and computers are *complicated* systems.

The direct examination of complexity has its modern origins in the field of cybernetics, itself an outgrowth of collaborative work between biologists and engineers during the Second World War. Cybernetics can be defined as the 'science concerned with how systems organise, regulate and reproduce themselves, and also how they evolve and learn'.[7] Recently, a more fundamental complexity science has developed as a multidisciplinary effort, its purpose described by the leading centre of this endeavour, the Santa Fe Institute, to '[understand] the common themes that arise in natural, artificial, and social systems [which] attempts to uncover the mechanisms that underlie the deep simplicity present in our complex world'.[8] Much of this work is expressed in mathematical terms and at the leading, abstract edge of the disciplines concerned, which is at some remove from the competences and interests of most social scientists. Nevertheless, a literature on complexity and its meanings for a less scientifically oriented readership has recently developed;[9] and studies of the applicability of complexity for some aspects of the social sciences have now appeared[10] (although notably, not in the global governance literature).

Complexity is not a fixed attribute, but a quality of and capacity for relatedness shared by biological, social and technological systems alike. Whether general laws can be discovered which will throw light on the mechanisms of markets as well as evolution; and whether complexity science will further both cognitive neuroscience and economic prediction is outside the scope of this enquiry. The subject here is the attributes which do appear to be common to all complex systems and their implications for both creating order and for generating disorder.

> Complex systems are not just complicated systems. A snowflake is complicated, but the rules for generating it are simple. The structure of the snowflake, moreover, persists unchanged, and crystalline, from the

moment of its existence until it melts, while complex systems change over time. It is true that a turbulent river rushing through the narrow channel of rapids changes over time too, but it changes chaotically. The kind of change characteristic of complex systems lies somewhere between the pure order of crystalline snowflakes and the disorder of chaotic or turbulent flow.[11]

Chaos and chaos theory are not included in this discussion. This is because it is not at all clear what the study of turbulence can add to the study of complex systems; its inclusion in social science contexts invites the kinds of reductionist relativism which have no bearing on this argument; and because it can be turned to what Terry Eagleton has termed, 'the political ambivalences of postmodernism'.[12]

What brings the properties of complex systems into play is that their many parts can be connected in multiple ways. Consider the road transport system of any developed country. Both infrastructurally and operationally, it is connected in innumerable ways to other systems, both domestic and foreign: raw materials extraction, manufacture and importation – not least the products of the oil industry; land use; the spatial arrangement and maintenance of urban spaces; the organisation and conduct of industry and commerce; health; social mobility. There are also environmental consequences, local and global; direct and indirect. As one study of the rapid development of motor vehicle traffic in China noted:

> For Chinese cities, the automobile means a whole new way of life for the residents of the world's most populous country, offering levels of personal mobility previously unthinkable. For global car manufacturers, China offers one of the biggest markets in the world. The benefits, will, however, exact a terrible toll on the urban environment and the quality of public spaces and human interaction in Chinese cities, as the automobile has in countless other cities. Accommodating the automobile will also have a big impact on China's land supply for agriculture and on its economy through a whole range of new costs.[13]

What soon becomes clear is that although complex systems can be thought of as 'nested' – each encompassing one smaller – their lines of significant relation are not hierarchically determined or limited. The insights from ecology are probably most instructive in this regard; and to the general insights it provides, we can add the now-common instances of exotic species introductions between distant ecosystems, with their disruptive and destructive potential.[14] The 'world without walls' promised by the champions of free trade[15] remains a world in which complex systems other than industry and commerce can be brought into close relationship by an intensification of globalised patterns of interaction. No one intends, say, that the potential for an infectious disease to become a pandemic should be heightened by trade or tourism, but that potential and many others are implicit in a great deal of the interaction between complex systems, much of which is unmediated – and unanticipated. The SARS virus is estimated to have cost Asian economies some US$28 billion.[16]

Complex system interaction is not confined to linear exchanges, in the manner of billiard balls. This is because they are subject to feedback: information about on-going processes is 'fed back' into the system so that any necessary adjustment can be made. The common example used to illustrate feedback is a room thermostat, which adjusts its output according to the feedback it receives – in this case, the temperature of the room in which it is sited, measured against the setting of the thermostat. Living organisms make similar adjustments: without feedback, homeostasis (the maintenance of stable internal temperature, acidity/alkalinity levels and other essentials) would not be possible. Governments will intervene in an economy to stimulate growth or to dampen inflation and will either ease or increase such measures according to the pertinent feedback, such as a cost of living index, house prices or consumer spending. Feedback is implicit in descriptions of complex systems as *self-regulating*; indeed, the well-known Gaia hypothesis argues that the planet itself is a self-regulating system for the maintenance of conditions necessary for the continuance of life.[17]

In addition to feedback, 'the diverse components [of complex systems] can interact both serially and in parallel to generate sequential as well as simultaneous effects and events'.[18] This can be illustrated by reference to one of the underlying causes of the 1987 stock market crash: the introduction of programmed trading. Computers in the larger trading houses were set to sell stocks at a preset price. Finalising as many as 60 transactions worth billions of dollars in a second, the fall in stock prices quickly developed a momentum detached from human judgement. The billions of transactions soon overloaded computers not designed to handle so much traffic.[19] These transactions were at first parallel (that is, each computerised system acted on the basis of 'normal' fluctuations of the stock market) and then serial (in a very rapid sequence, computers acted on the activity of other computers, with the cumulative effects triggering an avalanche of programmed trading). The simultaneous effects are what came to be known as Black Monday.

Three more formal characteristics of complex systems follow from the qualities outlined above.

Complex systems are open and adaptive

They are open in the sense that they are not isolated or sealed off from their environments. As described by Geoffrey Vickers,

> Open systems depend on and contribute to their surround and are thus involved in interdependence with it as well as being dependent on the interaction of internal relationships. This interdependence imposes constraints on all their constituents. Organization can mitigate but not

remove these constraints which tend to become more demanding and sometimes even more contradictory as the scale of organization rises. This places a limit, though usually not a predictable one, on the possibilities of organization.[20]

And the adaptability of complex systems is not confined to the maintenance of system integrity. Because they are open and interdependent, complex systems change themselves *and* their environments. For example, infectious disease agents are capable of mutating in response to the prolonged use of anti-microbial drugs with the result that new, multi-drug-resistant strains of tuberculosis are now a major global health threat;[21] and nosocomial infections from other drug-resistant microbes are increasing.[22] Moreover, the properties and capacities of complex systems in the natural world combine with our structured systems of interdependence in ways so complex that we sometimes become aware of them only after the fact. This was the case with the export of BSE – 'mad cow disease' as it is called – and the threat it carries of human infection in the form of vJCD. In the following, note the openness of microbial, agricultural and trading systems to one another and their adaptability – in this case, with deleterious consequences:

> It started out as a British disease, but the UK exported it and then its trading partners spread it even further afield. Now no country can be sure it has kept BSE out. Mad cows have gone global. To date, 24 countries have declared cases of BSE and it seems almost certain that many more are affected. BSE spreads when infected cattle are rendered into meat and bone meal (MBM), and fed to other cows. In 1991, at the height of its mad cow epidemic, the UK exported more than 25,000 tonnes of MBM. The stuff it sent to Europe did not contain brains, spinal cords or intestines (so-called 'specified risk materials') which carry most of the infection, but the MBM it sent outside Europe did. That year alone Thailand bought 6,240 tonnes. Other big buyers were Taiwan, Singapore and Indonesia. They sold some of it on to other countries, probably including China. After the UK stopped exporting MBM in 1996, other European countries took over the market, insisting they had no BSE – until 2000, when BSE exploded across Europe. Then the US, also denying it was at risk, took over Europe's markets. Last December, the US found its first mad cow.[23]

Complex systems are self-organising

The order of the natural world is neither designed nor brought about by purposive action. The wonder and beauty of the evolution of life is in its ability to assume increasingly complex organisational forms through self-organisation and adaptation; and in contingency, not teleological development.[24] The stark reality of processes that are powerful and directional but purposeless is difficult to confront and carries with it both the residual resistance to evolutionary theory and the larger philosophical questions that attend the frontiers of complexity science.[25]

> Since the self-organizing process is not guided or determined by specific goals, it is often difficult to talk about the *function* of such a system. As soon as we introduce the notion of function, we run the risk either of anthropomorphising, or introducing an external reason for the structure of the system . . . When a system is described within the context of a larger system, it is possible to talk of the function of the sub-system *only within that context*. We can talk of the 'function' of the endocrine system of a lion with reference to the lion, but then it is difficult to simultaneously talk about the function of the lion itself. We can talk about the 'function' of predators in an ecosystem, but then not the function of the ecosystem. The notion of function is intimately linked to our *descriptions* of complex systems. The process of self-organization cannot be driven by the attempt to perform a function; it is rather the result of an evolutive process whereby a system will simply not survive if it cannot adapt to more complex circumstances.[26]

The capacity of complex systems for self-organisation with structural outcomes is sometimes described as 'emergence':

> Sometimes . . . the properties of [a] system emerge simply as a result of the connectivity of very simple components in a network. In the most extreme cases the parts do not individually perform any activities that can be characterized in terms of what the system does. [. . .] The surprising feature of these networks is that the pattern of connections results in systemic properties that would not be anticipated by focusing on the contributions of component units.[27]

Self-organisation is also a feature of human organisations: the ability and conscious desire to learn and the independence of human agents accounts for some measure of this. An interesting study of the corrosive effects of the deliberate frustration of what can best be described as organisational learning in newly-automated factory processes concluded: 'Obedience has been the axial principle of task execution in the traditional environment of imperative control. The logic of that environment is reproduced when technology is used only to automate. When tasks require intellective effort, however, obedience can be dysfunctional and can impede the exploitation of information.'[28] The independence and responsiveness of people also manifests itself in larger and less directly managed human enterprises and can lead to self-organised groupings and outcomes. As we have seen, much of the history of human rights can be recounted in this way; and so too can the organisational and operational history of the UN, particularly by dint of the normative expectations it has created outside of its organisational boundaries. Governments need frequently to intervene in economies not only because of factors external to their routine functioning, but also because of outcomes brought about by self-organisation. The steady state equilibrium and rational actor of classical economics is in short supply everywhere.[29]

Much as evolutionary theory has replaced creationism, so has the necessity of governance replaced the notion of human 'dominion' over the earth. The domain is one of complex, self-organising systems – those we create as well as those we confront. However, the natural world is now subject to direct manipulation and re-ordering at the genetic level with possibilities for interaction and adaptation with complex systems of every kind that can scarcely be guessed at. In Canada, three pigs genetically modified to produce proteins for the pharmaceutical industry have been released into the food chain without tests for human safety. And according to Greenpeace, on a previous occasion, 'eleven genetically engineered pigs from the University of Guelph were fed to chickens in Southern Ontario'.[30] In light of the regulatory failures that led to the spread of BSE (above), these actions seem reckless in respect of immediate risks to human health; more profoundly, they suggest that we little appreciate that self-organisation and adaptation in the natural realm are blind to human welfare.

Complex systems co-evolve

The process of mutual adaptation has cumulative effects and systematic outcomes, so the fitness of organisms to their environment, and of an environment to the organisms it contains, are two expressions of a single reality: they co-evolve. In this context, the term 'evolution' applies both in the Darwinian sense and it also describes accommodation processes of many kinds, on very much shorter time-scales than the subjects of evolutionary science. The evolutionary metaphor is quite apt to describe the ways in which human communities have found a productive and sustainable balance internally and with their environment, even when this has involved extensive interventions such as the establishment of agricultural systems:

> In the coevolutionary explanation, experimental knowledge, both individual and collective, is maintained in the belief systems of each culture. Experiments with alternative social structure uncovered organizational forms which enhance people's ability to interact with their environment as well as with each other. Simultaneously, people intervene in the environment, and if the environmental response is favourable, they establish myths and forms of social organization to rationalize and encourage the intervention by individuals and thereby maintain the favourable environmental response. Hence myth and social organization are selected according to their fitness to the environment. At the same time, the fitness of environmental changes are determined in part by whether they fit people's myths and social organization. In this manner,

social and environmental systems coevolve such that environmental systems reflect the characteristics of social systems – their knowledge, values,
social organization, and technologies – while social systems reflect the
characteristics of environmental systems – their mix of species, rates of
productivity, spatial and temporal variation, and resilience.[31]

Coevolutionary development extends to processes within and between human
systems.[32] The advance of integration of computers into human systems of
every kind has required innumerable adjustments in employment patters, the
organisation and conduct of business, teaching and learning and scholarship.

There is also a negative side.

Complexity and global governance

The direct contribution of complexity theory to governance and global
governance is limited, but not negligible. Clearly, 'we lack a theory of how
the elements of our public lives link into webs of elements that act on one
another and transform one another';[33] and even the predictive potential of the
theoretical work on complexity would appear to be constrained by complex
systems' sensitivity to initial conditions (the so-called 'butterfly effect'). James
Rosenau rightly points out that

> it is when our panacean impulses turn us toward complexity theory for
> guidance in the framing of exact predictions that the payoffs are least likely
> to occur and our disillusionment is most likely to intensify. The strides
> that complexity theorists have made with their mathematical models and
> computer simulations are still a long way from amounting to a science
> that can be relied upon for exactitude in charting the course of human
> affairs that lies ahead. Indeed, to a large extent theorists continue to be
> confounded by the behaviour of complex systems.[34]

But the ability to discern the trajectories or to calculate the probabilities of
the interaction of many complex systems, invaluable though they might be,
would not lift us out of the human predicament. No theory or group of theories
could encapsulate or meaningfully eliminate or reduce what we take to be the
human essentials of the large-scale change we bring about: human need;
confected human wants; social psychology; and unparalleled numbers and
kinds of environmental, social and technological linkages. Uncovering the
mathematical and physical underpinnings of life processes, or laws of order
underlying system exchange will not, on their own, tell us how to live. The
contribution that evolutionary theory and of neo-Darwinian perspectives
within established disciplines can make to the conduct of life are similarly
oblique: we learn something of contingency; of the deep sources of human
impulses and cognition; of requisite variety; and perhaps, of limits. But we are
still faced with choice – and sometimes with dilemmas; and a good deal of

human behaviour is focused on immediate concerns, or is self-interested or non-rational. Perhaps much of this can be reliably modelled, but that informs rather than forces political choice. Our climate change predictions are imperfect but sufficient to indicate the direction and momentum of our ways of life, yet our efforts to reverse the trends are halting at best. Would scientific certainty, even if it could be secured, dramatically alter the political processes involved?

So what is the contribution of complexity theory to global governance? Its most immediate contribution is to deepen our understanding of the human condition. On first sight, the abstractions of complexity theory might seem remote from our most pressing concerns, but they offer us a more nuanced understanding of interdependence; and some insight into the wide-ranging, multiple lines of causation and adaptation at the heart of large-scale interactions within and between complex systems, both human and natural. In much the same way that the science of ecology has gradually been moving understanding of our relationship with the environment from hierarchy and dominance to web-of-life and interdependence, insights gleaned from the study of complexity can contribute to a clearer understanding of uncertainty and risk. Comprehending and acknowledging the extent of our ignorance is an important beginning.

In conjunction with quantifiable increases in globalisation, an awareness of complexity might also lend itself to a less compartmentalised understanding of our operating environments, now so easily and frequently conjoined, whatever we intend. Yet it is notable that some of the more robust defences of globalisation concentrate on economic globalisation[35] to the exclusion of a great deal of what follows in its wake, including the necessity of extending and refining governance mechanisms. To the extent that global governance facilitates or manages the machinery of globalisation – the WTO, for example – contradictions, dilemmas and trade-offs with negative implications for the human security of at least some groups, or for certain aspects of the environment, are certain to arise. Moreover, a great deal of the work of global governance is belated, remedial or a race to keep pace with new globalising dynamics, the consequences of which are sometimes disregarded, or tolerated as an acceptable or unavoidable price. At other times, these consequences are unanticipated; and sometimes intractable or unmanageable, at least in the short term or by already-established means. Complexity theory helps us to grasp that as the linkages between human systems grow in number and speed and as ecosystem resilience declines, feedback loops will be more numerous, more rapid and will have more immediate impact. Our global environmental crises with their varied consequences and threatening possibilities illustrate this. The sum of these points, to be discussed in the following chapters, is to make the governance enterprise much less sure-footed; less a technocratic, problem-solving endeavour in a world whose stability can largely be taken for granted, or righted by largely familiar means. There is much to applaud in the efforts being made to understand complexity and the wondrously rich but unforgiving relational webs that life sustains and humanity creates; and certainly further crises on the scale we have already endured will be a poor substitute for this kind of learning.

This brief introduction to formal understandings of complexity cannot do justice to complexity science, but it does qualify the way in which the phrase 'complex interaction of human and natural systems' is employed in what follows, here and in following chapters. The 'complex' in the phrase is intended to indicate the full weight and meaning of complex systems and their capacities; it is not merely a synonym for 'complicated' or 'difficult'. The delineation of complex systems into human and natural is a convenience which helps to distinguish our governance efforts in respect of the environment and environmental crises. An understanding of humanity being *of* the world as well as *in* it is implicit. Hereafter, the phrase 'global dynamics' is a generic term for interactions between human and natural systems. The sense in which 'global dynamics' is employed here denotes interactions of human and natural systems which, though rooted in familiar physical, social, industrial and political arenas, are considerably more than the background hum to human affairs; and also more than the issues or problems they routinely generate.

Global governance and the interaction of human and natural systems

A large part of what we understand to be the human condition rests on the expectation of the continuance of natural orders – 'natural systems' as the term is used here.[36] Their routine fluctuations, occasional volatility and even some degree of unpredictability occur within familiar and generally life-sustaining bounds. All human dramas are played out within this arena, however much our necessary abstractions might make the natural world appear as a static backdrop. There are also distinct human systems which, although they operate within and ultimately depend on natural systems, are functionally driven by human ends. On this characterisation, farming is a human system, while the soil ecology on which it is practised is a natural system; and on a much larger scale, the world trading and currency exchange systems are clearly human systems. As human numbers have grown, resource extraction and use has intensified, industrialisation and consumerism have expanded and ecosystem resilience has declined. In addition, the engineered complexity of much of our infrastructure has extended and grown. As a result, many of the larger global issues which now beset us – practically, politically and morally – either arise from the complex interaction of human and natural systems, or quickly impact on them.

A few qualifications are in order. The more ordinary forms of inter-state contention persist, instances of which are as global in their implications as they are international in their structure – one need only think of the nuclear arms race between the Soviet Union and the United States; and more recently, the nuclear rivalry between India and Pakistan. But there is also a legacy from years of atmospheric nuclear tests;[37] and the problem of disposal of the highly radioactive waste that has been generated as a result of these weapons programmes.[38] In the case of biological weapons research, the links between human and natural systems are more clear, even if the implications and malign possibilities are not. Likewise, resource geopolitics can usefully be abstracted from the dynamics of the natural world,[39] but the burning of fossil fuels and the depletion of the world's ocean fisheries soon make themselves felt, environmentally as well as politically. A second qualification is that although complex global dynamics sometimes manifest themselves in quite dramatic fashion, it would be misleading to think of these interactions as titanic clashes. For the most part, the quality of complex systems – openness, adaptation and emergence – mean that small-scale, incremental change is sufficient, over time and on a large enough scale, to bring about quite substantial changes, within human systems themselves (the collapse of the Soviet Union is instructive here), or in the physical environment.

We can identify three fundamental kinds of change brought about by global dynamics, each greatly reinforced by the still-accelerating processes of globalisation; and each fundamental to our prospects for conceiving and exercising global governance.

Systemic change

For the largest part of human history, ecosystem resilience in combination with relatively small and technologically unempowered populations made unsustainable ways of life possible – for some; and in the short term – instances of which persist, driven by political and economic interests and much abetted by technical prowess.[40] The now familiar catalogue of environmental degradation and destruction, its pace and extent, would once have been inconceivable, let alone achievable. Yet there is a huge qualitative difference between the mostly localised and incremental ecosystem damage that pre- and early-industrialised populations could wreak and the kinds of global change we have now brought about. The point is not merely that a body of water as considerable as the Aral Sea could be destroyed, but that we are now also capable of introducing *systemic* change – on a global scale. The full range of environmental systems subject to anthropogenic change interact with one another, vastly complicating both comprehension (the subject of Chapter 5) and political calculation, including varieties of global governance (Chapter 6).

There are, of course, fundamental natural processes – the physics, chemistry and biology which drive periodic geophysical and ecological upheavals[41] and more generally sustain the conditions for the continuance of life on the planet.[42] Given the size and distribution of the human species and our impact upon the global environment, from biodiversity to the ozone layer, it is doubtful that any of the planet's life-sustaining physical dynamics are unaffected by human activity. And although we cannot meaningfully consider the governance of natural global systems ('nature'), we do nevertheless profoundly impact them – not as 'damage' in a fixed sense, but as *alterations to their functioning and to their interactions*. For example, climate change is less an event than a threshold – a manifestation of (worsening) aggregate anthropogenic dynamics and their effects on atmosphere physics and chemistry. In turn, altered climate has already begun to drive a variety of large-scale changes in other fundamental global dynamics.

Altered and/or amplified natural dynamics can then cascade back into human systems of every kind, from huge disruptions in agricultural production to altered patterns of the transmission of vector-borne diseases.[43] More worryingly, disturbances to the balance of the planet's biological, oceanic, atmospheric, climatic and thermal dynamics present us with the possibility that positive feedback loops could create runaway global warming.[44] Although calculating the precise 'tipping point' for such a disaster might not be possible, this potential is inherent in our understanding of complexity and complex systems. From the perspective of global governance, what is most compelling in this and related scenarios is that the behaviour of these dynamics would no longer operate within familiar or predictable bounds. The necessary abstractions of International Relations and governance theorising do not imply that the essential orders of human life are fixed, or cannot or have not been disturbed; nevertheless, they necessarily encompass only willed activity rather than powerful natural dynamics which, once altered and/or amplified, can continue to shape the conditions for human security, outside of human agency.

Human systems are also susceptible to systemic change. Human systems are distinct from, although of course they operate within and are ultimately dependent on, natural ones. The functioning of the world trading system, and the world-wide, continuous, electronic exchange of currencies are at a sufficient remove from the natural dynamics which underpin them to warrant this abstraction. Yet because non-linear dynamics are not confined to the natural world, complex human systems can, like natural systems, also exhibit unanticipated system behaviours. This is not as widely appreciated as it needs to be. For example, as part of achieving his ideal of achieving 'friction-free capitalism', Microsoft Chairman Bill Gates is confident that 'The information highway will extend the electronic marketplace and make it the ultimate go-between, the universal middleman, thus bringing us efficient electronic markets that provide nearly complete instantaneous information about worldwide supply, demand, and prices.'[45] However, computer models suggest that because ' . . . [electronic] agents are not subject to the restraints that normally slow economic activity. . . . Economic booms and busts will become more frequent and more severe if . . . software agents control electronic commerce.'[46]

The combination of complexity and speed of many human systems, much abetted by computerisation, raises difficult, perplexing questions about our ability to exercise governance over many of the systems we ourselves have created. In his study of high-risk technologies, Charles Perrow noted,

Complex systems tend to have more elaborate control centres not because they make life easier for the operators, saving steps or time, nor because there is necessarily more machinery to control, but because components must interact in more than linear, sequential ways, and therefore may interact in unexpected ways.[47]

Not knowing and being unable to ascertain what risks and vulnerabilities are thereby entailed is itself problematic; and the ongoing consolidation of globalisation further extends and entrenches this facet of life. But what we wind up with is not only the risk that arises from complexity, but also *complex risk* – hazards, susceptibilities and uncertainties which are sometimes acknowledged and controlled as far as we are able; sometimes unwilled and unanticipated; of varying degrees of calculability; and within, between or altogether outside of existing modes of regulation and control. Risk does indeed feature largely in our lives, not as a looming, disabling shadow but as an integral, enduring feature of the human condition, now that the unco-ordinated and undirected activity of global humanity combines unprecedented speed and interconnectedness.

Once systemic change is brought about, it will not always be reversible – this is certainly the case with biodiversity loss; and it needs to be borne in mind that systemic change either in natural or human environments will engender adaptations in other, related complex systems and sub-systems. So on the largest scale, remedial action might not always be possible, a point familiar to those who remind us that species conservation cannot meaningfully be separated from habitat conservation.[48] Similarly, there is compelling evidence that some species require a 'critical mass' – high population densities in order to reproduce (the Allee Effect).[49]

Complex system interaction produces public policy problems of unprecedented complexity and difficulty

The engines of globalisation can variously facilitate, spread, amplify and complicate what might otherwise remain unproblematic or localised relations. Examples abound: the HIV/AIDS pandemic;[50] the introduction and dissemination of 100,000 synthetic chemicals in the last century;[51] the exigencies of intensive agriculture in developed and developing countries alike;[52] and, as we have seen, the spread of multi-drug resistant microbes;[53] and invasive species ('bio-invasions').[54] Alterations and stresses introduced into non-linear ecosystem dynamics, furthered by the efficiencies of globalisation, are visibly multiplying the number of global issues that now beset us. The 1999 World Disasters Report, predicting a 'decade of super-disasters', warns that widespread acknowledgement of ' . . . [the] environmental problems of global warming and deforestation on the one hand, and the social problems of increasing poverty and growing shanty towns on the other' only give us partial comprehension of what is probably in store, for ' . . . when these two factors collide, you have a new scale of catastrophe'.[55]

In addition, the possible dangers of more routine release of genetically modified plants and animals into the environment will present us with a further, profound risk of systemic change, no more calculable for having been engineered rather than appearing as the 'disregarded externalities' of industrial and consumerist pollution. And against what we already know of accident proneness in system design and operation, biotechnology presents us with ' . . . a far more fearsome potential for an ecosystem accident where little attempt is made to insure that human-created and human-imposed systems can remain in a proper equilibrium'.[56]

The kinds of issue to be found within relatively discrete human systems are no less vexed. The varieties of governance issues surrounding information, knowledge and knowledge products have burgeoned, still largely centred around possession, ownership and control. Now, copyright in everything from the human genome to the images of the famous have joined more familiar information-rich control issues, such as pharmaceuticals. But the recent anthrax terrorist outrages in the United States reveal a complex of human systems centred around biotechnology which are deeply embedded in our ways of life and widely dispersed. Biotechnology is a disseminative system[57] (discussed in full in Chapter 7). That is, fundamental research, data, knowledge, applications and infrastructure are widely held and easy to transmit, share, sell and acquire. The epistemic communities involved are transnational networks; the necessary materials and equipment are available in open markets; the knowledge and expertise is available at institutions throughout the world. We have long regarded this aspect of globalisation as being to the good of humanity at large – but what happens when we are faced with the dangerous misuse of biological knowledge? This is a novel and deeply perplexing issue. The misuse of physics by malign, non-state groups for the purpose of making nuclear devices was not feasible for much of the nuclear age, because the manufacture of fissile material was hugely expensive, technologically sophisticated and required highly specialised knowledge at the leading edge of the field – in short, it was relatively easy to control centrally, by states. The revolution in biotechnology reverses this, but the dangers – environmental, social and political as well as military – are every bit as profound. Against the dark possibilities opening up through the revolution in biological sciences and their highly dispersed competences and practical requisites, consider once again the following depiction of the growth of non-state governance mechanisms:

> [S]ystems of rule can be maintained and their controls successfully and consistently exerted even in the absence of established legal or political authority. The evolution of intersubjective consensuses based on shared fates and common histories, the possession of information and knowledge, the pressure of active or mobilizeable publics, and/or the use of careful planning, good timing, clever manipulation and hard bargaining can

– either separately or in combination – foster control mechanisms that sustain governance without government.[58]

There are numerous configurations of human activity for which this optimism is apposite – it could, for example, stand as a description of the dynamics which informed the campaign to ban landmines. However, the 'clever manipulation and hard bargaining' open to a vast array of human groups will not necessarily take benign form, or be directed toward a recognisable global public good, or be subject to any form of accountability.'[59]

Convergence of human, natural and technological systems

The convergence under discussion here is not to be confused with the 'convergence theory' that appeared in the 1960s. This was a perspective within development theory that worked on the assumption of Western technology being so 'superior' that it would bring all other forms of development onto the same path.[60] The most succinct expression of the way in which human, natural and technological systems have now begun to converge is Jeremy Rifkin's summary of the forces bringing about what he has termed the 'biotech century': ' . . . [T]he genetic revolution and the computer revolution are just now coming together to form a scientific, technological, and commercial phalanx, a powerful new reality that is going to have a profound impact on our personal and collective lives in the coming decades.'[61] This is already well advanced in the agricultural and pharmaceutical industries, but the kinds of convergence made possible by technological advance and urged upon us by various interested parties, although usually presented as efficient and safe, are very often soon embroiled in complicated governance wrangles, both within and between states: 'Anti-biotechnological resistance . . . has impacted multilateral trade and biosafety negotiations, international trade, research investments, intellectual property rights, and marketing decisions by major corporations, and intergovernmental agency relations.'[62] Technological advances, however benign, take their place within an array of complex systems; and the more these converge, the greater the number of interactions – and complications.

Other forms and degrees of convergence are visible in the way in which industrialised societies are now highly dependent on electronic and computerised control and communications systems for their routine functioning; and the way in which a great deal of the most critical environmental monitoring is (and needs to be) satellite-based. Within natural, human and technological systems, there are many further striking instances of convergence: the diminution of planetary biodiversity; loss of cultural and linguistic variety and non-urban ways of life; dependence on and standardisation of long-distance transportation, communication and commerce. US President Eisenhower's 1960 warning against the dangers of a military-industrial complex can be read as an awareness of the dangers of convergence (which also extended to warning about the threats posed by the technological revolution as it was then for the integrity of scientific research and scholarship more generally).[63]

One of the dangers of highly accelerated convergence is that it decreases adaptability, even as it introduces new operating environment variables against which systems must regulate themselves.

A runaway world?

The inventor Thomas Edison once declared, 'What man's genius can create, man's character can control.' As we continue the struggle to control nuclear, biological and other weapons proliferation, to decrease the quantity of atmospheric pollution driving climate change and to prevent ecosystem catastrophe in areas as large as the world's remaining rain forests, that spirit of late Victorian optimism could hardly seem more distant. But what would it mean to say that Edison was wrong, or that from the start of the twenty-first century, his confidence is no longer warranted? In a globalised world, the larger instruments of control are what we now term global governance. Can we say with confidence that what humanity can create, our institutions of global governance can control?

The most difficult challenges facing us do not arise from inventive genius, but from simple, even mundane activities – often, not intentionally destructive. The complexity and complex systems of the natural world that sustain life, variety, growth, resilience and adaptability also support human systems, but our uniqueness does not extend to a special standing in respect of the processes of the natural world. That is why globalisation has brought in its wake greater numbers of interactions between complex systems, with the object of our designs – free trade, wider consumerism, cheaper inter-continental travel, genetically modified life forms – trailing ever-longer and more vexed causal chains. The familiar aphorism, that 'there are in nature no rewards or punishments, just consequences' has real purchase in our present circumstances. The consequences of decades of intense carbon-emitting behaviours, widespread pesticide use and resource extraction are now upon us, as are a range of indirect consequences that follow from the first-order, systemic changes we have brought about. For example, the prospects for global health are impacted, indirectly, but nevertheless seriously, by the systemic alterations of climate change (including disruptions to the planet's hydrological cycle) and bio-diversity loss.[64]

Nor have the products of our inventiveness ever been a simple matter to control: it is difficult to find a single technological advance of significance that has not been weaponised. Now, though, the advent of genomics – something Edison would probably recognise as the product of human genius – places the hugely enabled life sciences at the centre of an array of human systems, including research into weapons development. This has necessitated a considerable span of treaties and regulatory bodies, covering matters as diverse as health, disease, development, trade and the environment, as well as drugs control –

and arms control.[65] Taken together, these prohibitive and regulatory instruments comprise what might generally be regarded as the global governance of biotechnology. But the pace of scientific research conducted in laboratories world-wide, various commercial pressures and the openness, or potential openness, to the natural world of the experiments and outcomes of this science pose quite fundamental questions for the nature and scope of this global governance. For example, in 2001, Imperial College London was fined for a violation of laboratory procedures:

> The prosecution related to laboratory work that was aimed at using genetic modification techniques to construct a hybrid virus by splicing together genes from Hepatitis C virus and Dengue fever virus. The work thus raised important safety considerations because it involved the construction of an artificially-created virus by combining together genetic material from two viruses that are hazardous to humans. In general, such hybrid viruses have been found to be much less virulent than naturally-occurring viruses, but because it is difficult to predict outcome of the modifications at the outset of the experiments, work of this kind is subject to tight regulatory control.[66]

However tight the regulatory controls on laboratory experiments, they exist to facilitate rather than to prevent such experiments; and even within the well-established lego-political framework of the EU,

> [t]he European Commission . . . decided to refer France, Luxembourg, Belgium, Netherlands, Germany, Italy, Ireland, Greece, Spain, Austria and Finland to the European Court of Justice for failing to adopt and notify national legislation implementing an EU law on the deliberate release of genetically modified organisms (GMOs) into the environment. [. . .] The EU law strengthens earlier laws and was adopted to help better ensure a safe, step-by-step approach to releasing GMOs into the environment.[67]

Meanwhile, transgenic plants are now grown commercially on a large scale, even as scientific research is continuing on the possible risks, including inadvertently created 'superweeds' and other unwanted outcomes as a result of genetically modified genes jumping the species barrier.[68] In 2002, 145 million acres in 16 countries were devoted to GM crops.[69] It would appear that the global governance of this one aspect of biotechnology is, like GM crops themselves, all over the map.

Three principal objections can be raised against the suggestion that a world of complexity and complex systems greatly enlarges and even transforms the arena in which global governance must operate.

The first is that in broad historical terms, there is little new in this. William McNeil correlated the rise and fall of empires with the incidence of infectious disease epidemics;[70] and more recently, Mike Davis has demonstrated the ways in which recurrent El Niño weather patterns facilitated British colonial domination in India and, more lastingly, the division of the world into developed and undeveloped though the interaction of world climate and the world economy.[71] What the insurance industry refers to as 'acts of god' are hardly the stuff of governance, and the business of governance includes the mitigation of risk, not the extinction of human vulnerability. However, the scale, intensity and immediacy of human-natural dynamics is of an historically unprecedented order. Ecosystem devastation and resource depletion with planetary implications are not static events, but also entail reconfigurations of the conditions for human life and development.

Second, it could be argued that complex dynamics do not necessarily deliver complex problems – that attending to the densely-woven fabric of the world does not entail tracing every thread. But one need only survey the range of implications of climate change to understand that selective governance to deal with the indirect consequences of unregulated and/or unco-ordinated human activity is already a full, pressing agenda.

Third, one could contend that the perception of limits on our ability to exercise global governance greatly underestimates our capacity for problem-solving; and that we can develop and extend our existing machinery of management and control. However, the limits of a problem-solving approach to governing the human condition are already manifest, not least because as crisis management absorbs a larger part of our energies, comprehension and problem-setting of the kind and on the scale required will move ever further out of reach. More broadly, the interactions of human and natural systems are not only generating relatively discrete problems, but also altered conditions. Our changed and changing environments, physical and political, are not themselves problems open to solutions: for better or worse, they comprise the human condition. The trajectory of unsustainable human activity and its links to the inertia of related globalising forces add to the daunting nature of conceiving coherent political responses to the world we have already made, and give some indication of the paucity of our conceptions of global governance.

A generation ago, Geoffrey Vickers observed that ' . . . both the Western way of life and its chief rivals are challenged by growing instabilities which exceed their regulative powers.'[72] Today, the regulatory challenges are more numerous and more urgent; and the arena is global, whilst the conceptual and practical difficulties, the subject of the next two chapters, are enormous.

5 Global governance
Conceptual challenges

The reassuring resonances of the phrase 'global governance' soon fade when its conceptual development is set beside the nature and scale of global issues – and beside the trajectories of global dynamics.[1] It would certainly be mistaken to conflate governance, global or otherwise, with crisis management. Our capacity to deal with quite serious and threatening crises is already strained; and even though further depletion of the planet's ozone has been halted, the slow progress and still-present contention over climate change is a sharp reminder of the difficulties experienced by our established means of political co-operation in dealing effectively and equitably even with identified and quantifiable threats to human well-being. This does not foreclose the possibilities for creative thinking and imaginative approaches to building humane social futures; however, if we are to do so, we are going to have to face the reality of a globalised human condition and the absence of anything politically effective that might answer to the name 'global polity' let alone world government.

As we have seen, a large portion of the theoretical literature on global governance is concerned with significant actors, the adjustment of power relations between them and their capacity for dealing with exchanges between complex systems, either as part of maintaining routine functioning (the global governance of international finance, for example); or as crisis response (the Asian financial crisis of 1997; ozone layer depletion). This chapter is not directly concerned with the theoretical considerations regarding institutional form or with which non-state groups or networks can claim significant status in the exercise of governance, or world politics more generally. Instead, the focus here is on the difficulties we face in comprehending the meaning and extent of complexity as part of framing and executing public policy.

Comprehending complex, dynamic systems

First of all, there are limitations to comprehensive understanding of the dynamics of open systems, including natural ones, as the following description of the historical development of the ecosystem concept makes plain:

a system's behaviour can never fully be determined, because it entails many interactions, and there are always stochastic elements to be considered. The only way to improve the predictability of a system's behaviour was to take the system out of nature and confine it to a controlled environment, where it could be manipulated experimentally. Ecologists used microcosms and meso-cosms to study ecosystems in this way, which solved one problem but created another. The isolation and closure of the ecosystem ignores the role of other systems that control system behaviour and introduce stochasticity [randomness]. Ecosystems are open systems. Thus, neither the laboratory nor the modelling analogies led to the anticipated advances in knowledge of the ecosystems.[2]

However, challenges to our comprehension of the behaviour of natural systems begin at still more fundamental levels. One difficulty is insufficient data. For example, according to E. O. Wilson, the number of species of bacteria could be as much as a thousand times greater than the number currently recorded.[3] This means that we cannot have any true reckoning of the full extent and meaning of habitat destruction or the disappearance of other, ecologically linked species – with clear implications for the compass of the governance of global biodiversity, particularly in terms of estimating risk. A second, related difficulty is that data alone is not sufficient for comprehending complex dynamics, sometimes because our research agendas and imaginative capacities are not attuned to what the data could reveal. A NASA satellite launched in 1978 made readings of the ozone layer which indicated the hole opening up over the Antarctic, but the computers programmed for the analysis of the data were set to parameters which relegated the low-end readings as 'noise'.[4] It took another six years before ozone layer depletion entered the scientific literature.

The larger point is that the various practical and cognitive limitations (including 'information overload') on our comprehension of open systems are also limitations on our ability to conceive and enact systems of governance. For all of our sophistication – not least, the ability to monitor the earth's atmosphere from space – the depletion of the earth's ozone came as a surprise. This is a sobering reality by which to measure the prospects for the 'global governance of the environment' and related conceptions of planetary management.[5]

The operation of large-scale human systems are no less subject to these constraints – something clearly visible in the interaction of financial markets as electronic networks usher in considerable and often unanticipated system behaviours. Although there remain voices arguing that ' . . . markets would be even more unstable than they are if it were not for the inertia created by laws and customs that supposedly impede markets',[6] a configuration of ideological and corporate interests see in deregulation and globalising technologies the promise of a 'coming global digital stock market' that 'will be available in an orderly, fair, well-regulated, and lower-cost environment, with improved high-tech electronic surveillance of trading to protect the integrity of the markets'.[7] Yet less than a year before this pronouncement was made, the largely unregulated hedge fund industry saw the collapse of Long-Term Capital Management (LTCM). The Chairman of the US Federal Reserve Bank was obliged to defend a publicly organised bail-out, on the reasoning that ' . . . [the fund's] failure could have caused substantial damage to banks and investors and might have impaired the economies of many nations, including the United States'.[8] Yet the subsequent government investigation revealed that even estimating the size of the industry was difficult;[9] and when asked how the collapse of LTCM could have occurred, the chairman of another hedge fund was given to wonder ' . . . how the banks and the brokerage industry lent $116 billion to one borrower with $4 billion of liquidity'.[10] This is not merely a tale of hubris and overreach, but also of an old game in a new environment; not so much that one hand didn't know what the other was doing, but that none of the scores of hands involved had any comprehension of the systemic meaning of the sum of their actions – that is, until Russia defaulted on its loan repayments and a system-level crisis was triggered.

On a global scale, the increase in the extent and intensity of human activity is creating a systems-rich environment in which, at certain levels of complexity, intensity and dynamism, much of what is taken as given in modes of regulation and control (including governance) soon become problematic: predictability within clear parameters; an appreciation of and a degree of control over the more important variables; and an adequate knowledge base or access to pertinent information. These combine with the difficulties involved in securing the more familiar requisites of governance: shared goals; authority; accountability. Geoffrey Vickers expressed our situation as follows:

> Men, far more than other creatures, anticipate the future; and because their greater understanding gives them greater power to intervene, they have used this power increasingly to adapt their environment to themselves, rather than to adapt themselves to it. These Promethean, even Faustian powers of understanding and intervening, which once seemed complementary, have proved to be mutually limiting in three main ways.[11]

The power to change restricts the power to forecast

As natural systems lose their resilience, they also lose their predictability. For example, the complex of human and natural systems implicated in the making of climate change are in turn subjected to a changed and changing physical and political environment. One high-profile instance is clearly indicative: 'The problem for insurers is that their rates and coverage policies are based on past trends and averages and historically-based probabilities that are rapidly becoming redundant. Climate change that results from global warming makes their predictions meaningless and poses a serious threat to their future profitability and viability.'[12] More insidiously, as discussed below, a staggering range of slow-onset and invisible hazards, arising from the cumulative and synergistic effects of unco-ordinated human activities are beginning to come to light, extending the meaning of 'the power to change' from willed outcomes to the unanticipated consequences of established ways of life.[13] With every diminution of predictability comes a corresponding (though not necessarily proportional) diminution of our ability to exercise governance.

Our power to change the future is shared by others, whose actions are harder to predict or control than the natural course of events

This can be seen most clearly in the growth and intensification of global financial markets, which are acquiring unplanned-for, unanticipated system behaviours and vulnerabilities, and in which the largest part of the activity is dispersed, narrowly focused, short-term and competitive. Much of what has passed as 'development' and its attendant environmental destruction, within states and also (directly and indirectly) to the global commons, is no less competitively driven. The ability to create and/or contribute to global environmental impacts is reaching an ever-increasing portion of humanity – a trend reflected in the capacity of small groups and even individuals to affect large-scale human systems. The result of these trends is that the human ability to alter global dynamics, by accident or design, is considerably in excess of our current capacity to exercise governance over them.

Even the power which any policy maker regards as available to the system which {s/he} is helping to manage is itself dependent on the coherence of that system

Much of the global governance literature sees in social, political and economic fragmentation the possibility of a broadening and strengthening of control systems, including but extending beyond states and the state system. The literature places a good deal of emphasis on shifting power relations and the emergence of non-state centres of competence and authority:

> [C]onsidered in a fragmegrative worldview, not only have states lost some of their earlier dominance of the governance system, but also the lessening of their ability to evoke compliance and govern effectively is in part due to the growing relevance and potential of control mechanisms sustained by transnational and subnational systems of rule.[14]

But the many sites of non-authoritative 'capacity to get things done'[15] which feature routinely as a characterisation of 'governance without government' can only make for global governance as a composite actor realm – essentially, such as we now have, despite its manifest deficiencies:

In short, global order is conceived . . . to be a single set of arrangements even though these are not causally linked into a single coherent array of patterns. The organic whole that comprises the present or future global order is organic only in the sense that its diverse actors are all claimants upon the same earthbound resources and all of them must cope with the same environmental conditions, noxious and polluted as these might be.[16]

But these arrangements, however 'organic' their sum, are indisputably struggling to keep pace with the number and range of global governance issues now extant. Part of the difficulty can be traced to problems of political co-operation, but there are also problems of comprehension which are much more extensive and serious than is generally acknowledged, especially given the principal research orientations of global governance studies at present. We need to consider the limits on our ability to predict, perceive and appreciate the full consequences of our actions, especially in aggregate terms, as an important limitation on our ability to conceive and enact systems of control. What soon becomes clear is that the requisites of management for small or closed systems cannot easily be scaled up for application to global dynamics. Problems of knowledge affecting the construction and maintenance of governance systems include:

- inadequate understanding of systems and systems behaviours; and insufficient or inconclusive data;
- scientific uncertainty, including the determination of causal relations; and scientific contention for which the long-running disputes over global warming are perhaps the best-known exemplar; and
- the burden of proof falling on those who argue change or restraint; and entrenched interests and competing priorities militating against the 'precautionary principle'.[17]

We are already familiar with systemic outcomes (and sometimes threats) outside our range of imagined possibility, many driven by numerous and highly dynamic forces – and often, of a complexity that is compounded by dynamism. The larger point to be grasped is that at certain levels of size and complexity, the determination of causation becomes very difficult, with the result that governance, both as controlling, stabilising oversight and as a restorative exercise, becomes highly problematic.

We can now review each of the themes above in turn.

Inadequate understanding of systems and systems behaviours; and insufficient or inconclusive data

This theme can be divided into a number of distinct though overlapping sub-themes. What lies at the heart of each is the innumerable interactions between complex systems. From a governance perspective, what is most difficult is that what we perceive and must deal with as issues are in fact manifestations of relations that are not always discernible – and in any event, which cannot easily be reduced to problem-solving configurations or manageable proportions. We are not always stuck with treating symptoms but, within the environmental field, actions and events locally generated and shrugged off as disregarded externalities can return in the form of quite dramatic systemic change. So, for example, there are now an estimated 150 oceanic 'dead zones' – areas of sea deprived of oxygen – ranging in size from 1 square kilometre to 70,000 square kilometres. As UNEP Executive Director Klaus Toepfer outlines:

> Human kind is engaged in a gigantic, global experiment as a result of the inefficient and often over-use of fertilizers, the discharge of untreated sewage and the ever-rising emissions from vehicles and factories. The nitrogen and phosphorous from these sources are being discharged into rivers and the coastal environment or being deposited from the atmosphere, triggering these alarming and sometimes irreversible effects.[18]

In abstract terms, designing and implementing governance mechanisms that would abate the debilitation of marine ecosystems is not outside the capacity of practical politics; however, this would involve working backwards from sites of aggregate environmental damage to sources that are often distant in space and time. This greatly complicates the determination of causation – and hence questions of liability, as well as of equity and justice. The same difficulty has also featured as part of the climate change negotiations.[19]

Diffuse causation

The functioning of large human systems cannot be reduced to the outcomes of managerial deliberation, willed action and easily traceable, linear cause-and-effect – and the same applies to interaction between human and natural systems. This is as true of inflation and world trade as it is of biodiversity loss. The causation involved in any of these conditions is frequently spread across a range of activities; over wide geographic areas and across jurisdictional boundaries; and across time. Staying with the example of world biodiversity loss, we have had extinctions driven by excesses in hunting and fishing; habitat destruction (itself driven by many other factors, from resource exploitation to urbanisation) and pollution, both direct and indirect. The pace and extent of biodiversity loss is accelerating, but it is not a contemporary or localised novelty; and because biodiversity loss is most often an unintended consequence of other activities, addressing the condition entails governance measures that impact across a wide range of interests and polities.

Multiple causation entailing quite separate complex system interactions can also be identified. For example, governance mechanisms to halt the serious depletion of fish stocks in the North Sea have agreed considerably reduced fishing quotas for the countries concerned. Now, however, it appears that a dramatic warming of the North Sea is impacting its entire food chain, including plankton and birds as well as cod. Conservation measures will not be sufficient to save the fisheries; and indeed, if the worst estimates are borne out, the conservation measures might be all but redundant. (And complex interactions continue in the same vein but with varying effects, over vast areas: marine species once largely confined to the tropics are now becoming common in northern waters.)[20]

Even within relatively discrete human systems, individual and group responses are difficult to predict and are often contrary to the wishes and intentions of planners, particularly when complex relations are simplified to linearity and subordinated to a single, exclusive objective, as James C. Scott's study amply demonstrated:

> The clarity of the high-modernist optic is due to its resolute singularity. Its simplifying fiction is that, for any activity or process that comes under its scrutiny, there is only one thing going on. In the scientific forest, there is only commercial wood being grown; in the planned city, there is only the efficient movement of goods and people; in the housing estate there is only the effective delivery of shelter, heat, sewerage and water; in the planned hospital there is only the swift provision of professional medical services. And yet both we and planners know that each of these sites is the intersection of a host of interconnected activities that defy such simple descriptions.[21]

The most important point to note about diffuse causation is that many systemic crises can effectively 'slip under the radar' of existing governance systems. These disturbances are not accidental in the ordinary sense, not deliberate and not the outcome of high-impact or high-risk activity (such as atmospheric nuclear testing). And many are consequences of long-established ways of life which have genuine benefits as well as unwelcome legacies. One current, disturbing possibility is the introduction of new strains of HIV-like viruses into human populations through the trade in bush-meat. SIV, the primate equivalent of HIV, 'has now been reported in 26 different species of African non-human primates, many of which are hunted and sold as food.'[22] At the same time, though, '[t]he dependence on bushmeat protein is emphasised by the fact that [at least] four . . . [African] countries . . . do not produce sufficient amounts of non-bushmeat protein to feed their populations'.[23] Multiple lines of causation would have to operate in order for an SIV-like virus to cross the species barrier, to develop as a human disease and then to spread from localised outbreaks up to the level of pandemic. This chain of events might seem so unlikely as to be improbable, but it is the story of HIV/AIDS. Moreover,

> The HIV virus has jumped from primates to people on at least seven separate occasions in recent history, not twice as is commonly thought.

And people in Cameroon are showing up with symptoms of HIV, but are testing negative for both the virus and its primate equivalent SIV, the virus from which HIV is thought to have evolved. That suggests that new strains of HIV-like virus are circulating in wild animals and infecting the people who eat them, sparking fresh fears that such strains could fuel an already disastrous global HIV pandemic.[24]

The combination of causation dispersed geographically and temporally, together with the character of complex systems mean that the following four kinds of outcome are now becoming common.

Slow-onset outcomes

Interaction between complex systems does not always immediately manifest itself visibly or significantly because the dynamism of the world is not uniform – an obvious enough point when comparing organic processes with changes that occur over geological time, but perhaps less clear when we try to calculate outcomes from the interaction of complex systems that are quite disparate in kind, speed or extent:

> Ecosystem ecologists . . . have made it plain for a long while that some of the most telling properties of ecological systems emerge from the interactions between slow-moving and fast-moving processes and between processes that have large spatial reach and processes that are relatively localized. Those interactions are not only non-linear; they generate alternating stable states and normal journeys of biotic and abiotic variables through those states. Those journeys – measured in decades and centuries – maintain the diversity of species, spatial patterns, and genetic attributes. They maintain the resilience of ecological systems.[25]

Slow-onset crises generate restorative or rectificatory governance initiatives – belated, of course, and considerably more difficult than stabilising or preventive measures. Systemic alterations are not always reversible; and if the determination of causal relations is scientifically difficult or politically contentious (as with the disputed evidence for climate change), then the crisis can easily spread and deepen. What has facilitated the emergence of so many slow-onset crises of global import is the tightening of the nets of relations linking all complex systems together. Globalised systems of production and distribution mean that quite complex systems anywhere in the world can be affected more quickly than ever before; an expanding, industrialising human population is making ever-greater demands on already stressed environments, both local and global; and, as discussed below, actions of little consequence in themselves can combine powerfully in ways unforeseen, unbidden and un- or under-regulated.

Cumulative and combinational outcomes of human activity

To gauge the additive power of what might generally be regarded as inconsequential human actions and human systems, consider that the stand-by switches on household appliances in the US alone consume electricity comparable to the output of four large generating stations per year; and that there are no reliable figures for the commercial and government sectors.[26]

Other examples are considerably more disturbing. PCBs (polychlorinated biphenyls), introduced in 1929, are a class of more than 200 synthetic chemicals. They are 'persistent' – that is, they do not easily decay naturally. At the time of their introduction 'PCBs seemed to have many virtues and no obvious faults. They are noninflammable and highly stable. Toxicity tests at the time did not identify any hazardous effects . . . [so they were] quickly moved . . . into production and onto the market.'[27] (The same was true of CFCs, which depleted the ozone layer.) PCBs were used in a wide range of manufactured products, including materials to preserve and insulate common household materials such as rubber, plastic and wood; and they were also widely used in industrial processes. PCBs quickly found their way into the environment not only as useful products but also as pollutants, through normal manufacturing and eventually, as disposed waste. The chemical persistence of PCBs means that they can easily move between environmental mediums (air, soil, water); and this combines with the fact that they are bioaccumulative – appearing in the body fat of living creatures, with the highest concentrations at the top of the food chain. Long after becoming a ubiquitous component of our built environment – and now found in the tissue of living creatures in even the remotest parts of the world – PCBs are widely recognised as 'hormone disruptors', which can mimic, stimulate, block, alter or destroy hormonal response. They are implicated in a range of deformities and dysfunctions in species ranging from reptiles to human beings, including impaired immune function, cancers, reproductive abnormalities and behavioural, neurological and cognitive effects.[28]

PCBs are now known to be harmful in minute concentrations, but it is their gradual, additive manufacture and dispersal over more than four decades that makes their existence a global threat. They also display slow-onset characteristics: manufacture of PCBs ceased in 1977, but of the one million tonnes produced, '[T]he best estimates of emissions suggest that the bulk of the PCBs manufactured/used (perhaps > 70 per cent) have not entered the environmental pool, because they are still associated with diffusive source materials'.[29] And their accumulation is present not only in rivers and industrial sites, but also throughout the animal kingdom. (In the 1980s, fish caught in the Rhine ' . . . often carried 400 times the concentrations of PCBs officially deemed safe to eat.)[30] As a governance issue, the problem of PCBs is but one of numerous toxicity problems coming to light from our extensive manufacture and use of synthetic chemicals. It is also clear that our regulatory systems are at the very least trailing behind the routine diffusion of substances capable of such pervasive and fundamental threats to the biosphere and to human well-being. Even as the United Nations Environment Programme's initiative on Persistent Organic Pollutants[31] attempts to grapple with the problem, a formidable legacy is already in place, made worse by inconsistent regulatory standards:

> The chemicals used to fireproof everything from computers to carpets are accumulating in the food chain at a frightening rate. The chemicals, called polybrominated diphenyl ethers, or PBDEs, are in the same family as polychlorinated biphenyls (PCBs) and have the same toxic effects in animal tests. [Scientists have recently] found that levels of PBDEs in arctic seals have increased exponentially over the past 20 years, and are set to overtake levels of PCBs in the area by 2050. [. . .] No one knows what effect the chemicals have on people. PBDEs are banned in much of Europe, but aren't regulated in the US and Canada.[32]

Synergistic outcomes of human activity

Synergy is 'co-operative action of two or more agencies such that the total is greater than the sum of the component actions'. This is a well-known phenomenon and the concept is now frequently applied in business and economic contexts to demonstrate how the adoption of new practices can have multiple, cross-sectoral benefits. But it is also applied to the negative impacts of global dynamics. For example, the depletion of the earth's ozone layer is very damaging to marine phytoplankton, which acts as an important 'sink' for carbon dioxide emissions. Thus ozone layer depletion can also accelerate climate change by diminishing the planet's ability to absorb greenhouse gases.

The potential for unwanted synergisms also explains why newly developed drugs are tested for their interactions with other drugs likely to be prescribed as part of a larger therapeutic regime. However, 'while [the US Food and Drug Administration] requires studies on drug–drug interactions before a pharmaceutical gets to market, no drug/pesticide and/or pesticide/pesticide interactions are required before commercialisation';[33] nor are tests for synergistic effects 'mentioned on Material Safety Data Sheets required for the sale of toxic chemicals in the United States by the Environmental Protection Agency'.[34]

Human activity is generating a vast increase in the potential number and kind of complex system interactions and, given the nature and extent of the harm brought about by the simple accumulation of PCBs in the world, the synergistic potential of our highly chemicalised environment is for practical purposes incalculable. Within the single field of chemistry, the Chemical Abstracts Service lists more than six-and-a-half million commercially available chemicals;[35] there are more than 300 widely used pesticides;[36] and the US government's priority list of 275 hazardous substances is not a list of 'most toxic' substances, but lists only those 'which are determined to pose the most significant potential threat to human health due to their known or suspected toxicity and potential for human exposure at [National Priority List] sites'.[37]

Invisible and non-quantifiable hazards

Diffuse causation and the potential for additive, cumulative and synergistic effects mean that hazards that are global in their extent or import (for biosphere integrity or human well-being) are difficult to anticipate and might only become discernible once they generate a serious and consistent pattern of symptoms, such as statistically significant clusters of abnormalities. Even then, inferring causation is often difficult and not definitive (see scientific uncertainty, below). In addition, the combination of multiple causation and time lag compounds our response to problems once they do appear:

> Once symptoms have arisen in the form of cancers, deformities, allergies and contaminations of marine life or meat, for example, it is exceedingly difficult and sometimes impossible to establish verifiable connections between those symptoms and their causes. During the invisible periods of latency the provable links have been broken, causal connections severed. This discontinuity has implications for the scientific definition of a problem, the understanding of causes, and the formulation of potential solutions.[38]

We are now accustomed to the rapid, world-wide distribution of everything from manufactured goods to information: the human world made global by the infrastructures we have set in place. But beneath these human systems are the dynamics of the natural world, ever capable of combining with human dynamics – and not always in ways foreseen, or quickly visible, or beneficial. In the case of many toxic substances, natural systems have three distinct means of global distribution within the non-human environmental realm and back into human systems. The first of these is bioaccumulation, familiar in cases where concentrations of toxic substances increase via the ordinary function of the food chain. The second is that once ingested, toxins can be transmitted down the generations through mother's milk. And finally, there is physical distribution, both direct, through the legal and illegal distribution of certain substances; and indirect, through planetary dynamics, such as ocean currents, winds and animal migrations. (By 1970, concentrations of DDT could be found in Arctic animals, Antarctic snow and in the upper reaches of the atmosphere.) The several modes of transmission mean that the accumulation of such substances is not static, either within geographic areas or within environmental realms; and a combination of natural dynamics and human agency means that the outward momentum towards globality is high. These processes – and their potential to store, concentrate and spread dangerous levels of toxicity – might often be both slow and unnoticeable, but they are nevertheless relentless and consequential.

Problems of comprehension for the maintenance of stable human-environmental relationships have their counterpart in the governance of human systems. F. A. Hayek gave this succinct expression in an article written in 1945:

> The peculiar character of the problem of a rational economic order is determined precisely by the fact that the knowledge of the circumstances of which we must make use never exists in concentrated or integrated form, but solely as dispersed bits of incomplete and frequently contradictory knowledge which all the separate individuals possess. The economic problem of society is thus not merely a problem of how to allocate 'given' resources – if 'given' is taken to mean given to a single mind which deliberately solves the problem set by these 'data'. It is rather a problem of how to secure the best use of resources known to any of the members of society, for ends whose relative importance only those individuals know. Or, to put it briefly, it is a problem of the utilization of knowledge not given to anyone in its totality.[39]

Hayek lamented that the 'character of the fundamental problem has . . . been rather obscured than illuminated by many of the recent refinements of economic theory, particularly by the many uses made of mathematics'. In our own time, complexity theorists have begun to clarify the structural and dynamic features of economies that frustrate the traditional mathematical approaches used in economics, as summarised in Box 5.1.

Box 5.1 Six features of the economy that together present difficulties for the traditional mathematics used in economics

Dispersed interaction. What happens in the economy is determined by the interaction of many dispersed, possibly heterogeneous, agents acting in parallel. The action of any given agent depends upon the anticipated actions of a limited number of other agents and on the aggregate state those agents cocreate.

No global controller. No global entity controls interactions. Instead, controls are provided by mechanisms of competition and co-ordination among agents. Economic actions are mediated by legal institutions, assigned roles, and shifting associations. Nor is there a universal competitor – a single agent that can exploit all opportunities in the economy.

Cross-cutting hierarchical organisation. The economy has many levels of organisation and interaction. Units at any given level – behaviours, actions, strategies, products – typically serve as 'building blocks' for constructing units at the next highest level. The overall organisation is more than hierarchical, with many sorts of tangled interactions (associations, channels of communication) across levels.

Continual adaptation. Behaviours, actions, strategies, and products are revised continually as the individual agents accumulate experience – the system constantly adapts.

Perpetual novelty. Niches are continually created by new markets, new technologies, new behaviours, new institutions. The very act of filling a niche may provide new niches. The result is on-going, perpetual novelty.

Out-of-equilibrium dynamics. Because new niches, new potentials, new possibilities, are continually created, the economy operates far from any optimum or global equilibrium. Improvements are always possible and indeed occur regularly.

From W. B. Arthur and S. N. Durlauf, 'Introduction', in W. B. Arthur, S. N. Durlauf and David A. Lane (eds), *The Economy as an Evolving Complex System II*, Proceedings Volume XXVII, Santa Fe Institute Studies in the Sciences of Complexity (Reading, Massachusetts: Addison-Wesley, 1997), pp. 3–4

Yet the promise of computer-assisted mathematical modelling is itself limited. We might readily agree that the 'conception of the economy as an adaptive nonlinear network – as an evolving complex system – has profound implications for the foundations of economic theory and for the way in which theoretical problems are cast and solved'.[40] But that will not necessarily make the governance of economies clearer or simpler. As a matter of practical politics, the making of a 'rational economic order' is not an agenda item in any polity, because economies are open systems – and in the contemporary world, they are open to quite powerful globalising dynamics. Governments and financial institutions do not confront economic problems that can be solved; rather, they attempt to negotiate their way through unstable and shifting situations. Even within well-managed national economies, the control of matters such as inflation and even consumer spending is hardly an exact science. And for the practical business of managing economies, the systems which comprise them cannot for long remain abstracted from their physical foundations – and the consequences of human actions upon them. In a world which can be transfixed by currency exchange rates, junk bonds and derivatives, a sudden surge in the price of oil, driven by non-economic variables, brings us down to earth with a bump.

Scientific uncertainty

The history of reductionist science and the technological advances it has brought about created an expectation of scientific certainty that persists, albeit much diminished: that from the atomic and molecular levels upwards, we can identify, define and measure the constituents of our world, trace causal relations, and make reliable predictions. With science so conceived, the facts can be uncovered; 'facts will speak for themselves'; and exactitude will clarify choice. This view of scientific endeavour is highly idealised if not fanciful, but one need not look to epistemology or philosophy of science to see that it does not accord either with scientific practice, political expectation or practical possibility. The 'precautionary principle' is a public policy orientation founded explicitly on the difficulties posed by scientific uncertainty.[41] Scientists and non-scientists engaged in policy-oriented work now routinely acknowledge scientific uncertainty as an important policy context[42] and an interest in how 'certainty is constructed and deconstructed' has become a feature not only of academic study, but also of political activism.[43]

Scientific uncertainty also features as part of the difficulties that attend the making of effective global governance. In this regard, the limits of reductionist science are most striking, as we begin to consider how to frame policies to regulate human–natural systems dynamics on the scale of ocean fisheries, rain forests or the earth's atmosphere:

> In a Newtonian world, the stability of cause-and-effect relationships makes it possible to pursue reductionist science. This stability makes the observation and measurement of system relationships reliable and, more importantly, allows us to accumulate useful knowledge and to intervene in the system with predictable outcomes at whatever scale we find appropriate to our needs. . . . [T]here is no doubt that many parts of our world fit this paradigm well. What is problematical about complex systems in this regard are their pervasive nonlinear, causal relationships. At any time a large number of factors may influence the outcome of a particular event, each one to a greater or lesser extent; at another time, the strength of those same causative factors on the same event may be very different. The result is a decline in predictability and/or often a shift in the scale or dimension of predictability.[44]

Of course, scientific expertise is not merely invoked for policy conundrums: scientific applications and predictions are central to many aspects of government policy-making as well as to highly competitive industries. Many of the risk assessments and decisions made about scientific processes and products now have truly global implications, apparent not least in the legacies of our miscalculations and risk-taking political priorities. (Stockpiles of nuclear waste as a product of both military and civil applications of nuclear power is a clear case in point.) With widening and intensifying globalisation, scientific research is now positioned on both sides of public policy debates: its predictive capacities are sought for estimating risk and its explanatory capacities are sought for making inferences, often about establishing causal links at variance with earlier risk projections. The difficulties that attend making scientific inferences, particularly with respect to suspected human harm, are considerable[45] and the combined effect of legal cases of this sort – together with suspicion of scientifically validated risk estimates and standards – is an erosion of public trust in government and governance. The controversy and conflict over the safety of genetically modified organisms – for the environment and for human health – is not confined to public suspicion, but has also featured as a particularly rich source of disputes between states. In this case, although potential risks have not been scientifically quantified, they have already been judged to be acceptable in many states. Beyond arguments about the labelling of food that contains GM products, there is a larger and more profound concern that we might unintentionally alter the genetic make-up of our environments, with synergistic and possibly very harmful results. This is a question that can be framed in abstract terms, but cannot be known in advance.

> Fundamental uncertainty results from indeterminacy, ignorance, or ignorance-of-ignorance. In the case of novel technologies, existing models might not apply. Moreover, if we are ignorant of the potential existence of a particular hazard, we might fail to consider it at all when attempting to estimate the potential harms or benefits of an activity. Molecular breeding by DNA shuffling, for example, will result in at least some outcomes that fundamentally are uncertain and always will be virtually impossible to predict. We will remain ignorant of them until they occur, and even then, might only identify them if we search in sensitive ways. Attempts to estimate the probability of harm (or benefit) from such a fundamentally uncertain activity must be undertaken with great care since ignorance-of-ignorance might lead to serious errors.[46]

We have now created a situation in which an important aspect of biotechnology has passed beyond the 'applications' threshold, albeit in some states but not others. So such global governance as we will now be able to exercise in this field must proceed from profoundly opposed understandings of risks already taken in some parts of the world, but not in others. It is clear that scientific uncertainty has not paralysed public policy-making, yet the challenges are no less daunting for all that. From a conservationist perspective:

> [The characteristics of] complex systems [raise] fundamental and difficult questions: How can we cope with or successfully intervene in ways that sustain the resources of those systems over the long run if we cannot predict the long-term consequences of our own actions? More importantly, how can we hope to make collective decisions in these circumstances? Won't honesty about our lack of knowledge lead to a situation in which groups

or individuals can honestly question and oppose restraint because it is costly in the short run with unproven benefits in the long run? In short, if we are in a world of complex systems, does the absence of predictability mean that we have no rational basis for making conservation decisions?[47]

Uncertainty can be used either to urge or to postpone decisions which prominently feature scientific risk-assessment and special interests are adept at shaping their arguments with or around scientific uncertainty, which is itself socially determined, not a fixed quality of data. Moreover, a great deal of scientific research is not disinterested and there is some evidence to suggest that although knowledge influences institutions, the reverse can also be true: that institutions shape the generation of knowledge.[48]

As discussed earlier, the more prominent risk society literature has a rather despairing attitude towards what has been termed 'the self-endangering momentum of global risk society',[49] but not all governance initiatives which are impacted by scientific uncertainty carry the risk of enlarging or deepening the span of human and environmental insecurity. Conservation efforts are notable in this regard, as are studies in public policy which attempt to formalise the way in which policy-making can be framed to take account of uncertainty in conjunction with social values, ethical considerations and group interests. Nevertheless, our willingness to undertake applications of scientific knowledge which combine uncertain outcome, possible (if unquantified) risk and global implications must be set against the reach of current and future configurations of global governance. Our willingness to continue to accrue dangerous radioactive waste in the absence of any viable means of disposal or safe storage[50] should give one pause over the prospect of scientific uncertainty as a serious restraint on the determination of powerful parties (including, but not limited to states), with serious implications for the practical prospects for comprehensive global governance.

There is a further interesting feature to scientific uncertainty and that is how, as the number and kind of both measurable and hypothesised causal relations in our various operating environments increase, our legal means of determining proximate causation and responsibility also become enmeshed, not only in the limits of scientific certainty, but also in striking a balance between legal sufficiency and scientific evidence. The combination of scientific uncertainty and redress sought for injury of uncertain origin appear to be mutually reinforcing:

> [There are] two intersecting problems. The first is the great disparity between the ease with which a controversy about a suspected hazard can begin and the difficulty in resolving the nature of the connection, if any, between the suspected hazard and the health effect. The second is the havoc the resulting confusion wreaks in the courts. The two problems cannot be separated: litigation may reflect scientific controversy, but it may also help to create it.[51]

This has historical roots and implications for the future, both of which can be seen most clearly in the development of tort law.

Agency, tort law[52] and negligence

Social and legal adjustments to complex and/or remote causation as a feature of individual injury and institutional liability are not a novelty of globalisation, but also featured significantly in the industrial revolution. Within Anglo-American law, and particularly in the United States, determinations of responsibility based on strict determinations of causation or formal relations could not be sustained in a rapidly industrialising environment. Enter the concept of blameworthiness:

> Distinguishing between blameworthy and unblameworthy behaviour on the basis of the kind of care taken during the act that resulted in injury introduced a much broader notion of responsibility. It assumed, in fact, that a certain level of care was owed to each individual, not just to specific individuals in specific status relations. And once the notion of ordinary care replaced status and causation as an arbiter of liability, liability depended on a definition of duties which, having been violated, would lead to a finding of fault. Indeed, in larger factories, and in more densely populated urban areas . . . accidents increasingly took place between people who had never met before and between whom there was no preexisting sense of obligation. In this new, highly industrialized and technologized climate, where the causes of accidents were uncertain, and the perpetrators and victims of accidents unknown, decisions about liability for accidental injury required both a new theory of liability, and a new calculus for distinguishing between a primary cause and a potential host of others.[53]

An interesting point in the quotation above is that the principal drivers for this socio-legal reorientation were the development and dissemination of human systems – factories, railways and steamships; while in our time, it is largely the fact of, or behaviour of, anthropogenically altered natural systems that is the source of dislocation. Yet if one substitutes 'damaging outcomes' for 'accidents', the parallels, though inexact, are striking. Although the development of negligence as an aspect of tort law was informed by cases of indirect or diffuse causation by which the human agent was acted upon, interest under globalised conditions must also extend to individuals and institutions as actors.

As industrialisation and its concomitant social changes continued apace, so too did the sociological, moral and legal conceptions of right conduct and responsibility:

> The concept of duty – the duty to exercise ordinary care when engaged in potentially hazardous activity – proved a paradox. Insofar as it assumed

a duty that was in Oliver Wendell Holmes's words, 'of all the world to all the world', it turned liability from a standard that applied to certain individuals because of their status either as actors or in certain occupations into a concept that applied to everyone indiscriminately. In short, liability went from being a specific designation for certain acts or actors to a universal standard. . . . Under negligence, for the first time, liability for accidents was based not on the status of the victim and perpetrator or on the fact of injury alone but on the question of fault and blameworthiness. Thus . . . [according to Chief Justice Lemuel] Shaw's [1850] decision, negligence was defined as the absence of 'ordinary care', or the 'kind of care prudent and cautious men would use . . . in the circumstances'. But if the concept of ordinary care and the invocation of the average, prudent, and cautious man paralleled a rise in democratic social relations, it did so in part by imposing a model of universal liability. In the nineteenth century, universal liability was especially problematic for it threatened to put an end to the taking of risks necessary for an expanding industry.[54]

How far can the duty of ordinary care, and a conception of a cautious and prudent person, usefully be applied to the intentions and actions of people and institutions in the contemporary world? Certainly within our current legal ethos, negligence cases comprise a substantial portion of tort law and a defendant's contention of 'reasonable care' would form the substance of the legal argument in specific cases. But what of our less immediate but still far-reaching and morally significant actions and omissions – particularly those not bound by law? One of the striking features of the notion of duty 'of all the world to all the world', is how easily it accommodates extended notions of environmental justice, including obligations to future generations;[55] and arguments concerning the moral significance of the non-human world.[56]

But duties undirected and unenforced by legal strictures, particularly in Holmes's declaratory, universalising terms, eventually come up against practical limits of various sorts, as do legal duties themselves – after all, perhaps unsurprisingly, the development of universal liability led shortly afterwards to the introduction of 'limited liability'. And although throughout the latter half of the twentieth century, negligence cases gained pre-eminence in tort law, they have generated tensions within the legal community and society at large:

> [T]ort law came under attack from those who believed that it had betrayed its moral purpose of promoting justice between individuals. In their eyes, tort law could only be seen as a part of private law, and it risked incoherence if it sought to pursue 'public' goals . . . [At present], these tensions show no sign of resolution. The past twenty years have seen, in society as a whole, a return to nineteenth century values of individual responsibility and self-reliance, and fears that tort law might undermine these by 'going too far' have caused the courts to cut back on the scope of liability in negligence in certain notable cases.[57]

And a 'duty of all to all' cast in moral terms is as unsupportable in practice as its personification is unbelievable. Here, for example, the idea of the Reasonable Man as the measure of human conduct is held up to ridicule in a piece written in 1927:

> This noble creature [the Reasonable Man] stands in singular contrast to his kinsman the Economic Man, whose every action is prompted by the single spur of selfish advantage, and directed to the single end of monetary gain. The Reasonable Man is always thinking of others; prudence is his guide, and 'Safety First' . . . is his rule of life. All solid virtues are his . . . he is the one who invariably looks where he is going, and is careful to examine the immediate foreground before he executes a leap or a bound . . . who investigates the *bona fides* of every mendicant before distributing alms, and will inform himself of the history and habits of a dog before administering a caress; who believes no gossip, or repeats it, without firm basis for believing it to be true. . . . Devoid, in short, of any human weakness, without one single saving vice, sans prejudice, procrastination, ill-nature, avarice, and absence of mind, as careful for his own safety as he is for that of others, this excellent but odious character stands like a monument in our Courts of Justice, vainly appealing to his fellow-citizens to order their lives after his example.[58]

Even so, when set against what we know about the global environment, many of our actions would count as negligent were they to fall under the jurisdiction of a 'world tort'. What would further mark them as negligent is our appreciation that the cumulative and synergistic impacts of human activity are creating injurious situations of considerable gravity. This is comprehensible to any moral agent, let alone the idealised Reasonable Person; and it is true of governmental and institutional decision-making as well as individual action. On the other hand, while we might understand the full implications of, say, using a range of chemicals now known to be damaging to the planetary environment, the many uses made of substances such as CFCs and PCBs over years and decades were done in good faith – backed by degrees of scientific validation. The question that then arises is, how much validation and what level of certainty must we achieve in order to avoid disasters in the future? The precautionary principle is a risk-averse policy orientation in the face of scientific uncertainty – laudable *as* a principle, but very difficult to enact, at least in its strongest forms, for many reasons.

The precautionary principle and the burden of proof

A survey of the largest and most vexed global environmental problems can easily suggest that precaution in the face of unknowns might have spared us the issues now absorbing so much of our current global governance: CFCs might not have been produced; GM crops and animals would remain at most a strictly-controlled laboratory matter; PCBs would not have been produced and integrated into our industrial and domestic infrastructures; DDT – still in use in the developing world as an anti-malarial measure – would not have accumulated in environments around the world; and various anti-microbials and hormones as growth stimulants in farm livestock would never have been permitted.

The incorporation of variants on 'precautionary principle' in a number of treaties and agreements (precautionary 'principles,' 'measures' and 'approaches' have all been used[59]) makes a simple definition difficult, but the general disposition is this: 'Forestalling disasters usually requires acting before there is strong proof of harm, particularly if the harm may be delayed and irreversible. [This] approach to scientific evidence and policy making . . . is part of what is now called the precautionary principle.'[60] The precautionary principle is also advocated on the argument that in its absence, legal redress will be disastrously belated:

> The tort-oriented non-precautionary approach postpones the regulation of activities until harm occurs and compels states to respond to environmental degradation rather than promote environmental protection.[61]

It is not difficult to appreciate this perspective. The essentially legal counters to it – that Anglo-Saxon tort law does allow pre-emptive action in cases of imminent danger; and that the prospect of fines and/or compensation creates strong incentives to do no harm[62] – do not have a great deal of purchase against the possibility of large-scale and pervasive harm that might be slow-onset or synergistic; and that in at least some cases, might be irreversible. The case of PCB contamination is relevant here. When set against the time-scale, the number of responsible agents and the nature of the environmental damage done by PCBs over the decades, determining responsibility – let alone negligence – would be a legal task of epic proportions. And the kinds of compensation that might meet the demands of rectificatory justice for individuals and communities in tort cases would be all but meaningless in the face of the diminution of male fertility now measurable in many species throughout the world, thought to be caused by PCBs. Proponents of the precautionary principle argue that situations of the magnitude of our global environmental crises represent a gap between uncertainty and risk that must be narrowed. But these and similar arguments do not mean that the precautionary principle, especially in its stronger forms, can easily be incorporated as a mainstay of global governance.

The interests and tensions surrounding estimates of risk and 'acceptable risk' also apply to the wording of 'precaution' in treaties and declarations. In fact, because the more prohibitive expressions of the precautionary principle would have immediate and profound impact across all of industrial and technological development – and because the burden of proof would strain at the limits of scientific certainty – the strong form is very contentious.[63] An example of the 'strong form' of the precautionary principle was expressed by Jeremy Leggett of Greenpeace with regard to the regulation of greenhouse gas emissions:

> For organisations like Greenpeace, what comes first must be the needs of the environment . . . the modus operandi we would like to see is: 'Do not admit a substance unless you have proof that it will do no harm to the environment' – the precautionary principle . . . the fact that proof of harm might come too late – or that proof is invariably hard to demonstrate with absolute certainty – only augments the licence given to polluters.[64]

The arguments against this and similar positions have a philosophical foundation:

> The demand that a technology should not be admitted until it has been proved harmless means an infinitely high standard of proof. Obviously such a standard cannot be achieved. It is epistemologically absurd; it demands a level of knowledge that simply cannot be reached. It is not possible to prove something is harmless, any more than it is possible to prove that there are no fairies at the bottom of one's garden. Wildavsky . . . observes: 'One could well ask whether any technology, including the most benign, would ever have been established if it had first been forced to demonstrate that it would do not harm.'[65]

Add to this the considerable interests (including national interests) behind scientific and technological innovation, and the resistance to the strong form of the precautionary principle is easy to appreciate. The Montreal Protocol which galvanised action to halt the depletion of the ozone layer was not precautionary: unusually, the damage could be quantified and without swift action, the trajectory and prognosis were clearly disastrous. The climate change debate is much more instructive. In this case, what is at issue is not untried, leading-edge technologies which might harbour unforeseen risks if applied and/or distributed. Carbon-emitting activities (principally power generation and transport) are central to developed-nation infrastructures; and the associated costs impact directly on the competitive edge of economies – concerns mirrored in Russia's stated reluctance to accede to the Kyoto standards.[66] What is most notable in this case is that the lack of scientific certainty cuts both ways: it can be used to argue against the application of stringent, precautionary measures as well as for them; and in conjunction with benefits both actual (the number of lives saved through anti-malarial applications of DDT) and possible (increased crop yields through genetic modification), arguments against the implementation of a 'strong' precautionary principle, even with respect to new processes and products, are very robust.[67]

In any event, the Framework Convention on Climate Change incorporates a weak version of the precautionary principle, which gives states ample room for manoeuvre:

The parties should take precautionary measures to anticipate, prevent or minimise the causes of climate change and mitigate its adverse effects. Where there are threats of serious or irreversible damage, lack of full scientific certainty should not be used as a reason for postponing such measures, taking into account that policies and measures to deal with climate change should be cost-effective so as to ensure global benefits at the lowest possible cost. To achieve this, such policies and measures should take into account different socio-economic contexts, be comprehensive, cover all relevant sources, sinks and reservoirs of greenhouse gases and adaptation, and comprise all economic sectors. Efforts to address climate change may be carried out co-operatively by interested parties.[68]

Given a high level of scientific and political consensus about the reality of climate change – including a recent Pentagon warning to the US President about the dangers[69] – the precautionary measures contained in the Framework Convention could hardly be described as stringent. They might be considered a better reflection of political realities than of scientific uncertainties, but in fact the two are closely linked: our perceptions of risk are informed by scientific investigation, but policy decisions that weigh possible benefits to be greater than unproven risks are political decisions, as the European Commission recognised quite directly:

Decision-makers need to be aware of the degree of uncertainty attached to the results of the evaluation of the available scientific information. Judging what is an 'acceptable' level of risk is an entirely *political* responsibility. decision-makers faced with an unacceptable risk, scientific uncertainty and public concerns have a duty to find answers. Therefore, all factors have to be taken into consideration.[70]

The precautionary principle cannot lever us out of problems of knowledge: it is wholly enmeshed in such problems and its use in strong form (which is both politically controversial and philosophically contentious) still requires us to rely on the uncertainties of scientific research and human, essentially political judgements about what counts as an acceptable balance of risks and benefits. We are familiar with this at lower levels of human activity, such as the introduction of new medicines that are largely beneficial, but might occasion a small number of deaths, but it has proven very difficult to strike a reasoned and acceptable balance between overregulation and underregulation, even of toxic substances.[71] But new technologies – and the growing number of states and other actors able to acquire them – usher in possible new dangers, unprecedented in kind or degree. Work has been under way for many years on articulating and enacting precautionary approaches to public policy-making that strike a balance between untenable prohibition and unwarranted risk.[72] But the history of climate change negotiations should temper any expectations that we could initiate a 'precautionary global governance'; indeed, as one study points out, 'Differences in international regulation are seldom a function of the differential threats posed by different risks. In fact, risks of similar proportion, all deriving from globalisation can generate quite distinct international regimes, suggesting that risk assessment and regulation are neither as technocratic nor as politically neutral as they sometimes appear.'[73] Whether these many disparate regulatory mechanisms can amount to a coherent global governance in a world of complex system interaction is open to question; and whether the balance between preventive and rectificatory governance efforts will favour the former may come to be decided by default.

6   Authority and accountability in a global arena

Are the worldwide prospects for democracy and accountability not merely extending, but also deepening? As we have seen, much of the turbulence and fragmentation which now besets the international system has also opened up new possibilities of political association – decentralisation, a profusion of new centres of competence and allegiance, new configurations of state and non-state actors – which is reflected in the burgeoning literature on governance and global governance. The governance literature combines powerfully with (and often includes) theorising about the role of civil society, global civil society, spheres of authority, transnational interest and protest groups and the beneficent possibilities on offer through 'globality' or in 'globalising space'. Taken together, these suggest unprecedented opportunities for democratic participation and accountability across many sectors and at every level of political organisation. James Rosenau has contended that, 'By decentralising authority in disparate and localised sites, fragmentation has greatly inhibited the coalescence of hierarchical and autocratic centres of power.'[1]

But has it? And in particular, has the fragmentation driven by globalising dynamics given us a glimpse of a *global* governance of benign character – or at least, of benign possibility? There is certainly good reason to be sceptical: in world politics, decentralisation is not a force of nature, but is the outcome of competition, shifting power relations and calculations of political and economic interest. The notion that the shards of the old order (within and between states) cannot be put back together again or that a new, global one will lack autocratic centres of power rests on a highly selective view of current affairs, not least of the drivers and outcomes of globalisation. The diminution of the authoritative reach of nation states (the extent of which is difficult to quantify), is hardly a guarantee against new concentrations of power in familiar forms. Yet the most frequently cited definitions of governance offer no suggestion that its exercise will of necessity be open to democratic scrutiny or public accountability – if anything, quite the opposite. Consider the following well-known definitions of governance and global governance:

- *Lawrence Finklestein*: 'Global governance is governing, without sovereign authority, relationships that transcend national frontiers. Global governance is doing internationally what governments do at home.'[2]

- *Ernst-Otto Czempiel*: 'I understand "governance" to mean the capacity to get things done without the legal competence to command that they be done. Where governments, in the eastonian sense, can distribute values authoritatively, governance can distribute them in a way which is not authoritative but equally effective.'[3]
- *James Rosenau*: 'systems of rule can be maintained and their controls successfully and consistently exerted even in the absence of established legal or political authority. The evolution of intersubjective consensuses based on shared fates and common histories, the possession of information and knowledge, the pressure of active or mobilizeable publics, and/or the use of careful planning, good timing, clever manipulation and hard bargaining can – either separately or in combination – foster control mechanisms that sustain governance without government.'[4]

What is striking about these definitions and much of the literature they have inspired is a conspicuous absence of considerations of agency. After all, 'governance' is not an agent; nor are 'capacity' and 'systems of rule'. Who will be exercising authority without legal competence, or establishing and exercising new systems of rule? Who – or what – will be 'doing' global governance? Governance is about the distribution and exercise of power or it is nothing at all, so it is reasonable to ask whether the emergence of governance systems promise anything in the way of democratic control and accountability.

But in the most prominent literature on governance to date, a great deal more attention is given to the accrual of power by non-state actors than to the qualities of the exercise of such power. Unless rather general calls for the 'democratic accountability' of governance mechanisms, 'democratic global governance' and 'democratising global space' are linked to detailed considerations of governance mechanisms and the power they wield, we will be left with James Rosenau's rather thin hope that ' . . . severe violations of democratic values cannot be readily concentrated in hegemonic hands'.[5] While the study of governance is still in its infancy, there is nevertheless the possibility that an emphasis on process above agency could lock it into a pattern of abstraction not dissimilar to Realist conceptions of International Relations. In the case of Realism, anarchy – the absence of world government – has been elevated from being a condition of state interaction to an arena, thus relegating many fundaments of international life and global dynamics to matters of secondary consideration. In much the same way that one might ask of Realist theory, 'Where is the environment in this picture?' (in other words, where is the place of a fragile and threatened global ecosystem in its conception of states competing for their survival), we might ask of governance studies, 'Where is *power* in this picture?'

Questions of power and accountability are going to become very important in the years ahead as the democratic deficit of a very large variety of inter-state, private and state/non-state arrangements come under scrutiny. The many calls now being voiced for more democratic control and accountability, most visibly in the Seattle and Prague anti-WTO protests, are founded on a perception about unjust power relations, including questions of legitimacy – the negative expression of 'clever manipulation and hard bargaining'.

Three points follow from this. The first is that our fascination with governance as an outcome of larger reconfigurations and pattern shifts in world politics obscures our view of new and established power interests. If a new global political space is opening up possibilities for the empowerment of the hitherto weak, this does not necessarily mean that the already powerful will suffer a corresponding diminution in their abilities. (Nor, as Jan Scholte points out, will the activities of 'civil society' actors – however one chooses to define these – necessarily be either democratic or benign.)[6]

The second point is that the urgency of conceiving new forms of accountability for the many new sites of governance is driving us towards a faith in the efficacy of democracy and democratisation that is rare in other corners of political theory, or political science more generally.[7] It hardly requires a cynical disposition or a selected reading of contemporary affairs to see that powerful agents – including states, of course – even democratic ones – are not above using, abusing, subverting or destroying democracy, sometimes in the name of democracy itself.[8] Against this hard reality, the prospects for democratised governance systems as characterised by James Rosenau seem more hopeful than likely: ' . . . the more densely populated the [domestic–foreign] Frontier becomes, thus promoting a greater sense of connectivity among widely separated peoples and groups, the more will its governance exhibit democratic tendencies'.[9]

The third point is whether 'civil society' will find a way to make governance more accountable, more democratic. Characterised as a unitary phenomenon, 'global governance' might well seem open to the demands of the similarly unspecific 'global civil society', but we should not forget that globalising processes are in large measure about power: about its extension and consolidation; and about the reconfiguration of significant actors. All configurations of power, governmental and non-governmental alike, are hugely resistant to encroachment, whether in the form of outright competition, challenges to legitimacy, or various forms of accountability, regulation and control. The long and continuing march of human rights, which began with the struggle to wrest absolute power from rulers, is a testament to this. It is also noteworthy that what gives struggles for human rights their purchase, even in the most unpromising circumstances, is the existence of a powerful international norm – widely held and deeply felt by individuals, but also reinforced in codified international law – to which local actors can appeal and against which repressive governments must negotiate their standing with the rest of the international community.[10] The formal authority of the international system is what makes human rights the norm that it is. It is this very lack of formal authority – combined with 'clever manipulation and hard bargaining' which carries with it the darker possibilities of global governance.

Global governance and public policy

From the definition of global governance offered in *Our Global Neighbourhood*[11] – and indeed, on any plausible view – governance can be understood as global by way of the nature and sum of many governance systems, across sectors and at levels high and low. In the sense that all of the world's human systems can be regarded as inter-connected, however patchy and incoherent in their entirety, 'global governance' is an established fact of the human condition. What gives the abstraction its force and attraction is the pace and extent of globalising forces; and a clear sense that the explanatory reach of more traditional International Relations theory cannot accommodate the growth and change of contemporary world politics.

To varying degrees, the 'of, by and for the people' of democratic government has met a critical challenge in an 'organisational society' whose contours are not state-based or directly subject to state control, and this has occasioned the liveliest and most detailed thinking about the implications of governance. But because the wider governance literature is less concerned with the diffusion of power and authority 'outward' from states to transnational and stateless actors than 'downward' to local levels of association and political organisation, the main lines of debate and analysis are devoted either to the extent to which states and non-state actors can work together, or to 'governance without government' largely but not exclusively intra-state. If within states, 'We need to rethink the notion of democratic government to fit the reality of organisational society,'[12] the problem generated by the combination of globalising forces and a rapidly evolving global governance is so much more difficult, because there are no democratic forms at the global level; no formal means to hold powerful actors to account; and widely separated human groups are not a coherent constituency. So although we can theorise meaningfully about how to mediate the relationship between government and governance within states, it is far from plain that *global* governance is something that can be shaped, controlled, adjusted.

So at present, the governance literature concentrates on the more visible actor configurations and a certain class of issue–area studies. These reinforce the outline picture of a profusion of governance agents as an essentially progressive phenomenon. Indeed, viewed as world politics first decentralised and then re-configured, there is at first sight every reason to suppose that the general trend is quite positive in terms of participation and accountability. However, as the authoritative reach and deployable power of states diminishes relative to a range of non-state actors – in other words, as a larger share of the fundamentals of public life move from government to become subject to governance – the power/accountability ratio diminishes in favour of private interests. Although the parameters of states, NGOs and corporations are quite clear, can the same be said of governance structures or agents? Does any effective accretion of non-state power, purposefully directed but outside of familiar categories, qualify as an agent of governance? If what determines a body capable of practising governance is merely 'the capacity to get things done', then does power confer legitimacy? The governance literature is surprisingly elusive on this point. This is made plain in the language used to describe governance as an activity. For example, Czempiel asserts that 'Governments exercise rule, governance uses power'.[13] The seeming elevation of 'governance' from a class of activity to effective agent is a curious but rather telling device. Grammatically, one might expect the subject of the second clause to be an agent – something like 'dictatorships', 'transnational companies' or 'stateless/ virtual financial organisations'. Instead, we are left with a curiously disembodied form of rule – the 'doing internationally' quoted above.

Of course, purposeful activity, whether it is government or governance, necessitates purposeful agents. But in the absence of formal authority or established systems of accountability, will the agents of governance feel obliged to temper their controlling, agenda-setting and command capacities for the public good? According to governance theorists, an important, distinguishing difference between governance and government is that governance mechanisms lack the coercive powers of states – that 'systems of rule cannot persist unless they enjoy the support of most of those they encompass'.[14] Within states, one can credit this with some plausibility, yet at the level of world politics, there are many systems of rule which, though they are not overtly coercive, could hardly be said to enjoy the support of most of the people they encompass. Could we meaningfully say this of the WTO, for example, with or without Chinese membership? Does the current network of transnational corporations, which are still subject to varying if diminishing degrees of national and international regulation, exhibit any interest in a 'global public good' such as would make their active participation in the consolidation of a global governance something democratic polities could embrace?[15] What portion of global governance now undergoing transformation will be subject to negotiation, public scrutiny, regulation, control or possible rejection? These and a range of related questions suggest that although the consensual nature of governance systems might well apply at local levels, it is open to question whether this characteristic scales up. Global governance 'of, by and for the people' might raise a smile, but how often does unaccountable power take a benign form?

A disjuncture has opened up between the non-legal, non-authoritative 'capacity to get things done' described in the governance literature and the perceived need for inclusiveness, public participation and accountability in much of the literature now devoted to globalisation. What Rhodes terms 'self-steering inter-organizational networks' are one thing within states, but quite another at the global level – as is the business of 'democratizing functional domains'.[16] If we take some of the more forthright characterisations of global governance at face value, the troubling question that arises from this disjuncture is this: What will become of public policy in a globalised world increasingly subject to governance arrangements and mechanisms?

Governance without accountability

Power and accountability are not antithetical, but where power accrues incrementally, outside of established control mechanisms and/or not visibly – that is, without direct public sanction – asserting authority and reclaiming accountability are tough tasks. Consider the anti-trust suits brought by the US government against IBM and, more recently, Microsoft, to get an idea of the scale of the problem and the kind of difficulty facing citizen groups – or even states – that might want to challenge powerful governance agents. The task would be still more formidable were the body in question exercising its governance ' . . . successfully and consistently . . . in the absence of established legal or political authority' as quoted above. Advances in communications technologies and everything they bring in their wake, together with the sheer scale of the (worsening) disparity between rich and poor, and a general trend towards the 'hollowing out of the state' are ideal conditions for the appearance of governance mechanisms which, alone and in combination, can establish and/or entrench capacities for the unaccountable exercise of considerable power.

Here, we need not ask what might be the necessary or sufficient features of a site of governance in order to come to an understanding of the possibilities open to effective but non-legal and non-authoritative actors in a globalised world. The idea of causal webs, of a blurred distinction between high and low politics and of permeable boundaries of every kind are both familiar and well documented. These suggest that various international and institutional provision can facilitate the growth of governance, even if, much as for the states that help to propel globalisation, the full range of outcomes is not always welcome. Any conceivable global governance will not be a matter of governance without government; instead, the interest will be in the balance between them – the extent to which states and peoples alike will be subject to arrangements made privately, for private purposes.[17] The prospect is less positive than definitions of governance and global governance might suggest, as the following three themes briefly outline.

New modes of possession, ownership and control

Wide-scale privatisation of publicly owned assets and the patenting of genetic resources, which extends from meningitis bacteria to human brain cells, is continuing apace. Recently, negotiations conducted in the hope of keeping the world's plant resources in an international system of publicly owned seed banks collapsed, leading to the fear that ' . . . the bedrock of world food security is now in jeopardy'. According to one report, 'The first assault on the open-access system came from some plant-breeding companies who felt that their right to patent key resources should be paramount. That desire is redoubled now that biotechnology offers the prospect of turning the genes of humble plants in seed banks across the world into billion-dollar magic bullets.'[18]

There is also the matter of the concentration of media resources. In our time, the importance of the ownership of the means of production has been supplanted by the control of information and its dissemination. Gerald Levin, Chief Executive of the recently merged AOL Time Warner, views the prospect in a manner that accords neatly with 'governance without government': 'So what's going to be necessary is that we're going to need to have corporations redefined as instruments of public service. It's going to be forced anyhow because when you have a system that is constantly available everywhere in the world immediately, then the old-fashioned regulatory system has to give way.'[19] Levin's remarks should be reviewed in the light of the powerful impetus towards the convergence of electronic media[20] (especially the IT and broadcast sectors) and the considerable concentrations of global media ownership.[21] The implications for accountability, professional journalistic integrity and freedom of the press are both worrying and perplexing. Of private corporations as 'instruments of public service': already, according to the *State of the News Media 2004*, 'Those who would manipulate the press and public appear to be gaining leverage over the journalists who cover them.'[22]

Trends in the concentration of media ownership and control are part of the much larger growth of the size and power of the corporate sector. A few statistical indicators will be sufficient to bring the more sinister implications to bear on the assertion that 'Governments exercise rule; governance uses power': fifty-one of the world's hundred largest economies are corporations, not states; and the two hundred largest corporations 'have almost twice the economic clout of the poorest four fifths of humanity'. Moreover, 'The top five firms have over thirty per cent of global sales in airlines, aerospace, steel, oil, personal computers and the media.'[23]

'Off-screen' and virtual initiatives

The existence of 'shell banks' which maintain no physical presence within any jurisdiction are thought to facilitate fraud and money laundering,[24] yet they and a variety of legitimate though 'virtual' financial bodies, including hedge funds, are proving very difficult to regulate. In testimony before the Committee on Banking and Financial Services, the US House of Representatives, the Chairman of the Federal Reserve Board, Alan Greenspan, argued that 'While [hedge funds'] financial clout may be large, [their] physical presence is small. Given the amazing communication capabilities available virtually around the globe, trades can be initiated from almost any location. Indeed, most hedge funds are only a short step from cyberspace.' Despite the global financial implications of the near-collapse of one hedge fund, Long-Term Capital Management (discussed in Chapter 5), Greenspan admitted that 'Any direct US regulations restricting their flexibility will doubtless induce the more aggressive funds to emigrate from under our jurisdiction.' According to the report of the [US] President's Working Group on Financial Markets, even estimating the size of the industry has proved difficult.[25] And in the midst of efforts by some developed states to mitigate the burden of debt in less developed states, a number of hedge funds are now buying third world debt at discount rates and then bringing suit against the governments concerned for their face value.[26] The possibility of morally driven normative change generated by globalisation and/or its resultant fragmentation must still find its way in a world of actors who reconfigure, quickly and purposefully, often for less benign purposes; and if the latter can be characterised as 'governance without government', then so much the worse for accountability, moral or otherwise.

The difficulty of securing global public goods

One of the most serious outcomes of fragmentation is the diminishing prospect of advancing global public goods.[27] Within the span of a single lifetime, we have seen human rights move from being declaratory and aspirational to their present status as fixtures of codified international law. Yet presently, even as the physical global environment deteriorates, the constituency for addressing crises as urgent and compelling as climate change and biodiversity appears to be shrinking. Richard Falk argues that part of the explanation for the poor standing of environmental concerns in world politics 'arises from the extent to which governments representing states have accepted as their own outlook the framework of ideas embedded in neo-liberalism and have acted accordingly, jeopardizing territorial interests in the process, including the interest in a clean and healthy environment. In this regard, it is important to realise the extent to which states have become *instruments* of the private sector, including its transnational outlook, with a loss of capacity and will to promote the *public good* in general, and its environmental aspects in particular.'[28]

According to Falk, the urgency of addressing the global environment 'prompts a revisionist view of the role of the state in improving the quality of global environmental governance'. His hope is for a 're-empowered state [that] would act alongside other political actors, including those representing civil society . . . '.[29] However, the apparent retreat to unilateralism by the United States in matters ranging from arms control to environmental protection, together with the larger developed world's commitment to the World Trade Organization and its provisions, leaves scant room for manoeuvre by 'civil society', at least in respect of taking action against what Falk terms 'economism'. The enabling conditions for active democratic controls – at least for those 'from below' – might be largely absent in our larger institutions of global governance, however democratic they are in terms of national representation:

A critical limitation of defending democracy through functional regimes such as WTO and NAFTA is the failure to reckon with the spatial aspects of democracy. For democracy to make sense, there should be identifiable power centres in a territorial entity coterminous with a community which is conscious of itself as a corporate, self-governing entity. There can be no democracy in amorphous space through which power is infinitely diffused.

> Whatever arrangements are made to recontextualise and defend democracy
> must emulate the nation state in terms of a discrete spatial and social entity
> and a specific power centre.[30]

In any event, under the rubric of governance as frequently portrayed, those
most likely to be empowered – the larger forces now shaping the global
governance of the twenty-first century – will be least willing to subject
themselves to democratic deliberation and public accountability. So the hope
that 'democracy from below' can reinvigorate eroded democratic controls[31]
must contend with already considerable forms of power and control that have
already emerged from 'below' or 'outside' of formal democratic processes.

Who shall govern the governances?

The chief difficulties facing the construction of comprehensive and coherent
global governance in a highly plural and expanding (if not fracturing) actor
realm include the determination of priorities, achieving consensus and devising
actionable programmes. These are not simple matters even within the international arena, as the example of state orientation and the global environment
(above) makes plain. The *raison d'être* of powerful non-state actors is for
competitive advantage, not systemic stability as such. Likewise, corporate and
other bodies are more likely to lobby governments and international
organisations for changes favourable to their operating environments, rather
than to take up roles as sanctioned or even quasi-legitimate governance actors
in partnership with authoritative agents.[32] Transparency and accountability
are ill-served thereby, of course; and more fundamentally, the private ends of
private actors can and often do add to the regulatory burden of public bodies.
The independence and purposes of powerful, independent actors should be set
against a consideration of the nature and scale of political authority needed to
exercise the most important varieties of global governance. Consider one,
comprehensive definition of sustainable development:

> To maximize simultaneously the biological system goals (genetic diversity,
> resilience, biological productivity), economic system goals (satisfaction of
> basic needs, enhancement of equity, increasing useful goods and services),
> and social system goals (cultural diversity, institutional sustainability,
> social justice, participation).[33]

If these goals seem highly aspirational, the alternatives, for the weak and
powerful alike, are not what any would freely choose. But the weaker the ratio
between power and accountability in governance agents, the less likely they
are to accommodate the public interest, our shared environment, or even the
long-term systems stability on which they rely.

In order to deal with the difficult and contested notion of power, Susan
Strange argued that we can best think of it in terms of outcomes – and

specifically, as either relational or structural.[34] What is most disturbing about the broadest and best-known characterisations of global governance is not merely that they pose profound (if frequently unacknowledged) challenges to democratic control and public accountability – the relational aspect of power – but they do so on a scale that is truly global: not only pervasive and encompassing, but also structural – in ways which threaten to foreclose the political options that might lead to a flexible, responsive and humane global order. As Strange expressed it, 'Those who have structural power are recognisable because they are able to affect the range of options within which others can choose what to do. It may seem that others choose freely, but the risks and penalties of going outside that range of options are so punitive that they are not seriously considered.'[35]

As globalisation opens up unprecedented possibilities for the exercise of considerable power by non-state and even stateless entities, it is curious that our concern for governance without accountability is not yet the equal of our wonder over 'governance without government'. It should be kept in mind that the fragmentation beloved of governance theorists, much as the larger globalising trends which in good measure generate and shape it, is not necessarily a force for either good or ill; and that it works on social cohesion as much as on political structures. A glancing familiarity with the globalisation literature will make plain the extent to which globalising forces have debilitated social coherence and resilience.[36] What chance participation, negotiation, control and accountability on matters of global import when democracy and accountability *within* states moves on to shifting and uncertain ground? In the face of the worst social, ecological and economic effects of globalisation, assumptions about the democratising energies released by fragmentation seem remarkably blithe. However, we have no reason to suppose that the unco-ordinated sum of hundreds and perhaps thousands of quite disparate governances will create and sustain a stable and equitable world, not least because they will be subject to the same interests and antagonisms as any other sphere of politics. In addition, as an ever greater number of these governances become sited in the private sphere, prospects for the accommodation of differences and some degree of transparency if not democratic accountability will shrink.[37]

The fracturing of politics, characterised as the emergence of sub-politics[38] in the risk literature, cannot wholly be ascribed to the corrosive effects of a growing awareness of risk. It is as credible to speak of the empowerment of a variety of non-state actors through globalisation as to suppose that we are witnessing the dissolution of 'high' politics into splinters of 'sub-politics' because risk has disabled or invalidated established institutions. However, a hierarchically ordered world, with nation states in full control of the actors within their borders, if it ever existed, certainly is no more; and it is clear that power and authority of various kinds are now invested in many non-state actors, whether or not this amounts to 'governance without government' in specific cases.[39] But as the actor realm becomes more plural, it also becomes less coherent, particularly if governance is exercised by private bodies for private purposes. And as at the top, so too at the bottom: James Rosenau has termed the sometimes contradictory dynamics of globalising forces 'fragmegration',[40] – a visible phenomenon in societies in the developed world; and one need only look at the poorest parts of the world to see that a sizeable portion of humanity stands little to gain by maintaining or consolidating the status quo. Against these trends, we need to think carefully about the 'retreat of the state' – that is, how far the authoritative reach and standing of states can be diminished, before we also diminish the possibilities for the accountable exercise of regulation and control over the range of global dynamics we have set in train.

7 Case study

Disseminative systems and global governance

Introduction

In the aftermath of the Cuban Missile crisis, the Pentagon initiated the 'Nth Country Project' – a small initiative to determine whether two amateurs (individuals with doctorates in physics, but with no nuclear expertise and no access to classified information) could design a feasible nuclear weapon. As one of the participants recalls, after thirty months, 'We produced a short document that described precisely, in engineering terms, what we proposed to build and what materials were involved. The whole works, in great detail, so that this thing could have been made by Joe's Machine Shop downtown.'[1] Thirty-five years later, in 1999, the Pentagon's Defence Threat Reduction Agency commissioned 'Project Bacchus'. With little more than a budget and commercial catalogues for laboratory equipment, a team was given the task of assembling a small but functional germ factory. It took them just over a year to produce two pounds of anthrax simulants. 'The project had proven its point – a nation or a bioterrorist with the requisite expertise could easily assemble an anthrax factory from off-the-shelf materials . . . probably without the intelligence agencies' knowledge.'[2]

At least where the life sciences are concerned, the risks are no longer merely in the realm of intelligence agency speculation. Two years after 'Project Bacchus',

> A virus that kills every one of its victims, by wiping out part of their immune systems, [was] accidentally created by an Australian research team. The virus, a modified mousepox, does not affect humans, but it is closely related to smallpox, raising fears that the technology could be used in biowarfare. The discovery highlights a growing problem. How do you stop terrorists taking legitimate research and adapting it for their own nefarious purposes?[3]

The problem is compounded by the routine practice of scientific endeavour in our time: publishing results for the scrutiny of the global scientific community:

Defence experts are also worried about preserving the freedom to publish medical findings while trying to stop the information falling into the wrong hands. According to D. A. Henderson, a former US presidential adviser, and director of the Center for Civilian Biodefence Studies at Johns Hopkins University in Baltimore, what are effectively blueprints for making microorganisms more harmful regularly appear in unclassified journals. 'I can't for the life of me figure out how we are going to deal with this,' he says.[4]

The dissemination of expert knowledge and the physical requisites for conducting scientific research are rightly regarded as global public goods,[5] but the potential for serious misuse of biological knowledge is a particularly striking example of a problem which is woven into the fabric of our globalised world: the nature and extent of disseminative systems which defy centralised control and in some instances, even comprehensive understanding. This chapter will review the variety and character of disseminative systems before turning to the vexed question of how systems so dispersed, accessible and adaptable can be regulated or controlled without disrupting their beneficent uses. Given that the extent and integration of disseminative systems is global, the regulatory problem, conceptually and in specific instances, is a problem of global governance, so the chapter concludes with a critical examination of the conceptual compass of the global governance literature as it has developed to date.

Disseminative systems

The disseminative systems under discussion here are human systems – that is, constructs of human striving; and manifestations of human culture. However, disseminative systems are not free-standing entities, but are also caught up in, and contribute to, the intensifying interaction of human and natural systems which now comprise an important aspect of the human condition.[6] So it is important to maintain an awareness first urged upon us by Geoffrey Vickers, of

> human beings as systems and [of] systems in which human beings are significant constituent parts; that is to say [of] human societies and organizations and with ecological systems in which the behaviour of human beings and societies cannot usefully be studied without taking into account the mutual influences exerted on each other by the human element and its milieu.[7]

Distinguishing human systems from the natural systems that support human life is a necessary abstraction and easy to sustain if we choose as an illustrative example that farming is a human system and that the soil ecology on which it is practised a natural one. However, as we have seen, the consequences of decades of pesticide and fertiliser use around the world[8] and the more recent introduction of genetically modified plants into commercial agriculture remind us of the limits of abstractions, particularly in a globalised and globalising world.

Many human systems are *disseminated* in the sense that they are widely dispersed. This dissemination can be purposeful (the siting of the world's airline infrastructure is integral to its purpose and functioning), or it can come about in a largely unco-ordinated manner, propelled by industrialisation and globalisation (motorised vehicle traffic is a case in point.) However, there is more to the nature of disseminative systems than the passive quality of being or having been disseminated: they are *disseminative* in the sense that they also facilitate very considerable interaction and exchange, both within the realm of human systems and between human and natural systems. This is the point at which the staggering complexity of the world we have made for ourselves becomes apparent. The airline industry, for example, 'disseminates' more than holiday makers and business people. It is also responsible for some novel and quite complex interactions of human and natural systems, such as furthering the 'bio-invasions' of plant and animal species into new environments[9] and more dramatically, assisting the spread of infectious diseases, as the recent SARS epidemic demonstrated.

Disseminative systems facilitate human movement, but also, perhaps more importantly, exchange: physical (illicit drugs as well as medicine; small arms and laboratory samples); symbolic (electronic currency exchange and share dealing); and ideational (small wonder that repressive regimes try to restrict access to the aptly named world-wide web.) But as the growth of the web illustrates, the physical properties and/or intended purposes of disseminative systems often give little insight into their potential, benign and malign, once global distribution and low levels of accessibility are reached. What is most interesting from a governance perspective is how easily and frequently the functions of disseminative systems exceed design – that is, how the full potential and actual uses of disseminative systems are often difficult to foresee and deliberate upon, let alone subject to regulatory frameworks within or between states. For example, it was never decided that the value of worldwide electronic currency exchange transactions should greatly exceed the entire world's gross domestic product, but the spread and integration of various electronic communications systems made this possible.[10] The more blithe characterisations of our world as 'wired' all too easily overlook the profound challenges disseminative systems offer to our conceptions of global governance.

Three types of disseminative systems can be identified. The first is *infrastructural* – what we might call the conduits of globalisation. These include highways and airports; ships and ports; pipelines, wires, cables, aerials, satellites and satellite dishes; and the near-ubiquitous computer. Each of these systems is discrete, but the largest part of their function and purpose is contingent upon the functioning of other systems, both disseminated and disseminative. Globalisation is furthered by, but also partly contingent upon, the interaction of many human and natural systems; and increasingly, upon systems of systems.

Even though these systems are routinely functional, the sheer complexity and geographic distribution of the elements that comprise them often place them outside of meaningful comprehension by monitoring and managerial authorities. As a result, the blind spots in regulatory oversight across the full range of disseminated and disseminative systems become apparent only after the fact. The network structure of Al Qaeda is frequently noted, but what made it effective is the careful use of disseminative systems – not least clandestine airline charters; illicit means of global cash transfers; and 'bulk cash smuggling and the global trade in gold and other commodities to move and store value'.[11]

Second, there are also *organisational* disseminative systems. It is not sufficient that objects, tools and infrastructural platforms are disseminated, since the systems they comprise are only systems to the extent that they are enabled. That is, in order to be globally disseminative, they must be dedicated to one or more purposes and configured accordingly; variously connected and/or co-ordinated; and subject to some degree of oversight and adjustment. The laws and conventions facilitating and regulating world trade fit into this category, as does the networked information that makes possible credit card use practically everywhere in the world; likewise, the protocols that ensure non-competitive use of broadcast bandwidth and the world-wide web. The material and non-material components of disseminative systems are integral to one another: witness the on-going struggle to deter credit card fraud, now that the information embedded in the cards (ever more usable remotely) is as easy to steal as the cards themselves.

The organisational aspect of disseminative systems is what makes possible uses which are also unplanned, unregulated and sometimes illegal. An example of this is *hawala*, an informal yet simple and efficient system of cash transfer via email or fax, used throughout much of the Middle East and the Indian subcontinent, often for the repatriation of foreign worker remittances, but sometimes for more nefarious purposes. The human links are more a matter of trust-based community than corporate organisation, although in technical terms, the principle behind *hawala* differs little from that of Western Union. What makes *hawala* possible is the existence of electronic communication as a disseminative system; however, in addition to the support of distant families and personal debts being honoured, money laundering and the financial dealings of criminal and terrorist activity are also enabled.[12]

The third type of disseminative system is *epistemic*. Data, information, knowledge, technical expertise and belief are all transferable, of course – this is the foundation for all human culture. But global, disseminative systems extend this by an order of magnitude that is difficult to appreciate even now. As the means to acquire and transmit information have expanded, epistemic communities have become disseminative systems in their own right – something that became plain when the encryption code of DVDs was cracked and subsequently posted on the web.[13]

This is not merely a tale of corporate loss: it also points to the kinds of regulatory difficulties that disseminative systems have begun to generate.

Our understanding of what counts as an epistemic community is misleading if it assumes shared values as well as common interests, technical competence and available information. This has far-reaching implications, even within the relatively narrow field of data storage, retrieval and transmission technologies as disseminative systems. It is now easy to transmit data and new research findings about viruses, whether this means gene sequences or logarithms, to anyone – and in effect, to everyone. In addition, now common but quite sensitive electronic communication – governmental, commercial and private – depends on utterly reliable, yet shared encryption standards. But the development and maintenance of encryption systems is not a closed world; and the larger epistemic communities of which it is a part share the same mathematics and increasingly, the same or sufficient computing power. Note that although the corporations concerned invested very considerable sums of money in developing the encryption system for DVDs, it was cracked by a teenager.

Characteristics of disseminative systems

In order to understand the formidable obstacles in the way of exercising governance over disseminative systems, three principal characteristics of their place in twenty-first century life must be grasped. The first is that the global distribution and accessibility of disseminative systems has made them not merely common but also deeply embedded in our ways of life. The degree of our dependence on disseminative systems is easiest to grasp when they fail, but vulnerability can also take sudden and surprising, albeit non-catastrophic forms. Governments throughout the world have every reason to be concerned about bio-safety and about what non-sanctioned agents might be sharing, either electronically or physically, but none is about to disable its stake in the global pharmaceutical industry or scientific research in the life sciences more generally. Nor, more tellingly, will they easily curtail electronic communication without also impacting so much of the ordinary functioning of states, societies and organisations. The accessibility and adaptability of disseminative systems create vulnerabilities which are particularly vexed not only because the systems exceed national and sometimes international jurisdiction, but also because their dangerous or undesirable uses and/or effects cannot simply be excised from the routine, benign purposes for which we build and sustain disseminative systems in the first place.

The second important characteristic of disseminative systems is that their connectivity and speed engenders surprising forms and degrees of risk and vulnerability. For example, because of the countless connections between the machines that comprise the web, a virus can be inadvertently circulated much more quickly than anti-virus software can be distributed.[14] In turn, to the extent that disseminative systems are dependent upon one another, vulnerability becomes a much broader and less calculable phenomenon. It is worth keeping in mind the range of what was affected by the massive 2003 power failure in the Northeast of the US and Canada: the New York stock exchange, airports and banks were unable to operate; hospitals were on emergency power; and computers and mobile phones would not work – two disseminative systems whose failure created a cascade of other failures and shut-downs.

The danger inherent in the tight coupling of human systems has featured in the sociological and disaster prevention literature for some time,[15] but its extension to highly intricate and dynamic disseminative systems introduces new challenges to comprehension, let alone control. So even as our dependence on computers and computerised systems is extended and consolidated, we might well be engineering what one author has described as a 'computer trap':

> the elaborate, long-term, collective effects of the possibly irreversible and largely unexamined drive to computerize and network everything and anything whose efficiency or economic performance might thereby be improved. In the process, those who re-design and re-engineer the large-scale social and socio-technical systems that are essential for managing the complexities and structures of modern life seem to have little understanding of the potential vulnerabilities they are creating. Such effects are already being noted in the similar, persistent search to eliminate from hazardous systems all possible sources and causes of 'human error'. Whether those systems be military or industrial, financial or bureaucratic, the increased tightness of coupling, lack of redundancy, and speed of response, will make human intervention or control difficult at best when (and not if) something goes wrong – particularly for those systems whose means and mechanisms of operation are so deeply embedded in the computers that operate them that no human being fully understands them.[16]

The third characteristic of disseminative systems is the unparalleled degree of complexity they introduce into human affairs. An array of disseminative systems is now central to the organisation and function of our lives and life support; and they are configured to one another; to natural systems and to other non-disseminative human systems. (The growth of international airline travel of 7 per cent per year over four decades – and its environmental, cultural, political and security outcomes and implications – is but one quite clear example.)[17] Every extension of disseminative systems will open the way for further change – not all of it either willed or desirable – within and between both human and natural systems. This is not difficult to predict in outline, because globalisation is essentially a human phenomenon, not a technological one; and the main drivers for the establishment and uses of disseminative systems are hardy perennials: profit, convenience, greed, relative advantage, curiosity, demonstrations of prowess, ideological fervour, malign destructiveness. None of these human impulses are likely to disappear, but on the largest scale, their manifestations now extend considerably beyond more familiarly empowered governmental and corporate actors to include even individuals: terrorists, computer hackers and rogue market traders. And the potential consequences – for national security, social well-being, the global environment and the uninterrupted functioning of the very disseminative systems on which we have come to depend – are considerable.

The engineered complexity of the contemporary world introduces challenges to our ability to exercise governance which go much deeper than the question of how we might best mitigate visible or calculable risk. This is because some quite fundamental disseminative systems are connected and used in ways which make system-wide comprehension, and hence management in any meaningful sense, highly problematic, as for example, the case of large systems comprising many sub-systems:

> Just as they did after major blackouts in the Northeast [US] in 1959, 1961, 1965 and 1977, investigators are trying to figure out exactly what set off the avalanche of failure [in August 2003]. . . . But what all the failures had in common is that the grid – complicated beyond full understanding, even by experts – lives and occasionally dies by its own mysterious rules. . . . The incomprehensible complexity of the grid comes with its own irreducible pathologies, experts say. The system brings power to every wall in the United States, but increasingly, as the scale of the grid grows, it can suddenly take away that power. And given the sensitivity of the grid to accidental power failures, the realization of what deliberate acts of terrorism could do is also raising new concerns.[18]

But the problem of comprehension goes much deeper: the vast, continuous volume and speed of electronic financial transactions could not be comprehended by any individual or group for the purpose of oversight, even if the data were gathered. When set against the number, configuration and dynamism of the electronic systems now at the heart of global financial dealing, the attempt to make considered judgements about the hour-by-hour functioning of this system of systems would have as little purchase as a snapshot for the purpose of refereeing a football game. The significance of complexity and systems behaviour is as yet little appreciated within the social sciences,[19] but the extent to which our systems have begun to manifest them is gradually becoming apparent. In the following example, the matter is trivial but indicative, particularly in light of the description of the US electricity grid (above):

> Airline pricing has grown so complex that it is now technically impossible to design an algorithm that will find the cheapest fare. In mathematical terms, the problem of finding the cheapest airfare between two locations is actually unsolvable. Even if you specify the route or the flights, the problem of finding the lowest fare could take the fastest computers billions of years to solve. [. . .] The problem was that all the different rules interact in ways that not even those who designed the systems could begin to understand.[20]

This discovery surprised the researchers involved – much as each new, pernicious or fraudulent use of the world wide web appears to come as a shock; or as we experience failures of disseminative systems that no one was able to foresee. Yet the peculiarities or emergencies that emerge from the workings of our disseminative systems are in a profound sense, 'accidents waiting to happen', as has been clear for some time to those working within the field of cybernetics: 'Outcomes are latent in the dynamic structure of the systems we have or may adopt: they will inexorably emerge.'[21] The inexorability here is not to be confused with the 'inevitability' that is a feature of some of the 'risk society' literature.[22] The point is that the intensifying, complex interaction of human and natural systems mean that few of our larger public policy choices or defaults will have merely linear consequences; and that some of these will not be open to correction. So it is that the physical properties of atmospheric pollutants and the oceans' thermal inertia mean that saving the Maldives from flooding is no longer open to us;[23] and that scientific thinking has begun to converge around the view that 'It is now more sensible to think about *adapting* to [climate change]'.[24]

Disseminative systems and global governance

The most remarkable outcome of the emergence and spread of globally disseminative systems is the speed with which they have been absorbed into social and economic life – or perhaps, the rate at which long-established modes of human interaction have been transformed. The succession of technological innovations and social changes in the twentieth century is a common enough observation in the globalisation literature, but of particular note is the *pace* of change, because it is historically unprecedented. By comparison, the validity of written text over oral testimony ' . . . occurred over more than three centuries of early English history'.[25] Something so basic to the social intercourse and governance of the time was not merely met with resistance, but also by modes of adaptation commensurate with social coherence. Now, disseminative systems impact on all societies, directly and indirectly; rapidly, fundamentally and all but inescapably; for purposes both pre-determined and subsequently adapted; and with multiple effects, sometimes unforeseen and often difficult to discriminate.

Throughout the world, societies or significant aspects of their form and workings have been transformed (and sometimes debilitated) by disseminative systems; and the momentum of globalising change very often makes 'adaptation' the euphemistic form of 'change or die'.

This is important because the adaptive capacities of societies are a critical indicator of their ability to formulate and exercise governance – that is, to the extent that what comes within the compass of their needs or concerns is also within their authoritative reach. However, the sheer scale, power and diffusion of disseminative systems are at least in some instances able to override or elude control systems that have featured as part of functioning societies for centuries.

Recently, this has begun to feature in the literature analysing the diminution of state power in the face of various transnational and global dynamics.[26]

On the other hand, adaptive capacity can be turned to the full range of human purposes. So, for example, the scale and extent of illicit trade can be regarded as a form of social adaptation because even though the infrastructural features of disseminative systems are sited within political communities, the purposeful functioning of these systems is to act as though the world were borderless – or to make it so. The UN Global Report on Crime and Justice notes that:

> There is some overlap among the various [illegal] markets, partly because some criminal organizations traffic in a variety of products. Once the trafficking infrastructure is in place, the product line is virtually irrelevant. [. . .] There has to be an acknowledgement that in many . . . sectors of activity . . . there is no sharp disconnect between licit business activities and illicit or criminal activities. There are significant grey areas populated by unscrupulous entrepreneurs who move from the licit to the illicit and back again as circumstances and opportunities dictate.[27]

What, then, does it mean to speak of global governance in a world in which various kinds of smuggling are routinely characterised as parasitic upon the world political economy, but may in some instances and to some degree be integral to it – and in any event, which make effective use of the same disseminative systems on which regulated trade depends? These illegal/illicit enterprises are estimated to entail values in the trillions of dollars and they are plainly well-regulated, albeit informally.[28] Curiously, they conform to some of the better-known characterisations of global governance, such as Lawrence Finklestein's, 'Global governance is governing, without sovereign authority, relationships that transcend national frontiers. Global governance is doing internationally what governments do at home.'[29] Similarly, Ernst-Otto Czempiel takes ' . . . "governance" to mean the capacity to get things done without the legal competence to command that they be done. Where governments, in the eastonian sense, can distribute values authoritatively, governance can distribute them in a way which is not authoritative but equally effective.'[30]

Yet few would suppose that a world in which *any* effective exercise of competence or power for private purposes would be secure, equitable and sustainable – for all that it might be well-ordered, sectorally or geographically. Likewise, conceptions of global governance as a summative phenomenon[31] – that is, the totality of many governances, high and low; state and non-state – implicitly entail the darker possibilities of effective, but non-authoritative and unaccountable power.[32] The promise of 'governance without government'[33] therefore carries with it risk that is at least the equal of its benign possibilities.

A conception of global governance that ignores, or is abstracted from, disseminative systems can be 'global' in a variety of ways, but in view of the

extensive and rather worrying possibilities now emerging from the intensification of globalising dynamics, we are still left with the question: What
would an adequate global governance be the governance *of?* To date, the largest
part of the global governance literature concentrates on what is often described
as the 'current system', or the 'architecture' of global governance (most often,
the larger UN system, including the IFIs);[34] or on various sectoral concerns:
global finance; trade; health; the environment.[35] The importance of such work
is indisputable, but is it sufficient for a world in which disseminative systems
are so powerful, extensive, accessible and adaptive?

Any effective governance of disseminative systems would of necessity
be global, at least in extent, because the distribution, connectivity and uses
of them are global, too; and also because some of the most powerful and
potentially most threatening globally disseminative systems also shape and
sustain aspects of the international and global systems on which even the most
powerful states depend. At an abstract level, then, we might suppose that the
global governance of disseminative systems would be an exercise (albeit a
remarkably difficult one) in practical politics, but the conceptual problems
alone extend far beyond the compass of the global governance literature as
it has developed thus far. The conceptual challenges can best be seen by
examining the extensive and detailed web of global business regulation, since
there is no shortage of business regulation that pertains to various aspects of
our larger disseminative systems. The airline industry, for example, is regulated
by a variety of actors and mechanisms both national and international for a
variety of purposes, including air worthiness and the harmonisation of traffic
control.[36] But it is not governed as a disseminative system; and it is difficult
to see how it could be. Typically, disseminative systems display many if not all
of the following qualities, which make the exercise of governance after the fact
a daunting prospect:

- They are integral to ways of life, both structurally and operationally, not
  least for the most powerful and wealthy constituencies.
- Routine, thoroughgoing and detailed scrutiny of disseminative systems
  for regulatory purposes would render the disseminative function(s)
  inoperative, and would quickly impact on other, connected disseminative
  systems. A typical parcel delivery company in the United States now
  delivers more than 2 million parcels per day.[37] And how thorough can we
  make airport security, while still maintaining the global airline industry
  as a disseminative system?[38]
- The technology is simple. (Adolescent computer hackers are not a scarce
  commodity.)
- Access to information and products (or to the processes that produce them)
  is also simple – at times, alarmingly so. (Dangerous applications of
  biological expertise are pertinent here.)
- Beneficial uses are more apparent – or more important – than possible
  risks.

- Conceiving and enacting governance over established disseminative systems would entail a daunting array of considerations: kinds and extent of regulatory authority (supranational; national; multilateral; bilateral; state-internal; state-perimeter); degrees of formalisation (institutions; laws; regimes; standard-setting); and range of purposes (prohibition; exclusion; regulation; taxation; monitoring).

Resistances from a very large number of concerned parties, both state and non-state, would be very difficult to surmount. A Rand Corporation study of the global governance challenges posed by the revolutions in communications and the biological sciences concluded:

> a 'top-down' approach to governance of these technologies would not be practical. In the realm of standard-setting, a bottom-up, informal approach could prove workable, given the incentives for participants to converge in a singe standard. However, regulation is more challenging. Enforcement across a wide variety of countries is likely to present problems, especially when top-down intergovernmental mechanisms lack force or fail because governments are unwilling to pressure one another. Moreover, the extent of control of these technologies and their applications that is or will be in the hands of individuals makes regulation particularly difficult. Given that many decisions about the use and application will be made on an individual basis, it is hard to imagine any regulatory structure without wide 'buy-in' from the polity.[39]

The hope expressed by the authors of that study in the regulative possibilities of citizen councils, NGOs and other 'stakeholders' to develop 'global governance norms or structures', seems not only belated but also oddly removed from the outcomes of disseminative systems already extant. Similarly, 'global civil society' is a meaningful abstraction, but not a deliberative, authoritative or purposeful agent.[40]

In any event, for all that the term 'disseminative systems' has meaning and analytical purchase, our public policy machinery is ill-suited to conceiving global governance – or even regulation – for infrastuctural and relational matters that are so closely and intricately woven into our infrastructures. The considerable array of regulatory mechanisms that pertain to the operation of disseminative systems exist primarily to facilitate their intended purposes,[41] but how they combine and come to be used is, like so much of what comes under the 'globalisation' rubric, a source of wonder, or alarm – and subsequently, public policy as fire-fighting. A report by the US National Research Council on the role of science and technology in countering terrorism noted

> the interconnected, highly technological nature of modern civilizations' basic systems. Market forces and a tradition of openness have combined to maximize the efficiency of many of our vital systems – such as those that

provide transportation, information, technology, energy and health care. However, economic systems, like ecological systems, tend to become less resilient (more prone to failure when strongly perturbed) as they become more efficient, so our infrastructures are vulnerable to local disruptions, which could lead to widespread, catastrophic failures. In addition the high level of interconnectedness of these systems means that the abuse, destruction, or interruption of any one of them quickly affects the others. As a result, the whole society is vulnerable, with the welfare and even the lives of significant portions of the population placed at risk.[42]

In addition, the speed of new discoveries and developments – and their entry into our physical and political environments – can and often does outpace our deliberative mechanisms. For example, it was the day *after* the appearance of the first cloned mammal that President Clinton asked the National Bioethics Advisory Commission to '... undertake a thorough review of the legal and ethical issues associated with the use of this technology'.[43] And national legislation and international covenants, belated or not, are enacted in a world of fracturing political and moral constituencies, noted in the global governance literature as new centres of power, competence and allegiance.[44]

Because a considerable portion of global governance theorising is rooted in International Relations and International Political Economy, there has been an understandable emphasis on the authority, competence and adaptability of states and state-based institutions to deal with a range of global and other non-state dynamics. As a result, the largest part of the global governance literature appears to rest on an assumption that our various governance mechanisms are sufficient, or sufficiently adaptable, to allow us to maintain a problem-solving disposition, even as we continue to fashion a world that in many important respects no longer conforms to the capacities of states, individually and collectively. In addition, disseminative systems might well be too diffuse, embedded, adaptable and open to rapid development or technological advance to be subjected to any conceivable global governance, at least as it is generally conceived.

Addressing the question of what an adequate global governance might or should comprise is therefore unlikely to be a reassuring intellectual exercise, but it is nevertheless curious that it has not yet found its place beside the questions that inspire so many fine actor- and sector-specific studies. Whether and to what extent we can exercise control over the world we have already created, for purposes collectively and accountably determined must surely be confronted directly as part of the theoretical development of global governance; and the concept of disseminative systems introduced here offers a rationale for that enterprise, if not a starting point.

In the first instance, a reckoning of the global governance of disseminative systems will pose some considerable conceptual problems. This is because the kinds of challenges offered to global governance by disseminative systems are not problems with solutions. They will routinely manifest themselves not as technological conundrums or reversible trends, but as deeply impacted issues of human relations, which will require calculations of the requirements for social coherence and environmental sustainability against the pull of special interest and individual empowerment, as well as more familiar international competition.

And the conceptual problems will be closely aligned to the political challenges, in all probability obliging us to face what has been described as ' . . . the extraordinary delusion which has dominated the Western world for two hundred years, equating individual liberty with universal peace'.[45] Any attempt to exercise global governance of at least some disseminative systems is likely to involve limits on human freedom that will be deeply objectionable in a world grown accustomed to a high degree of personal autonomy; technologically assisted mobility and access; and the expectation of ever-increasing and/or ever-widening economic prosperity. There are considerable differences between the US administration declaring a category of 'sensitive but unclassified' scientific information,[46] with its implications for information exchange and collaborative scientific work; and the Chinese government's clamp-down on legal but sensitive web access and electronic communication.[47] But both are belated attempts to control outcomes of the use of disseminative systems, not the systems themselves. The political difficulty for the Chinese government is its ' . . . quandary in trying to promote the economic, modernising side of the web, while suppressing its political and subversive nature'[48] – while in the US case, it is scientific advance versus national security. As disseminative systems continue to proliferate, is it plausible that their negative impacts can be dealt with on a case-by-case basis, nationally and/or internationally? On the other hand, exercising control over the systems themselves is a daunting political prospect, even setting aside the conceptual problems.

Meanwhile, there are countervailing pressures, some quite benign in intent. For example, bridging the 'digital divide' – even if one accepts that this is an important element in addressing the plight of the world's more impoverished peoples[49] – will create further difficulties and complications, increasing the inherent risks and the regulatory burden. Much the same can be said about the continuing expansion of trans-continental flights.

Finally, a consideration of disseminative systems highlights a need for the acknowledgement of cognitive limits as a condition of our potential to conceive and enact a global governance, since how much can be managed is in part a function of how much can be grasped. Human systems that defy timely comprehension because of their complexity or speed are not confined to computer-assisted data transmission. Whether or not we have created a runaway world through the complex interaction of human and natural systems (and disseminative systems most of all) might best be faced by asking, 'What are the limits of global governance?'

8   The limits of global governance

The sum of the orders we have created and sustained – global governance as we now have it – is certainly impressive. Turbulence in the international system persists, but it remains a system; and there are highly developed governance arrangements at state, regional and local levels. Social, political and legal systems underpin urban infrastructures, technologically assisted behaviours and much of what comes under the heading 'globalisation'. Very large and complex human systems such as world trade are regulated with some degree of success – or at least for sufficient stability and predictability to satisfy the interests of the most powerful constituencies. In addition, several other areas of human activity central to state interests, such as international finance, are variously regulated, controlled or co-ordinated by international organisations that balance the need for systemic order against the competitive standing of individual states. There have also been a good many initiatives concerned with adjusting and regulating the interaction of some human and natural systems on the largest scale, albeit often in response to crises. On an individual level, those of us privileged to enjoy the ease of world-wide travel, communication and consumer choice are aware that we are the beneficiaries of systems of governance which are global in their extent and/or connectedness. And to the more familiar governmental and institutional forms of governance, an 'association revolution'[1] adds new possibilities for the inclusion of peoples, issues and values which do not feature in – or indeed, may run contrary to – established modes of governance.

As we have seen, some detailed arguments have made the case that a combination of formal and informal arrangements (the governance of national and international actors, together with the 'governance without government' phenomenon) will at least provide the possibility of a global governance that is more extensive, more plural and more effective than one left to 'top-down' internationally led organisations alone. There is certainly abundant evidence that we now have what James Rosenau has termed 'the proliferation of governance':

> With the wide dispersion of authority at every level of community . . . recent decades have witnessed a vast expansion of rule systems and steering

mechanisms. Nor is there any lack of variety in the extant systems of governance. [. . .] New forms of government have been developed, and old ones have either added new layers or transferred their authority downward to subnational levels or upward to supranational levels. The result is an ever-widening realm in which governance is undertaken and implemented, a development that suggests the world may indeed be adapting to the ever-greater complexity of community, national, regional and global life.[2]

As the realm of significant and/or empowered actors widens, it is at least possible that new forms of association will add to and strengthen our already established modes of governance. And the proposition that informal co-operation can create significant, ordered outcomes – and may in fact be a necessary counterpart to top-down government and other forms of governance – is familiar in long-standing debates within the field of public administration. These debates neatly parallel the arguments advanced for 'governance without government':

> [D]espite the absence or weakness of central co-ordination of the partici-pants, their mutual adjustments of many kinds (of which bargaining is only one) will to some degree co-ordinate them as policy makers. In many circumstances their mutual adjustments will achieve a co-ordination superior to an attempt at central co-ordination, which is often so complex as to lie beyond any co-ordinator's competence. Such a proposition does not deny the obvious failures of co-ordination that mark government . . . It merely claims that such co-ordination as, with difficulty, our govern-ments achieve will often owe more to partisan mutual adjustment than to attempts at central co-ordination.[3]

Recent global governance scholarship has brought a searching scrutiny to the particulars of the steering, controlling and ordering imperatives of global institutions, with an emphasis on structural imperfections and operational shortcomings.[4] The established literature on globalisation and democracy now has its complement in work devoted to the democratic deficits of global governance.[5] Also, the way in which state, supranational, sub-national and non-state actors configure to exercise governance has necessitated 'multi-level governance' and 'complex multilateralism' perspectives and case studies.[6]

These and a host of other, related works are important and worthwhile lines of investigation. Across a field of study so rich in subject matter, what these disparate studies share is an understanding that the sum of governance arrangements at all levels of human activity amount to a global aggregate. This suggests an awareness of the interconnectedness of all human and natural orders – and by extension, the necessity for a minimal coherence, if not co-ordination of human systems. (Our growing concern with globalisation and its impli-cations greatly reinforces the idea of global governance as something necessarily as extensive and inclusive.) To ask whether our current arrangements are adequate is to invite the question, 'adequate for what and for whom?' But since the viability of planetary ecosystems is under threat, we need at least to ensure the conditions necessary for further political contention. Are the numerous, varied systems of governance we now have in place sufficient to secure the human future? A good portion of the global governance literature appears to offer a qualified 'yes'. The recommendations in the report of the Commission on Global Governance mostly entail running adjustments to existing institutions, particularly the UN (with the addition of an Economic Security Council and an endorsement of the idea of a global tax), and a further promulgation and strengthening of already existing norms. The message appears to be 'more of the same, but better.'[7]

For all the differences across the span of global governance scholarship, the works that comprise it strongly suggest (in keeping with the Commission's report), that the many forms of governance now at work in the world, together with our capacity for creativity and responsiveness, will keep pace with the larger consequences of human activity. However critical, either theoretically or with respect to particular governing institutions, the global governance literature carries an unvoiced assumption: that our institutions of governance are sufficient and/or sufficiently adaptable to address the vexed issues already facing us, as well as those we are clearly capable of generating in the near future. The evidence presented in the preceding chapters suggests the opposite. The argument can be summarised in three thematic points, discussed in turn below.

There is no logical reason to suppose that we will be able to control the outcomes of our creations and activities

In fact, there is abundant evidence in our many global crises that our capacity to create hugely complex, intractable problems is advancing beyond the reach of our policy-making machinery and in some cases, our predictive capacity. The limits of our global governance are not merely logical limits, but are already manifest. To add to the difficulty, these limitations are not merely a matter of political recalcitrance, nor confined to the difficulty of organising, negotiating and enacting appropriate multilateral agreements and regimes, contested and prolonged as these matters are. Much of what is coming to pose global governance challenges will, in all probability, not be confined to the jurisdictional confines of single states or come within the authoritative reach of existing multilateral and other current modes and levels of governance. What makes this trend so clear is the pervasiveness and speed of our disseminative systems; and the pace and extent of scientific advance – both of which are expanding and opening up new combinational possibilities as a large portion of humanity races to industrialise.

At the same time, already established human systems are placing enormous stresses on both the natural world and our existing systems of governance, in everything from resource scarcities to the pollution emitted by our transportation infrastructures, to the problems of securing the stability and coherence of an international financial system now in continuous, high-speed electronic exchange. And although there is a clear distinction between the cumulative impacts of familiar human activity that drive resource scarcities and environmental debilitation on the one hand, and the range of risks associated with new technologies on the other, the world-wide diffusion of scientific expertise, its technological and commercial uses and industrial-level applications have already begun to bring these two realms closer together, with consequences none can predict. For example, 'China has planted more than a million genetically modified trees in a bid to halt the spread of deserts and prevent flash floods. But a bureaucratic loophole means that no one knows for sure where all the trees have been planted, or what effect they will have on native forests.'[8]

There are two features of leading-edge scientific discovery and technological advance that illustrate the limits of our ability to conceive and enact global governance – over these human systems themelves and, by extension, over the consequences of their use. For this purpose, the most recent scientific marvel – nanotechnology – provides a clear illustration.

The potential for accident and malign applications applies at remarkably low organisational levels

The risks are integral to the research, development and applications of nanotechnology, not something that can be filtered out. According to the recent Royal Society policy document:

> [M]uch of the basic knowledge and technology needed to achieve military capabilities using applications of nanotechnologies will be produced within the civil sector, and hence is potentially available to a very wide range of parties, including non-state actors. Joy suggested that 'The 21st century technologies – genetics, nanotechnology and robotics (GNR) – are so powerful that they can spawn whole new classes of accidents and abuses. Most dangerously, for the first time, these accidents and abuses are widely within the reach of individuals or small groups. They will not require large facilities or rare raw materials. Knowledge alone will enable the use of them.' This factor also makes proliferation of weapons development programmes much harder to detect because the line between non-military and military industrial activity becomes blurred. In this way, nanotechnolgies may increase the range of asymmetric power relations.[9]

(These considerations are in addition to the health, environmental, social and ethical impacts examined in the report.)

Entrenched political and economic interests militate against strict regulatory and control regimes

This is now familiar enough in the resistance and foot-dragging that has attended the Kyoto protocol and is likely to remain a central feature of any issue that pertains to the management of the global commons, but it also applies to the appearance of new technologies. Indeed, the nature of contemporary scientific advance and its applications, both publicly validated and private (or secret), opens up the question of whether a reckoning of risks and uncertainties can ever find expression that is at once both duly precautionary but not restrictive of human betterment, and that is globally applicable and verifiable. This is difficult enough in matters where globalised disseminative systems do not directly or immediately undercut national legislation, as in matters pertaining to the legal and ethical limits of embryological research.[10] But in other cases, the global governance of new techniques and practices is both more important and more difficult – and the voices arguing that a permissive approach is the only pragmatic option, for all that they often have a vested interest, are not without merit. An early industry advocate of pressing ahead with nanotechnology acknowledges only one of the risks – its clear military potential – but other national competitive concerns, including commercial dominance, maintaining an up-to-date scientific-industrial base and profit must also figure prominently behind this and similar argumentative stances:

> It is worth considering the possibility of simply banning nanotechnology altogether, in which case we would avoid the need to expend further effort on technology policy questions. There will be enormous pressures to develop nanotechnology because of the potential benefits to society, as well as the threat of others gaining military superiority should they develop it first. It does not seem likely that *all* nations would agree to ban development. Even if they did, verification would be nearly impossible because research efforts could be easily hidden in small laboratories. And because of the mutli-disciplinary nature of nanotechnology, one would have to ban a large fraction of scientific research because so many areas will impact on developing nanotechnology, e.g. – scanning tunneling microscopes or computational chemistry. So it seems unlikely that we could implement a verifiable worldwide ban.[11]

Fundamental limitations on public policy-making do not begin when an increase in the number, complexity and connectivity of human systems reaches a critical threshold, but the consequences and risks greatly increase *because* of those limitations. In a classic article written in 1959, Charles Lindblom argued:

> Ideally, rational-comprehensive analysis leaves out nothing important. But it is impossible to take everything important into consideration unless

'important' is so narrowly defined that analysis is in fact quite limited. Limits on human intellectual capacities and on available information set definite limits to man's capacity to be comprehensive. In actual fact, therefore, no one can practise the rational-comprehensive method for really complex problems, and every administrator faced with a sufficiently complex problem must find ways drastically to simplify.[12]

He added:

Making policy is at best a very rough process. Neither social scientists, nor politicians, nor public administrators yet know enough about the social world to avoid repeated error in predicting the consequences of policy moves. A wise policy-maker consequently expects that his policies will achieve only part of what he hopes and at the same time will produce unanticipated consequences he would have preferred to avoid. If he proceeds through a *succession* of incremental changes, he avoids serious lasting mistakes in several ways.[13]

Nearly half a century later, the limits of our knowledge about the social world has been joined by the limits of our knowledge of the natural world: we cannot model the world's weather on a par with our ability to affect it – and the interaction of human and natural systems has thrown up numerous other nasty and quite large-scale surprises. 'Wise policy-makers' must weigh up costs and benefits which sometimes pit the immediate interests of political communities against local and global environments; against the interests of other states and peoples; and sometimes, in respect of unquantifiable scientific risks, against the security and health of future generations. This range of responsibilities attends our choices, whether or not we choose to exercise them in a form that could credibly be termed 'global governance'.

The number of governance arrangements that are wholly inclusive of all states and peoples will almost certainly remain limited in number as well as effectiveness – hence our reliance on the 'global' character of various subject-specific governances, many of them central to the interests of powerful states, either directly or through the maintenance of the international system. In the absence of global government, or policy making which is both authoritatively and practically global, policy-makers within states are faced with a combination of rising expectations and a growing number of inter-linked issues and crises, the origins of which can be both distant and diffuse. Nevertheless, our expectations of policy-makers remain high, as described by Geoffrey Vickers:

The policy-maker is expected not merely to balance but to optimize, to achieve, within the limits of the practicable, some state chosen as desirable or least repugnant. The mere existence of policy-making attests to the will to impose on the flux of events some form other than that which the interplay of forces would give it. Whatever scientists, as scientists, may

say, men as political animals expect from their policy-makers – at least in
our present society – not merely balance but artistry; the realization of
social form, in redesigning cities, in enfranchizing minorities, in many not
necessarily consistent ways. These demand consensus focused and sustained
for decades . . . if they are ever to be reflected in changes in the actual state
of the milieu.[14]

But as Vickers goes on to point out, 'No human society has ever achieved these
things, even in much more favourable circumstances.' As the variables and
uncertainties for policy-makers within states increase, their own difficulties
contribute to the problem of trying to secure a coherent and equitable global
order.

The weight of the evidence is that our capacity to produce unwanted and
sometimes dangerous conditions on a global scale is running greatly in excess
of our deliberative and control mechanisms. In some ways, this is not a surprise.
First, the wider and more inclusive the control regime, the greater the number
of interested parties, special interests – and resistances. In addition, organising,
convening and agreeing in very large international forums is a slow process,
often much slower than the processes they would seek to control. (It took twelve
years to bring the Law of the Sea Treaty into effect.) Second, any number of
technological innovations and their unregulated uses can be brought about
within relatively small working groups – genetic manipulation for a very
wide range of purposes is a case in point; and nanotechnology holds this prospect, too. Third, problems of comprehension are not going to go away: complex
system interaction is both a feature of globalisation and a catalyst for its
furtherance – and we can add to that momentum much more easily than we
can control it.

Globalised relations of all kinds are continuing
to multiply

As nets of globalised relations increase and intensify, demands on our systems
of governance will not only vastly increase in number – they will also pose
fundamental challenges to our ability to bring about a global governance that
is both comprehensive and equitable.

One reason for the assumption that our present array of global governance
arrangements are adequate is implicit in the disciplinary boundaries and
perspectives that comprise or inform the majority of global governance studies.
But at a deeper level, it is also difficult to confront the prospect that more of
the same might well fail us. This point is grasped at least partially by those
who document the ways in which our systems of global governance already fail
tens of millions of human beings and who highlight the human and environmental costs of some aspects of global governance as it is now constituted.
As Caroline Thomas argues, 'In an increasingly co-ordinated fashion, key
global governance institutions, and the interests they represent, are overseeing

a process of increased economic, political and social stratification.'[15] The argument here, however, extends beyond our necessary engagement with the global governance 'of, by and for whom?' question; and beyond a frank recognition that many of the most perplexing problems facing humanity actually arise from the orders we create and sustain.

We need not abandon hope, but we do need to recognise the relationship between many of the discomfiting particulars of the human condition and our global governance arrangements. In outline terms, a global governance premised on the same assumptions and conceived on many of the same understandings, values and interests that inform the fundamentals of international relations will be no less subject to the often surprising outcomes of the globalising forces that affect states and peoples. Moreover, one of the principal outcomes of globalisation (easily overlooked in our fascination with the world's larger dynamics and infrastructures) is a vast multiplication and intensification of relatedness. This includes the all-but-constant permeability of all cultures and all locations; wholesale transformations in centuries-long ways of life; the alteration or destruction of lands and their ecosystems, together with pressure on the oceans' resources; and the direct and indirect consequences of accelerating resource extraction and industrialisation. It is open to question whether the ways in which these innumerable dynamics emerge and combine can be comprehended in such causal and consequential detail as would be necessary for a comprehensive global governance, but the stresses are plain enough:

> An ever more scientific world was never less predictable. An ever more technological world was never less controllable. A world dedicated to majority rule is increasingly run by militant minorities. 'Free' individuals, increasingly dependent on each other, are subject to increasing demands to share the commitments, accept the constraints and accord the trust required by multiplying systems and subsystems to which they belong and on which they wholly depend. And these distribute their favours and still more, their responsibilities, with the equality of a battlefield. For good and ill, the ideology of the Enlightenment has worked itself out, paid its dividends and revealed its shortcomings.[16]

The wealth, ease and security enjoyed by some of us can be counted as successes of our social, political and economic organisation; and in our globalised circumstances, as successes of global governance. However, planetary-level threats to human well-being are not incidental to these splendours and nor are the human and ecosystem costs. Beneath the range of structural, cognitive and other limitations on our ability to exercise global governance is something more basic: because global governance as currently construed is informed by the same interests and values that drive the most problematic global dynamics, it is also limited by them. One analyst terms our predicament as an outcome of 'Enlightenment fundamentalism', described as that religion-like dogmatic belief that the principles on which we believe the unprecedented success in understanding, explaining, predicting, and utilizing the world for our human purposes was achieved, must be continuously and universally abided by. It is the belief that the cluster of values which consensually is at the basis of our science, technology, medicine, social science, and even some of the humanities is an absolute prerequisite for our continued success; it is a belief that the cluster of values is everywhere and always valid – or, in other words: that the world is manageable for our benefit if we only stick to those values. In one other formulation: it is the belief that if we do what we have been doing so far (or think that we have been doing) and only do it better, everything will turn out to our satisfaction. That cluster of values consists of: universalism, rationalism, objectivity, value-freedom, context-independence, unquestioned experimental and mathematical methodology, freedom from all political considerations, etc.[17]

The ordinary, non-governance activity of six and a half billion human beings now has very considerable weight and momentum. Much of it is technologically propelled; its aggregate and sometimes synergistic effects can be considerable (whatever individuals might be aware of or intend); and its lines of causation move easily within and across both the human and natural realms. By this combination of factors, little of the rapid and worsening diminution of biodiversity is deliberate. On the other hand, a great deal of purposeful activity both depends upon and contributes to large human systems – the purposes, implications and outcomes of which are outside of many actors' comprehension and most actors' ability to influence in fundamental ways. This is certainly the case with global capitalism. Like so much human activity on the largest scale, global capitalism is not a single phenomenon or even a unitary one, but an aggregate. Nevertheless, both its continued growth and routine functioning require forms of global governance which are designed to maintain the larger systems responsible. The logic of global capitalism, the interests and values it represents (by no means strictly ideological and political) and its practical trajectories are as implicit in the present institutions of global governance as they are in world-wide resource extraction, manufacturing and commercial enterprises. The human condition is as it is not because our systems of global governance are operationally deficient – or not merely because they are – but because they are deeply embedded in familiar social structures and organisations of political community.

In view of the above, there has been a surge in interest in the normative dimensions of global governance – in the academic literature,[18] in activist politics[19] and in serious, high-level investigations and discussions – the most notable recent endeavour being the Commission on Human Security. Entrenched human suffering and quite visible structural inequalities are hardly a novel feature of our world: they are the background to and impetus behind the establishment of the Commission. Yet its report, *Human Security Now*[20] succinctly articulates and reinforces perspectives that have been extant for decades.[21] The perspectives and prescriptions contained in the report are so morally compelling and so widely and routinely voiced that it becomes tempting to suppose that the wealthy and secure have experienced the counterpart to 'donor fatigue' in respect of awful and extensive human insecurity – a kind of moral habituation. What is one to make of the worthwhile but nevertheless generalised injunctions contained in the report?

This is not to question the considerable merit in the stance adopted: 'By placing people at the centre, the human security approach calls for enhancing and redirecting policies and institutions.' However, as with most such high-level reports, *Human Security Now* is quite ambivalent about the role of the state; unspecific about the deeply embedded sources of human insecurity and debilitating inequality; and – partly as a consequence of these two – largely admonitory in respect of the way forward. So although the aspirations are clearly set out, there remain the dishearteningly familiar injunctions that organisations of political community of every size and disposition 'ought' 'should' and 'must' expand, empower, encourage and advance the various goals of human security. To whom or to what are these laudable injunctions addressed? If what is at the heart of re-orienting the world's priorities is what the report terms, 'enhancing and redirecting policies and institutions', can we then assume that the fault lies with what is generally characterised as 'lack of political will' – and specifically (though not entirely) with states? In fact, the larger institutional forms of global governance – the Bretton Woods institutions and the World Trade Organization – evince very considerable political will. The efforts made by NGOs and others to make these bodies more accountable and more sensitive to the human impacts and environmental costs of their initiatives[22] are certainly praiseworthy and might well count as what the Commission on Human Security terms 'enhancement', but it is far from clear that they can re-orientate organisations of such size, power and importance. Global governance is not the governance *of* the world, in the sense invoked by the phrase 'the human condition' or 'human security'. Instead, we have governances on a world-wide scale, for the most part co-ordinated functionally, but not directed normatively. So it is not surprising that such global governance as we have that is inclusive of humanity in its entirety deals with crises of the planetary environment or infectious diseases.

Ethical considerations combine with the practical aspirations of millions who desire to achieve ways of life currently enjoyed by only a small portion of the world. If as seems likely 'sustainable development' – or at worst, 'survivable development'[23] – comes to be at loggerheads with the ethos of unlimited economic growth which our global governance now supports, our systems of global governance will be faced not merely with the need to work better, or more efficiently – and the prospect is not an inviting one:

Communities, national, sub-national and supra-national, will become more closely knit in so far as they can handle the political and cultural problems involved – and, in so far as they cannot, they will become more violent in their mutual rejections. The loyalties we accept will impose wider obligations and more comprehensive acceptance and will separate us by a wider gulf from those who reject them. These tendencies multiply around us now. A world in which interaction increases does not thereby necessarily become a more integrated world. On the contrary, these interactions may generate such tensions and pressures as to disrupt it. The worse the strains, the more demanding will be those societies which survive. Technology cannot unify the world. Unification, integration, are the fruits of political action; and the limits of political action are in the character and coherence of the cultures within which that action is taken, and in the rate at which those cultures can grow and change.[24]

Increasing interdependence can drive politics, but not determine its direction. Our global governance is furthering interdependencies of all kinds, without the means or the political willingness on the scale required to deal with even the predictable consequences of our ways of life.

The current 'architecture of global governance' is not a neutral, technocratic exercise: it is an expression of power and interests

This also places a limitation on global governance, its span and purposes – and, as is evident from the point above, its outcomes.

One need not adopt a Realist perspective to appreciate that the state-based international organisations that comprise the larger fixtures of global governance will also be arenas in which they also individually manoeuvre for advantage. Yet the compass of activity in which there remains sufficient resilience in international and global life to accommodate both self-interested and systemic outcomes – indeed, the extent to which they are easily compatible – is rapidly narrowing. As recently as the years immediately following the Second World War, which witnessed a great surge in multilateral endeavour, national interests and international order were felt to be synchronous. So, for example, given the war-ravaged condition of the European economies and their relative powerlessness, the reasonable expectation of the pursuit of national interest which US Treasury Secretary Henry Morgenthau anticipated in his remarks to the closing session of the Bretton Woods Conference in July 1944 must have sounded unremarkable to the assembled European delegates:

> I am perfectly certain that no delegation to this conference has lost sight for a moment of the particular national interest it was sent here to represent. The American delegation . . . has been, at all times, conscious of its primary obligation – the protection of American interests. And other representatives have been no less loyal or devoted to the welfare of their own people. Yet none of us has found any incompatibility between

devotion to our own country and joint action. Indeed, we have found on the contrary that the only genuine safeguard to our national interests lies in international co-operation.[25]

Yet even then, Harry White, one of the framers of the Bretton Woods Agreements, said of US domination of the World Bank and IMF that it 'resembles too closely the operation of power politics rather than of international co-operation – except that the power employed is financial instead of military or political'.[26]

Of course, even today, the most powerful states must make provision for various kinds of systemic stability: after all, they have the most to gain by maintaining the contours of the status quo (for all that it is both stressed and highly inequitable). Nor is it an historical novelty for national economic interests to be given priority over forms of international co-operation. But when the substance of international co-operation is global warming, the meaning cannot be confined to the familiar tension between state interests and the international system. It is becoming clear that global systems, both natural and human, are directly implicated in the governances practised at national and international levels. The lines of causation between quite distinct and once distant realms – international economic stability and environmental quality; large-scale system maintenance and cultural norms; international financial stability and the viability of communities – are now shorter and more direct than at any time in human history; part of our 'shrinking world'. The differences are more often overlooked or contested than reconciled. This is because a large portion of global governance as we now have it remains dedicated to state interests and to the stability of the international system – and insofar as possible, to favour the more powerful states – a point clearly visible in the weighted voting system of the Bretton Woods institutions.[27]

Again, it hardly requires a Realist disposition to see the pursuit of state interests as both certain and important, sometimes in competitive, exclusive ways. At the same time, the existence of human and natural global orders necessitates governance institutions of the sort that only states can provide. However, governments have only partially grasped the meaning of a global arena which is now highly responsive to the historical and contemporary consequences of human activity. If this were not the case, our response to climate change would be of a different order from our current, rather halting efforts. And the 'architecture of global governance' – a curiously static metaphor – does not yet provide a common home for the many impoverished millions. To the important aim of making our necessary global governance institutions more effective must be added the tasks which follow from the 'of, by and for whom?' question – as expressed by Robert O Keohane, '[H]ow can we gain benefits from institutions without becoming their victims? How can we help design institutions for a partially globalised world that perform valuable functions while respecting democratic values? And how can we foster beliefs that maintain benign institutions?'[28]

Emerging limitations on global governance

Some systemic changes are irreversible

The consumption of non-renewable resources, the generation of high-level nuclear waste material, the release of genetically modified organisms and the loss of plant and animal biodiversity are all irreversible. In addition, the persistence of the chemicals we have deposited in the atmosphere, together with the oceans' thermal inertia mean that the uncertainties associated with climate change would only diminish gradually, even if we were to cease industrially assisted atmospheric pollution altogether. Together, these and other matters constrain our policy choices by variously reducing predictability, diminishing ecosystem resilience, committing us to long-term, costly and unproven remedial activity and reducing the room for political manoeuvre and compromise in the international system.

In addition to permanent physical alterations such as the extinction of species must be added the ordering of human systems on such large scales that their reversal on the basis of anything short of catastrophic collapse would be highly unlikely. Most notable in this regard is unprecedented urbanisation, which continues to accelerate. On current trends, some two-thirds of humanity will soon be urban dwellers, a trend that has global implications. For example, as a result of its astonishing rate of urbanisation, China has now become a net importer of food, driving up international prices of its once staple crops.[29] The links between poverty and urbanisation – 80 per cent of the world's urban residents will live in developing countries by 2025 – and the implications for governance within and between states in matters extending from disease control to resource demands of every kind are very likely to grow in number and complexity.

It requires only a few such examples to see that the many trends which together comprise globalisation originate and combine in ways which place a top-down 'governance of globalisation' outside the realms of political possibility. Many of the more important infrastructural and organisational aspects of globalising activity are controlled and regulated, but they are done so most often for purposes which themselves either require certain globalised conditions, or which are designed to further them. This is one of the features of global capitalism. At the same time, ingenuity, aspiration, carelessness and a host of other human impulses shape our world by default and thereby frequently place global governance in a catch-up position.

The integration of human and natural systems is continuing apace

In some cases, particularly in the more developed parts of the world, this has advanced to the point that the division between human systems and natural ones has all but disappeared – a condition that must be sustained and fortified in keeping with the further growth and development of human systems. The following depiction of the river Thames, written 35 years ago, has even more salience today:

> For many millennia the river Thames has earned its name as a continuing entity. It is in fact the way in which water from a stable catchment area finds its way to the sea. . . . Throughout this time until very recently its valley provided a habitat for many species, including men, who long ago learned to live above its floodmarks and to cultivate its alluvial soil. Then we began to incorporate this river, once an independent variable, into our own man-made socio-technical system. We controlled its floods with barrages and dykes. We adapted it for transportation. We distributed its water. We used it as a sewer. Our demands rose and began to conflict with one another, making necessary, for example, the control of pollution. Now these demands have begun to conflict in total with the volume of the river. We plan to supplement it by pumping out the deep reservoirs. Soon, unless some other solution appears, we shall be supplementing its flow by pumping desalted water from the sea. By then the Thames as an independent physical system, part of the given environment, will have virtually disappeared within a socio-technical system, dependent on new physical constructions, new institutions and a new attitude to the use of water and the regulation of the whole water cycle.[30]

In the intervening years, vast tracts of lands and natural systems have been incorporated into human systems all over the world. Staying with the example of controlling water resources, the World Commission on Dams[31] was convened to examine the use of dams as a world-wide phenomenon – not only their physical and environmental aspects, but also the economic, developmental and political implications, as their building and use have now engendered various regional tensions as well as a range of injustices. As our human systems grow in number and affective capacity, so too must our systems for the governance of the environment, many of them belated. But there are, as we have seen, limits on our ability to manage physical environments and there is a considerable gap between those abilities and the kinds of alterations we can now so readily make.

Technological systems convergence is on the horizon

The first steps towards the convergence of existing technologies has already begun and, even allowing for exaggerated predictions, the practical possibilities are potentially transformative – an adjective aptly suggestive of the governance challenges. Combinations of computing power, IT, robotics, genomics and nanotechnology hold the prospect of challenging or confounding fundamental assumptions about what it means to be human, the boundaries of ethical behaviour and moral responsibility, and the bases of social order and governance. As is the case with our current disseminative systems, there is no reason to suppose that these advances will be confined to the leading edge of scientific research and confined to government-sanctioned and monitored laboratories. Nor is it reasonable to suppose that the military applications and a range of other malign uses will not appear. Perhaps most worrying is not only whether the diffusion of such technologies will be difficult to control in themselves, but also whether their uses will offer a challenge to sites of governance that are at once both authoritative and comprehensive.

The interactions of complex systems will continue to surprise us

And it is plain that few of these surprises will be welcome.

> In 1987, for example, geochemist Wallace Broecker reflected on recent polar ice-core and ocean-sediment data: 'What these records indicate is that Earth's climate does not respond to forcing in a smooth and gradual way. Rather, it responds in sharp jumps which involve large-scale reorganization of Earth's system. . . . We must consider the possibility that the main responses of the system to our provocation of the atmosphere will come in jumps whose timing and magnitude are unpredictable.'[32]

With every diminution in ecosystem resilience, increase in human numbers and activity and addition of new technologies, the predictability of our human and natural orders are likely to decrease – and with them, our ability to exercise kinds and levels of governance adequate to human security.

Political limitations

The provision of global public goods outside of pressing emergencies will not easily displace national and other interests

In view of the continuing reluctance of the worst polluting states to engage climate change on the scale required, the injunction that states should at least 'mainstream' the provision of global public goods through international co-operation would appear to be a dim prospect, at least in the generalised terms expressed in the following:

> [R]eform needs to go beyond controlling [global] bads. Patchwork corrections to the present system will not be sufficient. In order to move beyond constant crisis prevention and management and to be able to set our sights on positive, constructive development, we need to review the fundamental principles of policy-making. Two basic changes are called for. First, international co-operation must form an integral part of national public policy making. Clearly, the dividing line between internal and external affairs has become blurred, requiring a new approach. Second,

international co-operation must be a fair proposition for all if it is to be successful. With consensus on these two points, the rest might even be quite easy to achieve.[33]

And beneath generalised calls for international co-operation and enlightened self-interest, states both weak and powerful retain serious concerns about the basis of co-operation in everything from conceptions of sustainable development for what they will mean in terms of national obligation, to the terms of trade – and aid. International co-operation is not a threshold, after which things 'might even be quite easy to achieve': it is highly conditioned by interests and perceptions of relative advantage which often cut across many issue areas. In that sense, such co-operation as we have witnessed over climate change – as clear a 'global bad' as can be imagined – stands more as an exemplar than an anomaly.

This does not preclude the possibility for genuine international co-operation for other than directly self-interested purposes. The eradication of smallpox referred to earlier is a case in point. But that initiative, 25 years ago, stands in contrast to international response to the HIV/AIDS pandemic. And it is worth recalling that in November 1974 at an emergency World Food Conference in Rome, then-US Secretary of State Henry Kissinger promised that 'within a decade no child will go to bed hungry'.[34] Twenty-two years later, the UN World Food Summit declared the aim of *reducing* the number of malnourished human beings from 800 million to 400 million by the year 2015. 'This goal is, just for its modesty, a shame,' Cuban President Fidel Castro told the Summit.[35] The shame applies not merely to the paucity of the vision, but also because of what our imaginative and practical capacities could accomplish were the end deemed to be sufficiently important.

And when states come under pressure of various kinds, they are least likely to further international co-operation of the sort that furthers the provision of global goods, however they may present the matter. As the Jubilee Debt Campaign reports, the IMF, at the urging of the United States, supported cancellation of almost all of Iraq's $120bn debt, even as Jubilee and other campaigning groups continue to argue the case for a 100 per cent cancellation of *all* poor countries' debt to the IMF – a total of $5bn.[36]

The power and influence of progressive non-state actors will in all probability remain limited; and transnational and global constituencies are likely to remain fragile and shifting

The emergence of transnational groups and coalitions that work to further human betterment in a wide range of issue areas – and that seek to make the larger institutions of global governance more responsive to human need, and generally more accountable – are both welcome and noteworthy. However, it is unclear whether in any particular issue area or in aggregate, these groups possess or can attain sufficient coherence, persistence, power and standing to bring about structural change in global governance. For instance, the growth of neoliberal economics and its governance mechanisms have generated many forms of protest and resistance, but these are by no means either homogeneous or even entirely compatible. Similarly, a degree of scepticism is warranted over some of the claims made for global civil society – itself a contestable concept. In practical terms,

> [e]stablishing the precise influence of civil society on *specific* outcomes in global governance is no easy matter. For one thing, questions of causality raise complex methodological problems. In particular, it is difficult – if not impossible – to disentangle the role of civil society in a given global governance scenario from the impacts of many other forces in play: numerous actors, multiple social structures, and various historical trends. [. . .] It is even harder to determine whether certain organizational forms, capacities, objectives or tactics have allowed civil society to exert more influence than others, and under what circumstances.[37]

In addition, as Sidney Tarrow points out, there have long been three fundamental problems faced by all forms of transnational mobilisation, from which the latest are not excepted:

> [t]he problem of linking diverse and disconnected actors through organizations, networks, and means of communication they do not control; the problem of seizing opportunities for collective action offered by events, opponent and institutions without becoming hostages to routine politics; and the problem of identifying master frames for collective action that will detach activists' identities and claims from the limitations of their national origins.[38]

Nor should the power and adaptability of states and other powerful, interested parties be underestimated.

Global North/South disparities are going to make global governance even more difficult

The movement of peoples fleeing violence, poverty and scant opportunity in the shadow of globalisation's glittering wares is but one of the more visible outcomes of the severe and widening gap between rich and poor – a phenomenon that also has its counterpart within states in the developed world. On any humane reckoning,[39] the degree of absolute poverty in the world, to say nothing of statistical disparities, is itself a failure of global governance. In addition to its core human meaning, poverty brings with it a host of social, environmental and economic costs, which further expands the remit of global governance while straining practical capacity and political willingness.

War and violence remain a striking feature of international order

Studies of the persistence of war in the international system and the academic literature examining the proposition that democracies do not go to war against one another are both dwarfed by the Iraq war in 2003 and its continuing aftermath. American and British defiance of the UN and of international law for the purpose of invading Iraq is the worst but by no means the only significant retreat from law-based international order. The rule of law is fundamental for international peace and security – and clearly, also for the prospects for global governance: If powerful states adopt an instrumental approach to international law and to our most inclusive forum for global governance, the UN, the prospects for other forms of global governance are seriously weakened, if not damaged outright. Genuine hopes for a level of international co-operation that will foster the provision of global public goods seem a thin hope against the estimated financial cost of the Iraq war for the US alone in excess of US$100 billion.[40]

None of the trends above imposes a fixed limit on the possibilities open to global governance, but at the very least, they should temper our expectations that what will need to be governed can be confined to the direct outcomes of our willed actions; that our institutional forms can keep pace with our actions and defaults; that globalising dynamics can be kept within bounds both manageable and acceptable; and that improvements in the efficiency, inclusiveness and justice of our governance institutions will suffice to deliver an equitable, stable and sustainable world order. While it is true that 'stability is a special case of change, not the natural order of things',[41] there are, in addition to the stability we set our governing institutions to create and maintain, forms and degrees of stability that global governance requires. So, argues Geoffrey Vickers,

> like so many seemingly factual words, stability especially in connection with human affairs, proves to be structured by [many kinds of] value . . . It is structured by our interests, which determines what we shall regard as relevant; and notably by the range of time and space which we are accustomed to regard as relevant to the here and now. It is structured by our expectations, which determine what we accept as normal or abnormal variation. It is structured by our standards, which determine what changes we shall regard as unacceptable.[42]

These considerations are not typically the stuff of our studies of global governance. However, in another context, Vickers goes on to explain:

> [T]he minimal conditions which must be satisfied to enable a developed society to survive in the contemporary world . . . are primarily cultural, not technological. They require from societies, interest groups and individuals

an ability to reset their appreciative systems, their standards of what to expect, what to attempt and what to put up with, to an extent which our kind has not previously achieved or needed.

This insight does not supplant the need for detailed analyses of the actors and dynamics pertinent to global governance – and especially of the 'top-down' variety – but it does contextualise them or, perhaps, restore them to the fundamentals of human relating and co-existence which must, after all, comprise both the means and the ends of any sustainable and humane global governance.

Reconceptualising global governance

The social sciences in a highly dynamic world

Each of us is faced with the profusion and variety of the human and natural worlds and the multiplicity of human purposes. We construct the world that we purport to see objectively; and we select what appears to be important or relevant and filter out or disregard what is not – a process that extends from mundane, daily activity to the highest levels of theoretical abstraction. Comprehending the world we have made for ourselves, for any purpose, is that much more difficult in a greatly expanded arena – our globalised condition – with its unseen variables, remote actors and structures and plethora of powerful, complex dynamics not readily comprehensible. At the highest levels, then, understanding a world transformed not only in terms of the structures and patterns of human interaction, but also in terms of environmental setting and resilience, is a daunting prospect – particularly for those who would seek to exercise a greater degree of control over matters that affect the well-being and security of communities and polities, including states. We do not (and indeed, could not) start afresh with every anomalous or worrying development, but must first see whether our existing conceptions retain their explanatory purchase, enabling us to find our way.

The social sciences are on the front line, because the physical sciences can only inform but not address the fundamental themes of human co-existence: security; power; equity; justice. We look to the social sciences because their disciplines investigate the sources and configurations of human interaction, both interpersonal and organisational.

Understanding human dynamics, societies and institutions is difficult enough, even in abstract terms, since conceptual matters are at once both the foundation and a principal source of contention within the social sciences. Nearly every key concept is contested: society; state; power. And what is true about the structures of social life is also true of dynamics and relational matters: democracy; interdependence; hegemony. The debates are no less sharp when there is abundant empirical evidence, both historical and contemporary – evident in the debate about war: whether it is a single phenomenon; what are its causes; how to explain its persistence (or in the case of the democratic peace theory, its absence). These debates are fundamental to political and social life as well as to intellectual discourse.

For example, the difficulties and tensions involved in trying to reconcile quite different, perhaps conflicting objectives is the business of politics. But the necessity of doing so at the largest scale of political organisation – the international system – with a view to humanity as a whole, is neatly captured in the concept of 'sustainable development', conceived by the UN Commission on Environment and Development in 1987 as 'development that meets the needs of the present without compromising the ability of future generations to meet their own needs'.[43] Its critics might concede that sustainable development is a noble ideal, but even its advocates recognise that the concept leaves open whether all or most of what counts as 'development' is sustainable; and whether sustainable development is identifiable, quantifiable and actionable – all conceptual matters that precede the difficult if more familiar issues of power, authority and responsibility.[44] In this case as in so many others, what is at issue in the first instance is not poor levels of engagement or lack of political will, but the comprehension necessary to inform action. It might seem something of an indulgence to concentrate on problems of comprehension when there are so many urgent practical matters to hand; however, this is not an academic preference for abstraction over practical problems, but an assertion that in the absence of our ability or willingness to meet the intellectual challenge posed by rapid, accelerating and complex change, the considerable inertia of our existing world view – with its attendant structures – will prevail and fail us. Clearly, ' . . . the alternatives to seeking comprehension are too noxious to contemplate, ranging as they do from resorting to simplistic and ideological interpretations to being propelled by forces we can neither discern nor influence'.[45] But the task is a form of 'up the down escalator' because although globalisation is not a force of nature, an increasingly complex, dynamic and incoherent world will not wait or pause.

The largely unspoken assumptions which underpin the tradition of university research and education suggest a world largely knowable, at least in outline; and, for practical purposes, our categories of knowledge serve us quite well and assist us in the construction and maintenance of ways of life at every level.[46] To be sure, there remain great swathes of unexplored territory; and although the interesting intellectual endeavours of our day may excite, fascinate or disturb us, we generally expect to accommodate new discoveries more or less neatly within the prevailing intellectual order. Notwithstanding the occasional paradigm-shifting insights such as those of Darwin and Einstein or the emergence of new disciplines, we remain closely wedded to the notion of progress: to the steady acquisition of knowledge and understanding, despite the promptings of postmodernism.

Recently, however, even within single fields of endeavour, the problem is not merely one of accommodating new data, but of aligning new information, insights and events to structures of knowledge that once seemed secure, but which now often prove to be inadequate as explanatory frameworks for the world we can readily observe.[47] This applies generally – but most noticeably where strict disciplinary boundaries are defined and defended:

> It took long enough for [International Relations] neorealism to come to terms with economic variables . . . [but] . . . even neorealism is intellectually incapable of embracing questions of ecological interdependence. Realism makes positivist claims to objective knowledge and explicitly excludes values not associated with national interest. It would not admit that universalist values of the type associated with the preservation of the biosphere can have political relevance in a world of selfish and competing states.[48]

The multi-disciplinary nature of the task

Established theories of International Relations are now being confronted by matters as varied as the power of markets, their stability and their relationship with states; the threat of pandemics; and the social, economic and security implications of greatly enabled travel and electronic communications. And as dynamics of these kinds grow in number and variety, the conceptual foundations and disciplinary boundaries of all of the social sciences themselves become sources of debate, as in the following depiction:

> [M]ost significant phenomena that the so-called social sciences now deal with are in fact hybrids of physical *and* social relations, with no purified sets of the physical and the social. Such hybrids include health, technologies, the environment, the Internet, road traffic, extreme weather conditions and so on. These hybrids . . . are central in any analysis of global relations.[49]

The trajectory of unsustainable human activity and its links to the inertia of related globalising forces add to the daunting nature of conceiving coherent political responses to the world we have already made, and give some indication of the paucity of our conceptions of global governance as they now stand. The fragmentation and compartmentalisation of interest groups has its counterpart in the orientation of research communities in the social sciences, particularly where these are both inward- and backward-looking. The scope and meaning of the perennial 'How might we live?' becomes ever more perplexing and difficult under the strain of how we – humanity – *do* live. So there is an urgent need to begin more collaborative work on the possibilities and limits of governance, within the social sciences and between the social and physical sciences. Much as Geography is able to accommodate both physical and human perspectives,[50] we might best begin by finding ways to adopt Ecology as a social science. Even as we continue work on what have become the fixtures of global governance studies – the Bretton Woods institutions, global finance, transnational NGO advocacy, global civil society – the essential contexts of human relatedness, within and between communities and between the human and natural realms, need to be brought to the fore. Our abstractions are necessary, but their contexts should be made explicit.

Returning to Geoffrey Vickers' concern with human values as the basis for stability: rather than a normative politics of global transformation – the work of the few on the structures and institutions of the elite – we might instead ask whether world-wide normative transformation – that is, changes in lived expectation by the many, is possible. It is inconceivable that any number of technological 'fixes' will enable the entire human population to live as the prosperous currently do; and the conditions of the hundreds of millions worst off is unsupportable as well as unconscionable. It is clear that any truly inclusive global governance will have as its work not only the regulation of world-encircling physical and organisational infrastructures, but also the reconciliation of conflicting values and competing claims.

Scholarship on norms and norm shifts as an aspect of international life is much more advanced than changes in cultural norms, even under conditions of globalisation. The links between norms at the popular and state levels and between states themselves is well established, especially in the human rights field.[51] This holds some promise for helping us to understand how the accumulation of expectation – by no means always linear in its development – can bring about a change in the orientation of quite powerful organisational forms. But aside from the growth, universalisation, formalisation and inter-nalisation of the human rights ideal, have normative shifts on such a scale ever been witnessed before or since? Are other transformations on this scale possible? The human rights regime might rightly be regarded as a form of global governance: it first altered and now is crucial to protecting the life chances, freedom, safety and security of individuals and communities throughout the world. If the reality falls far short of the ideal, it is nevertheless remarkable that the ideal itself is undimmed – and if anything, strengthened by its many setbacks. The individuals, nations, communities, institutions, laws and norms that incorporate human rights continue to reinforce expectations at all levels and in all places. This is as close as anything in our world to global governance 'of, by and for the people'. This historic achievement is all too easy to lose sight of, but at the same time, the failures and other limitations of human rights might be highly instructive for the purpose of gauging our ability to deal with the expression of human values in an ever-globalising world.

The following passage could stand as a social sciences remit for the study of global governance. It suggests that, in addition to continuing investigations into our existing institutions of global governance, we must not lose sight of the larger human condition, nor shun a reckoning of the pressures that inform our comprehension and our choices:

> Since we depend on communication, within societies, between societies and between generations, developments which threaten these commu-nications with failure are a lethal form of trap. By failure of communication

I do not mean failure in the means to transmit, store and process information. Of that we have already more than we can use. I mean failure to maintain, within and between political societies, appropriate shared ways of distinguishing the situations in which we act, the relations we want to regulate, the standards we need to apply, and the repertory of actions which are available to us. This fabric, on which communication depends, is itself largely the product of communication. Demands on it are rising. We need to consider what chance there is of meeting them at what cost.[52]

Limits on our ability to conceive and enact global governance already apply even to some of our largest and most urgent concerns. Confronting these limits directly is an essential part of the task of finding what ways are open to us.

Notes

1 The human condition

1 Helena Norberg-Hodge, *Ancient Futures: Learning from Ladakh* (London: Rider, 2000).

2 See Martin E. Marty and R. Scott Appleby (eds), *Fundamentalisms and Society: Reclaiming the Sciences, the Family and Education* (Chicago: University of Chicago Press, 1993).

3 L. Wolfenbarger and P. Phifer, 'The Ecological Risks and Benefits of Genetically Engineered Plants', *Science*, 290 (2000), pp. 2088–93.

4 Geoffrey Vickers, *Freedom in a Rocking Boat: Changing Values in an Unstable Society* (London: Penguin Press, 1970), pp. 125–6.

5 A notable exception is Zygmnt Bauman, *Postmodern Ethics* (Oxford: Blackwell Publishers, 1993).

6 Daniel C. Dennett, 'Information, Technology and the Virtues of Ignorance', in *Brainchildren: Essays on Designing Minds* (London: Penguin Books, 1998), p. 381. For a hard look at the moral meaning of ubiquitous, urgent pleas for help, see Peter Unger, *Living High and Letting Die: Our Illusion of Innocence* (Oxford: Oxford University Press, 1996).

7 See Stanley Cohen, *States of Denial: Knowing About Atrocities and Suffering* (Cambridge: Polity Press, 2000); Nancy (Ann) Davis, 'Moral Theorizing and Moral Practice: Reflections on Some Sources of Hypocrisy', in Earl R. Winkler and Jerrold R. Coombs (eds), *Applied Ethics: A Reader* (Oxford: Blackwell Publishers, 1993), pp. 164–80.

8 This point is all too easily lost within International Relations theorising – at least with the predominant Realist school, which scales up from an assumed selfish, violent human nature to the anarchic international system. For a brief but thought-provoking counter to this assumption, see Stephen J. Gould, 'Ten Thousand Acts of Kindness', in *Eight Little Piggies* (London: Jonathan Cape, 1993).

9 'Biotechnology – Military Applications', The Strategic Assessment Center, Science Applications International Corporation (December 1995), p. 3. SAIC is ranked 294th on the *Fortune 500* list.

10 Andy Coghlan and Emma Young, 'Grave expectations: Rumours of a human clone pregnancy spark health fears and horror', *New Scientist*, 13 April 2002, p. 4. A useful and wide-ranging consideration of the topic is Martha C. Nussbaum and Cass R. Sunstein, *Clones and Clones: Facts and Fantasies About Human Cloning* (New York: W.W. Norton & Company, 1998).

11 James Meek, 'Special Report, The Ethics of Genetics: The Race to Buy Life', *The Guardian*, 15 November 2000. According to the report, 9,364 patents relating to the human body have been filed. The applications made cover 126,672 genes or partial gene sequences.

12 Malcolm R. Dando, *Preventing Biological Warfare: The Failure of American Leadership* (Basingstoke: Palgrave, 2002).

13 A recent report from the Nuffield Council on Bioethics, insists that 'Western scientists [should] always get their overseas research cleared by independent ethics committees in their own countries first. At present fewer than a quarter of US companies bother to do this.' Editorial, 'Double standards: Scientists must obey the same ethical standards wherever they work', *New Scientist*, 27 April 2002, p. 3. 'The Ethics of Research Related to Healthcare in Developing Countries': Online. Available HTTP: <http://www.nuffieldbioethics.org/publications/pp_0000000013.asp>(accessed 30 April 2002).

14 Lagdon Winner, 'Citizen Virtues in a Technological Order', in Earl R. Winkler and Jerrold R. Coombs, op. cit., p. 47.

15 See Michael Barnett, *Eyewitness to a Genocide: The United Nations and Rwanda* (Ithaca: Cornell University Press, 2002).

16 Elizabeth Wolgast, *Ethics of an Artificial Person* (Stanford: Stanford University Press, 1992), p. 35. See also Brian W. Hogwood and B. Guy Peters, *The Pathology of Public Policy* (Oxford: Clarendon Press, 1985).

17 Toni Erskine (ed.), *Can Institutions Have Responsibilities? Collective Moral Agency and International Relations* (Basingstoke: Palgrave, 2003).

18 Quoted in Jean Porter, *The Recovery of Virtue: The Relevance of Aquinas for Christian Ethics* (London: SPCK, 1994), p. 102.

19 Barbara Adam, *Timescapes of Modernity: The Environment and Invisible Hazards* (London: Routledge, 1998).

20 For example, Richard Rosencrance's assertion that 'territory is passé' in 'The Rise of the Virtual State', *Foreign Affairs* 75, No. 4 (1996), pp. 45–62. However, Jan Aart Scholte usefully points out that 'The end of territorial*ism* owing to globalization has not meant the end of territoria*lity*', *Globalization: A Critical Introduction* (Basingstoke: Palgrave, 2000), p.59.

21 For example, see Fernand Braudel, *The Wheels of Commerce* (Volume II of *Civilization and Capitalism, 15th–18th Century*), (New York: Harper & Row, 1982).

22 'One of the world's greatest rivers [the Mekong] has been reduced to a trickle in places by a series of dams and engineering works which are threatening the livelihoods of up to 100 million people in south-east Asia.' John Vidal, 'Damned and dying: the Mekong and its communities face a bleak future', *The Guardian*, 25 March 2004.

23 Paul Rogers, *Losing Control: Global Security in the Twenty-first Century* (London: Pluto Press, 2002).

24 D. Betham, 'What Future for Economic and Social Rights?' *Political Studies*, Special Issue, 1995.

25 M. Anne Brown, *Human Rights and the Borders of Suffering: The Promotion of Human Rights in International Politics* (Manchester: Manchester University Press, 2002), p. 204.

26 For a brief but useful survey, see Peter Drahos, 'Negotiating Intellectual Property Rights: Between Coercion and Dialogue', in Peter Drahos and Ruth Mayne (eds), *Global Intellectual Property Rights: Knowledge, Access and Development* (Basingstoke: Palgrave, 2002), pp. 161–82.

27 David P. Fidler, *SARS, Governance and the Globalization of Disease* (Basingstoke: Palgrave, 2004).

28 David Kaimowitz, Benoit Mertens, Sven Wunder and Pablo Pacheco, 'Hamburger Connection Fuels Amazon Destruction: Cattle Ranching and Deforestation in Brazil's Amazon', Center for International Forestry Research. Report: Online. Available HTTP: <http://www.cifor.cgiar.org/publications/pdf_files/media/Amazon.pdf (accessed 15 April 2004).

29 Cited in Richard Critchfield, *The Villagers: Changed Values, Altered Lives and the Closing of the Urban-Rural Gap* (New York: Anchor, 1994), p. vi. The adaptive strains involved in this transformation are particularly well captured in this volume.

30 Stephen Wurm (ed.), *Atlas of the World's Languages in Danger of Disappearing* (New York: UNESCO, 2001). On some estimates, as many as a quarter of the world's minority languages are under threat of extinction.

31 J. K. Galbraith, *The Culture of Contentment* (New York: Houghton Mifflin, 1992); Arthur O'Sullivan, Terri A. Sexton, Steven M. Sheffrin, *Property Taxes and Tax Revolts: Legacy of Proposition 13* (Cambridge: Cambridge University Press, 1995).

32 For a detailed consideration of this topic, see James N. Rosenau, *Along the Domestic–Foreign Frontier: Exploring Governance in a Turbulent World* (Cambridge: Cambridge University Press, 1997), especially Chapter 7, 'Boundaries', pp. 118–43.

33 John Braithwaite and Peter Drahos, *Global Business Regulation* (Cambridge: Cambridge University Press, 2000).

34 Geoffrey Vickers, unpublished manuscript on Western culture, science and technology, written in 1976, p. 135.

35 Indicative works include Jeremy Rifkin, *The Biotech Century: The Coming Age of Genetic Commerce* (London: Victor Gollanz, 1998); Mark A. Rothstein (ed.), *Genetic Secrets: Protecting Privacy and Confidentiality in the Genetic Era* (New Haven: Yale University Press, 1997); Bette-Jane Crigger (ed.), *Cases in Bioethics: Selections from the Hastings Center Report* (New York: St Martin's Press, 1998); Andrew Kimbrell, *The Human Body Shop: The Engineering and Marketing of Life* (New York: HarperCollins, 1993).

36 E. Richard Gold, *Body Parts: Property Rights and the Ownership of Human Biological Materials* (Washington, DC: Georgetown University Press, 1997).

37 Paul Brown, 'EU races to thwart influx of GM food from East', *The Guardian* 14 February 2004.

38 Geoffrey Vickers, *Human Systems Are Different* (London: Harper & Row, 1983), p. xxiv.

39 Ulrich Beck, 'Risk Society and the Provident State', in Scott Lash, Bronislaw Szerszynski and Brian White, *Risk, Environment and Modernity: Towards a New Ecology* (London: Sage, 1996), p. 27.

40 Ibid., p. 28 (italics original).

41 For example, Ruth N. Hull, Glenn M. Ferguson, Janine D. Glaser and Robert Willis, 'Risk Around the World: Risk Assessment Resources on the World-Wide Web (WWW)', *Human and Ecological Risk Assessment*, Vol. 8, No. 2 (2002), pp. 443–57; Christopher Hood, Henry Rothstein and Robert Baldwin (eds), *The Government of Risk: Understanding Risk Regulation Regimes* (Oxford: Oxford University Press, 2001); and Julian Morris (ed.), *Rethinking Risk and the Precautionary Principle* (Oxford: Butterworth, 2000).

42 Nan Goodman, *Shifting the Blame: Literature, Law, and the Theory of Accidents in Nineteenth-Century America* (Princeton: Princeton University Press, 1998).

43 Kenneth R. Foster, David E. Bernstein and Peter W. Huber, *Phantom Risk: Scientific Inference and the Law* (Cambridge, Massachusetts: MIT Press, 1994).

44 Julia Black, *Critical Reflections on Regulation* (London: Centre for Analysis of Risk and Regulation, London School of Economics and Political Science, 2002); Christopher Hood, Henry Rothstein and Robert Baldwin, *The Government of Risk: Understanding Risk Regulation Regimes* (Oxford: Oxford University Press, 2001).

45 Ulrich Beck, *World Risk Society* (Cambridge: Polity Press, 1999).

46 Ulrich Beck, 'Industrial Fatalism: Organized Irresponsibility', in *Ecological Politics in an Age of Risk* (Cambridge: Polity Press, 1995), p. 67.

47 Ibid., p. 66.

48 Ibid., p. 67.

49 Beck, 'Risk Society and the Provident State', op. cit., p. 38.

50 Barbara Adam, Ulrich Beck and Joost Van Loon (eds), 'Introduction', to *The Risk Society and Beyond: Critical Issues for Social Theory* (London: Sage, 2000), p. 3.

51 Ulrich Beck, 'Risk Society Revisited: Theory, Politics and Research Programmes', in Barbara Adam, Ulrich Beck and Joost Van Loon (eds), ibid., p. 223.

52 John Tulloch and Deborah Lupton, *Risk and Everyday Life* (London: Sage, 2003).

53 See William H. McNeill, *The Human Condition: An Ecological and Historical View* (Princeton: Princeton University Press, 1980); Hannah Arendt, *The Human Condition* (Chicago: Chicago University Press, 1958).

54 See Paul Farmer, *Infections and Inequalities: The Modern Plagues* (Berkeley: University of California Press, 1999).

55 The limited, generic sense of 'global society' is captured in the following: 'The most basic [way in which the term "society" is used] is as a generic term for social relations, which are the essential subject matter of sociology. In this sense, society is the totality of complex of social relations. Since social relations of all kinds are increasingly global, and all forms of social relations everywhere in the world are, at least in some indirect sense, bound into global networks, society in this sense is now necessarily global.' Martin Shaw, *Global Society and International Relations* (Cambridge: Polity Press, 1994), p. 5. Alternatively, consider the term 'global polity', defined as 'that totality of political structures, agents and processes, with transnational properties, that in the current historical context have developed a high level of *thick* interconnectedness and an element of *thin* community that transcends the territorial state'. Richard Higgott and Marten Ougaard, 'Introduction', in Richard Higgott and Marten Ougaard (eds), *Towards a Global Polity* (London: Routledge, 2002), p. 12 (italics original).

2 The development of the 'governance' concept

1 Harold Wilson, *The Governance of Britain* (London: Weidenfeld & Nicholson, 1976), p. 1.

2 Oran R. Young, 'Global Governance: Drawing Insights from the Environmental Experience', (Hanover, New Hampshire: Occasional Paper from the Dickey Center, Dartmouth College, 1995), p. 1, fn. 2.

3 James N. Rosenau, 'Governance in the Twenty-first Century', *Global Governance*, Vol. 1, No. 1, Winter 1995, p. 14.

4 Jan Kooiman (ed.), *Modern Governance: New Government-Society Interactions* (London: Sage, 1993), p. 2.

5 Jan Kooiman, *Governing as Governance* (London: Sage, 2003), p. 4 (italics original).

6 'According to the [UK] National Crime Intelligence Service . . . gangs opted to work together because it made sound economic sense. "The gangs have realised that fighting among themselves only draws police attention. What they really want to do is make money, and it makes much more sense for them to work together" said a spokesman.' Tony Thompson, 'Supergang ceasefire on ethnic feuds,' *The Observer*, 18 January 2004.

7 Mats Berdal and David Malone (eds), *Greed and Grievance: Economic Agendas in Civil Wars* (Boulder: Lynne Rienner, 2000).

8 R. A. W. Rhodes, 'The New Governance: Governing Without Government', *Political Studies*, Vol. 4, No. 4, (September 1996), pp. 652–68.

9 W. Kickert, 'Autopoiesis and the science of (public) administration: essence, sense and nonsense', *Organization Studies*, 14 (1993), pp. 261–78.

10 'According to *The Wall Street Journal*, between September 2000 and September 2002, [the US Federal Home Mortgage Corporation, known colloquially as Freddie Mac] raised its derivatives-based trading positions by almost half, to US$700 billion. That makes the company one of the largest holders of derivatives in the world during a period which has seen a sharp and sustained increase in financial market volatility of all kinds. [. . .] The assumption is that Freddie Mac has been tinkering with its profits over recent years in order to smooth out the spikes of profit and loss caused by its huge derivative exposure.' '$700bn, and nobody even blinks,' *The Guardian*, 21 June 2003. Online. Available HTTP: <http://www.guardian.co.uk/Print/0,3858,4605011,pp.html> (accessed 25 June 2003).

11 R. A. W. Rhodes, *Understanding Governance: Policy Networks, Governance, Reflexivity and Accountability* (Buckingham: Open University Press, 1997), p. 4.

12 James N. Rosenau, 'Governance in the Twenty-first Century', op. cit., p. 15.

13 Respectively: Robert A. G. Monks and Nell Minow (eds), *Corporate Governance* (Oxford: Blackwell Publishing, 2003); Michael T. Miller and Julie A. Caplow (eds), *Policy and University Faculty Governance in the 21st Century* (Information Age Publishing, 2004); B. Guy Peters and Donald Savoie, *Revitalizing the Public Service: Governance in the Twenty-first Century* (Montreal: McGill-Queen's University Press, 2001); Francis Oakley and Bruce Russett (eds), *Governance, Accountability and the Future of the Catholic Church* (Continuum International, 2004); Margaret A. Arnot and Charles D. Rabb (eds), *The Governance of Schooling: Comparative Studies of Devolved Management* (London: Routledge/Falmer, 2000); Paul Burgess, *et al.*, *Devolved Approaches to Local Governance: Policy and Practice in Neighbourhood Management* (York: Joseph Rowntree Foundation, 2001).

14 Alexander King and Bertrand Schneider, *The First Global Revolution: A Report of the Council of Rome* (New York: Pantheon Books, 1991), pp. 181–2.

15 Geoffrey Vickers, *Human Systems Are Different* (London: Harper & Row, 1983), p. 2.

16 Susan Strange, 'The Defective State', *Dædalus: Journal of the American Academy of Arts*, 124 (2), pp. 55–74.

17 Fritz Scharpf, *Governing in Europe: Effective and Democratic?* (Oxford: Oxford University Press, 1999).

18 See Susan Strange, *The Retreat of the State: The Diffusion of Power in the World Economy* (Cambridge: Cambridge University Press, 1996), chapters 6–12.

19 The descriptive term 'self-exciting' is used frequently by Geoffrey Vickers in a number of his works, including *Human Systems Are Different*, op. cit.

20 For a consideration of the limitations of performance effectiveness criteria as a measure for the viability of social systems, see C. Lynn Jenks, 'The Well-Being of Social Systems', *Systems Research and Behavioural Science*, Vol. 21, No. 3 (May/June 2004), pp. 209–17.

21 Jon Pierre, 'Introduction: "Understanding Governance"', in Jon Pierre (ed.), *Debating Governance* (Oxford: Oxford University Press, 2000), p. 2.

22 For a full account of the span of Realist theorising, see Jack Donnelly, *Realism and International Relations* (Cambridge: Cambridge University Press, 2000).

23 Mark Duffield, *Global Governance and the New Wars: The Merging of Development and Security* (London: Zed Books, 2001), p. 2.

24 Mark Rupert, *Ideologies of Globalization: Contending Visions of a New World Order* (London: Routledge, 2000).

25 B. Guy Peters and Jon Pierre, 'Is there a governance theory?' (Paper presented at the XVIIIth Congress of the International Political Science Association, Quebec City, 1–5 August 2000).

26 Saskia Sassen, 'The State and Globalization', in Rodney Bruce Hall and Thomas J. Biersteker (eds), *The Emergence of Private Authority in Global Governance* (Cambridge: Cambridge University Press, 2002), pp. 91–112.

27 Rodney Bruce Hall and Thomas J. Biersteker, 'Private authority as global governance,' ibid., pp. 203–22; James N. Rosenau, *Along the Domestic-Foreign Frontier: Exploring Governance in a Turbulent World* (Cambridge: Cambridge University Press, 1997).

28 Robert C. Paehlke, *Democracy's Dilemma: Environment, Social Equity and the Global Economy* (Boston: The MIT Press, 2004).

29 See for example, Software & Information Industry Association, 'SIIA applauds FBI's effort to combat piracy', 19 February 2004. Online. Available HTTP: <http://www.prnewswire.com/cgi-bin/stories.pl?ACCT=105&STORY=/www/story/02-19-2004/0002113006> (accessed 23 June 2004).

30 David Korten, *When Corporations Rule the World* (London: Earthscan, 1996).

31 Transparency International, *Global Corruption Report 2004*. Online. Available HTTP: <http://www.globalcorruptionreport.org/> (accessed 12 June 2004).

32 For an historical survey, see Cornelius F. Murphy, Jr., *World Governance: A Study in the History of Ideas* (Washington, DC: The Catholic University of America Press, 1999).

33 Christian Wiktor, *Multilateral Treaty Calendar, 1648–1995* (Dordrecht: Martinus Nijhoff Publishers, 1998). A useful, succinct summary is Charlotte Ku, 'Global Governance and the Changing face of International Law' (New Haven: Academic Council of the United Nations System, ACUNS Reports & Papers 2001, No. 2).

34 But not entirely: see Philip Allott, *Eunomia: New Order for a New World* (Oxford: Oxford University Press, 1990).

35 A pioneering and still pertinent work in this regard is James N. Rosenau, *Turbulence in World Politics* (New York: Harvester/Wheatsheaf, 1990).

36 NASA News Stories Archive, 'NASA Observations Confirm Expected Ozone Layer Recovery,' 29 July 2003. Online. Available HTTP: <http://earthobservatory.nasa.gov/Newsroom/NasaNews/2003/2003072915079.html> (accessed 4 June 2004).

37 Clearly conveyed by Robert O. Keohane in *Power and Governance in a Partially Globalized World* (London: Routledge, 2002).

38 Of course, assertions about the centrality of the international system can and do accommodate the reality of transnational dynamics – for example: 'Transnational activities are a striking feature of our era which signal some of the ways and directions in which human relations on the planet are changing at the present time. These changes are important. They are technological, economic or social circumstances that statespeople must deal with. They may adversely affect state institutions and may even undermine them or weaken them in certain ways. But they do not constitute or involve moral or legal claims that challenge the authority of state sovereignty. They do not constitute a global political institution that is a rival or alternative to the society of states. At the present time, there is no rival or alternative to the society of states for organizing and conducting political life on a global scale.' Robert Jackson, *The Global Covenant: Human Conduct in a World of States* (Oxford: Oxford University Press, 2000), p. 36.

39 Jim Whitman, 'The Map is Not the Territory: Reconceiving Human Security', in Andrew T. Price-Smith (ed.), *Plagues and Politics: Infectious Disease and International Policy* (Basingstoke: Palgrave, 2001), pp. 151–63.

40 James N. Rosenau, 'Governance, Order and Change in World Politics', in James N. Rosenau and Ernst-Otto Czempiel, *Governance Without Government: Order and Change in World Politics* (Cambridge: Cambridge University Press, 1992), p. 7.

41 Daphné Josselin and William Wallace, *Non-State Actors in World Politics* (Basingstoke: Palgrave, 2001); Seamus Cleary, *The Role of NGOs Under Authoritarian Political Systems* (New York: St. Martin's Press, 1997); Sarah E. Mendelson and John K. Glenn (eds), *The Power and Limits of NGOs: A Critical Look at Building Democracy in Eastern Europe and Eurasisa* (New York: Columbia University Press, 2002).

42 Ruth Philips, 'Is Corporate Engagement an Advocacy Strategy for NGOs? The Community Aid Abroad Experience', *Nonprofit Management and Leadership*, Vol. 13, No. 2 (Winter, 2002), pp. 123–37.

43 For example, see Ann Marie Clark, *Diplomacy of Conscience: Amnesty International and Changing Human Rights Norms* (Princeton: Princeton University Press, 2001).

44 Union of International Associations, *Yearbook of International Organizations 2003/2004: Guide to Global and Civil Society Networks* (Munich: K. G. Saur Verlag, 2003).

45 Mary Kaldor, 'The Idea of Global Civil Society', *International Affairs*, 79, 3 (2003), pp. 583–93; Marlies Glasius, Mary Kaldor and Helmut Anheier (eds), *Global Civil Society 2002* (Oxford: Oxford University Press, 2002).

46 'Why then should we study the neoliberal ideology with its world-wide significance, the growing network of both public and private regimes that extend across the world's largest regions, the system of global inter-governmental organisations and the transnational organisations both carrying out some of the traditional service functions of global public agencies and also working to create regimes and new systems of international integration? It is primarily a question of justice.' Craig N. Murphy, 'Why pay attention to global governance?' Foreword to Rorden Wilkinson and Steve Hughes (eds), *Global Governance: Critical Perspectives* (London: Routledge, 2002), p. xii.

47 Ronnie D. Lipschutz with Judith Mayer, *Global Civil Society and Global Environmental Governance: the Politics of Nature from Place to Planet* (Albany: SUNY

Press, 1996); Mary Kaldor, *Global Civil Society: An Answer to War* (Cambridge: Polity Press, 2003).

48 Louise Amoore and Paul Langley, 'Ambiguities of global civil society', *Review of International Studies*, Vol. 30, No.1 (January 2004), pp. 89–110; Lawrence Hamilton, '"Civil Society": Critique and Alternative', in Gordon Laxer and Sandra Halperin (eds), *Global Civil Society and its Limits* (Basingstoke: Palgrave, 2003), pp. 63–81.

49 Ann-Marie Slaughter, *A New World Order* (Princeton: Princeton University Press, 2004), p. 4.

50 Ibid., p.18.

51 Richard Higgott and Morten Ougard, 'Introduction: Beyond system and society – towards a global polity?' in Morten Ougard and Richard Higgott (eds), *Towards a Global Polity* (London: Routledge, 2002), pp. 3–4. The authors then go on to offer the following definition of 'global polity': 'that totality of political structures, agents and processes, with transnational properties, that in the current historical context have developed a high level of *thick* interconnectedness and an element of *thin* community that transcends the territorial state' (p.12, italics original).

52 Franz Nuscheler, 'Global Governance, Development and Peace', in Paul Kennedy, Dirk Messner and Franz Nuscheler (eds), *Global Trends and Global Governance* (London: Pluto Press, 2002), pp. 156–83.

53 The Department of Political Science and International Relations at the University of Delaware has compiled a useful bibliography, organised under the various IR and other schools of thought, 'Contending Perspectives on Global Governance'. Available HTTP: <http://www.udel.edu/poscir/gg/bib.htm> (accessed 4 February 2004).

54 Paul Cammack, 'The mother of all governments: the World Bank's matrix for global governance', in Rorden Wilkinson and Steve Hughes (eds), op. cit., pp. 36–53.

55 Henk Overbeek, 'Global Governance, Class, Hegemony: A Historical Materialist Perspective', Working Papers in Political Science No.2004/01, University of Amsterdam. Online. Available HTTP:<http://politicologie.scw.vu.nl/wpps/wpps200401.pdf.> (accessed 5 July 2004)

56 Anthony McGrew, 'Cosmopolitan Global Governance', (draft). Online. Available HTTP: <www.demes.dk/html/modules.php?op=modload&name=UpDownload&file=index&req=getit&lid=10> (accessed 8 June 2004).

57 For example, one study suggests that globalisation studies can be categorised on the basis of four research clusters, or approaches: world-systems; global culture; global society; and global capitalism. See Leslie Sklair, 'Competing Conceptions of Globalization, *Journal of World-Systems Research*, Vol. V, No. 2 (1999), pp. 143–62.

58 The best-known and most frequently cited definition is that supplied by the Commission on Global Governance in *Our Global Neighbourhood* (Oxford: Oxford University Press, 1995), pp. 2–3.

59 S. Maxwell, 'Food security: a postmodern perspective,' *Food Policy* (21) 2 (1996), pp. 155–70, cited in C. Ford Runge, Benjamin Senauer, Philip G. Pardey and Mark W. Rosengrant, *Ending Hunger in Our Lifetime: Food Security and Globalization* (Baltimore: Johns Hopkins Press, 2003), p. 5.

60 An example of which is Jonathan Michie and John Grieve Smith (eds), *Global*

Instability: The Political Economy of World Economic Governance (London: Routledge, 1999). The full listing for 'governance' in the index comprises the following: capital account; foreign investment alternatives; the world economic role of the Tobin Tax; and the World Trade Organization.

61 Volker Rittberger (ed.), *Regime Theory in International Relations* (Oxford: Clarendon Press, 1995); Nazli Choucri (ed.), *Global Accord: Environmental Challenges and International Responses* (London: The MIT Press, 1995); David G. Victor, Kal Raustiala and Eugene B. Skolnikoff (eds), *The Implementation and Effectiveness of International Environmental Commitments: Theory and Practice* (London: The MIT Press, 1998); Miranda A. Schreurs and Elizabeth C. Economy (eds), *The Internationalization of Environmental Protection* (Cambridge: Cambridge University Press, 1997).

62 This distinction is made in Jon Pierre, op. cit., p. 3.

3 Is governance global or just all over the map?

1 Robert O'Brien, Anne Marie Goetz, Jan Aart Scholte and Marc Williams, *Contesting Global Governance: Multilateral Economic Institutions and Global Social Movements* (Cambridge: Cambridge University Press, 2000).

2 For example: 'Activists in advocacy networks are concerned with political effectiveness. Their definition of effectiveness often includes some policy changes by "target actors" such as governments, international financial institutions like the World Bank, or private actors like trans-national corporations. In order to bring about policy change, networks need to pressure and persuade more powerful actors. To gain influence the networks seem to have leverage (the word appears often in the discourse of advocacy organisations) over more powerful actors. By leveraging more powerful institutions, weak groups gain influence far beyond their ability to influence state practices directly. The identification of material or moral advantage is a crucial strategic step in network campaigns.' Margaret E. Keck and Kathryn Sikkink, *Activists Beyond Borders: Advocacy Networks in International Politics* (Ithaca: Cornell University Press, 1998), p. 23.

3 James Rosenau, *Turbulence in World Politics: A Theory of Change and Continuity* (New York: Harvester Wheatsheaf, 1990); and subsequently, *Along the Domestic-Foreign Frontier: Exploring Governance in a Turbulent World* (Cambridge: Cambridge University Press, 1997).

4 James Rosenau, *Along the Domestic-Foreign Frontier*, ibid., p. 412.

5 For example, see R. A. W. Rhodes, *Understanding Governance: Policy Networks, Governance, Reflexivity and Accountability* (Buckingham: Open University Press, 1997).

6 James N. Rosenau, summary of presentation made to the Second Meridian Conference on Global Governance, 'Global Governance in a Turbulent World', Bolinas, California, 4–6 February 1994. Online. Available HTTP:<http://meridianinternational.org/global_governance.htm> (accessed 18 January 2002).

7 Martin Hewson and Timothy J. Sinclair, 'The Emergence of Global Governance Theory', in Martin Hewson and Timothy J. Sinclair (eds), *Approaches to Global Governance Theory* (Albany: State University of New York Press, 1999), p. 6; James N. Rosenau and Ernst-Otto Czempiel (eds), *Governance Without Government: Order and Change in World Politics* (Cambridge: Cambridge University Press, 1992).

8 Respectively, see Andrew Herod, Gearóid Ó Tuathail and Susan M. Roberts, *Unruly World? Globalization, Governance and Geography* (London: Routledge, 1998); Rorden Wilkinson and Steve Hughes, *Global Governance: Critical Perspectives* (London: Routledge, 2002); Ernst-Otto Czempiel (eds), *Governance Without Government: Order and Change in World Politics* (Cambridge: Cambridge University Press, 1992).

9 Craig N. Murphy, 'Global governance: poorly done and poorly understood', *International Affairs*, Vol. 76, No. 4 (2000), p. 799.

10 Jim Robbins, 'Lessons from the Wolf: Bringing the top predator back to Yellowstone has triggered a cascade of unanticipated changes in the park's ecosystem', *Scientific American*, 24 May 2004.

11 Julian Davis, 'The Campaign to Ban Landmines: Public Diplomacy, Middle Power Leadership and an Unconventional Negotiating Process', *Journal of Humanitarian Assistance*. Online. Available HTTP: <http://www.jha.ac/articles/a134.htm> (accessed 6 July 2004).

12 See Robert O'Brien, Anne Marie Goetz, Jan Aart Scholte and Marc Williams, op. cit., especially Chapter 1, pp. 1–23 for a summary of these perspectives.

13 W. Andy Knight, 'Engineering Space in Global Governance: the Emergence of Civil Society in Evolving "New" Multilateralism', in Michael G. Schechter, *Future Multilateralism: The Political and Social Framework* (Basingstoke: Macmillan, 1999), pp. 255–91. A worthwhile single case study is Ann Marie Clark, *Diplomacy of Conscience: Amnesty International and Changing Human Rights Norms* (Princeton: Princeton University Press, 2001).

14 Margaret E. Keck and Kathryn Sikkink, op. cit.; Sanjeev Khagram, James V. Riker and Kathryn Sikkink (eds), *Restructuring World Politics: Transnational Social Movements, Networks, and Norms* (Minneapolis: University of Minnesota Press, 2002).

15 This is clear in the self-description of the Bretton Woods Project, contained on their website: 'The Bretton Woods Project works as a networker, information-provider, media informant and watchdog to scrutinise and influence the World Bank and International Monetary Fund (IMF). [. . .] It monitors projects, policy reforms and the overall management of the Bretton Woods institutions with special emphasis on environmental and social concerns.' Online. Available HTTP: <www.brettonwoodsproject.org/index.shmtl> (accessed 4 October 2003). There are numerous others, concentrating on a wide variety of issues and concerns, including: Human Rights Watch (http://www.hrw.org); Corporate Watch (http://www.corporatewatch.org.uk/); People's Health Movement (http://www.phmovement.org/campaigns/GHEW/); and GM Watch (http://www.gmwatch.org/welcome.asp).

16 Sandra Halperin and Gordon Laxer, 'Effective Resistance to Corporate Globalization', in Gordon Laxer and Sandra Halperin (eds), *Global Civil Society and its Limits* (Basingstoke: Palgrave, 2003), p. 1.

17 Michael Edwards, *NGO Rights and Responsibilities* (London: The Foreign Policy Centre, 2000), p. 2.

18 L. David Brown and Jonathan A. Fox, 'Accountability within Transnational Coalitions', in Jonathan A. Fox and L. David Brown (eds), *The Struggle for Accountability: The World Bank, NGOs, and Grassroots Movements* (Cambridge, Mass.: MIT Press, 1998), p. 441.

19 Gordon Urquhart, 'That's not faith, that's provocation: Catholics and Muslims are uniting in a pernicious new alliance', *The Guardian*, 12 November 1999.

20 For example, see Jedrzej George Frynas and Scott Pegg (eds), *Transnational Corporations and Human Rights* (Basingstoke: Palgrave, 2003).

21 John Braithwaite and Peter Drahos, *Global Business Regulation* (Cambridge: Cambridge University Press, 2000).

22 For an instance of which, see the US Government's Trade Portal on WTO-authorised EU sanctions of US$4 billion against US exports. Online. Available HTTP: <http://www.export.gov/eu_tsatus.html> (accessed 4 July 2004).

23 John Braithwaite and Peter Drahos, op. cit., p. 123.

24 See Table 20.1, 'Some of the most influential actors in the globalization of regulation', in ibid., pp. 476–7. However, the authors also quote the Australian Ambassador for the Environment: 'The role of NGOs in the negotiation and implementation of agreements (which has increased dramatically during and since the UNCED process), will continue to grow. Two weeks ago, in Geneva, I was startled to find that the Chairman of a meeting of the *ad hoc* Committee on [*sic*] Parties to the Basel Convention giving the floor to the representative of Greenpeace to negotiate as an equal with the governments on the drafting language – something which I never before witnessed in twenty years of involvement with multilateralism.' (Quoted on p. 574.)

25 Ibid., pp. 605–6.

26 Nick Paton Walsh, 'Putin adviser calls Kyoto protocol a "death treaty"', *The Guardian*, 15 April 2004. '[President Putin's top adviser on the treaty] likened the protocol's restrictions on normal economic freedoms to an "interstate gulag".'

27 For the UN's own evaluative summary of these developments, see Office of the President of the Millennium Assembly, 55th session of the United Nations General Assembly, 'Reference document on the participation of civil society in United Nations conferences and special sessions of the General Assembly during the 1990s', (Version 1 August 2001). Online. Available HTTP: <http://www. un.org/ga/president/55/speech/civilsociety1.htm#earth> (accessed 25 January 2004).

28 Report of the Panel of Eminent Persons on United Nations-Civil Society Relations, 'We the peoples: civil society, the United Nations and global governance', A/58/817 (2004). Online. Available HTTP: <http://www.un.org/ reform/a58_817_english.doc> (accessed 1 August 2004).

29 W. Andy Knight, op. cit., p. 256.

30 Nicholas Bayne, 'The G7 Summit's Contribution: Past, Present and Prospective', in Karl Kaiser, John L. Kirton and Joseph P. Daniels, *Shaping a New International Financial System: Challenges of Governance in a Globalizing World* (Aldershot: Ashgate, 2000), p. 27.

31 Kelly Loughlin and Virginia Berridge, 'Global Health Governance: Historical Dimensions of Global Governance,' Centre on Global Change and Health, London School of Hygiene and Tropical Medicine and Department of Health and Development, World Health Organization (March, 2002).

32 See David Fidler, *International Law and Infectious Diseases* (Oxford: Oxford University Press, 1999); Kelley Lee (ed.), *Health Impacts of Globalization: Towards Global Governance* (Basingstoke: Palgrave, 2003).

33 David Fidler, *SARS, Governance and the Globalization of Disease* (Basingstoke: Palgrave, 2004).

34 A. J. McMichael, A. Haines, R. Slooff and S. Kovats (eds), *Climate Change and Human Health: an assessment prepared by a task group on behalf of the World Health*

Organisation, the World Meteorological Organisation and the United Nations Environment Programme (Geneva: World Health Organisation, 1996); Tony McMichael, *Human Frontiers, Environments and Disease: Past Patterns, Uncertain Futures* (Cambridge: Cambridge University Press, 2001).

35 Ronald J. Glasser, MD, 'We Are Not Immune: Influenza, SARS, and the collapse of public health', *Harper's Magazine*, July 2004. Online. Available HTTP: <http://www.longwoods.com/opinions/WeAreNotImmune.pdf> (accessed 2 August 2004); Laurie Garrett, *Betrayal of Trust: The Collapse of Global Public Health* (Oxford: Oxford University Press, 2003).

36 Ronald J. Glasser, ibid., p. 4.

37 Carlos Correa, 'Integrating Public Health Concerns into Patent Legislation in Developing Countries', Geneva South Centre (October 2000). Online. Available HTTP: <http://www.southcentre.org/publications/publichealth/toc.htm> (accessed 13 November 2003); see also Peter Drahos and Ruth Mayne (eds), *Global Intellectual Property Rights: Knowledge, Access and Development* (Basingstoke: Palgrave, 2002).

38 The Commission on Global Governance, *Our Global Neighbourhood* (Oxford: Oxford University Press, 1995).

39 For a discussion of which, see Geoffrey Vickers, *Human Systems Are Different* (London: Harper & Row, 1983).

40 Geoffrey Vickers, *Freedom in a Rocking Boat: Changing Values in an Unstable World* (London: Penguin Press, 1970), p. 125.

41 Ibid., p. 123.

42 James N. Rosenau, 'Change, Complexity and Governance in a Globalizing Space', in Jon Pierre (ed.), *Debating Governance* (Oxford: Oxford University Press, 2000), p. 172.

43 Wolfgang H. Reinicke and Francis M. Deng, *Critical Choices: The United Nations, Networks, and the Future of Global Governance* (UN Vision Project on Global Public Policy Networks), www.globalpublicpolicy.net, p. viii.

44 W. Andy Knight, *A Changing United Nations: Multilateral Evolution and the Quest for Global Governance* (Basingstoke: Palgrave, 2000), p. 3.

45 Fiona Macmillan, *The WTO and the Environment* (London: Sweet & Maxwell, 2001).

46 Peter Laslett, 'Environmental Ethics and the Obsolescence of Existing Political Institutions', in Brendan Gleeson and Nicholas Low (eds), *Governing for the Environment: Global Problems, Ethics and Democracy* (Basingstoke: Palgrave, 2001), pp. 165–80.

47 This is less evident in environmental and scientific studies. For example: 'We have entered an era characterized by syndromes of global change that stem from the interdependence between human development and the environment. As we attempt to move from merely causing these syndromes to managing them consciously, two central questions must be addressed: What kind of planet do we want? What kind of planet can we get?' William C. Clark, 'Managing Planet Earth', in *Managing Planet Earth: Readings from Scientific American* (New York: W. H. Freeman and Company, 1990), p. 2.

4 The interaction of human and natural systems

1 Michael Perelman, *The Natural Instability of Markets: Expectations, Increasing Returns and the Collapse of Capitalism* (Basingstoke: Macmillan, 1999), p. 25.

2 'Sinking feeling', *New Scientist*, 21 February 2004, p. 5.

3 Jean-François Rischard, 'A Crisis of Complexity and Global Governance', *International Herald Tribune*, 2 October 1998.

4 Geoffrey Vickers, *Human Systems Are Different* (London: Harper & Row, 1983), p. 14 (italics original).

5 R. Alan Hedley, 'Convergence in natural, social and technical systems: a critique', *Current Science*, Vol. 79, No. 5, (10 September 2000), p. 592.

6 Geoffrey Vickers, op. cit., p. 17.

7 *The Hutchison Dictionary of Science* (second edition, 1998), p. 176. For a fascinating account of the formal origins of cybernetics and the long-standing philosophical themes that informed it, see Jean-Pierre Dupuy (translated by M. B. Debevoise), *The Mechanization of the Mind: On the Origins of Cognitive Science* (Princeton: Princeton University Press, 2000).

8 Online. Available HTTP: <http://www.santafe.edu/> (accessed 6 February 2004).

9 Stuart Kauffman, *At Home in the Universe: The Search for Laws of Complexity* (London: Viking, 1995); M. Mitchell Waldrop, *Complexity: The Emerging Science at the Edge of Order and Chaos* (London: Penguin, 1992); and Roger Lewin, *Complexity: Life at the Edge of Chaos* (New York: Macmillan, 1992).

10 David Byrne, *Complexity Theory and the Social Sciences: An Introduction* (London: Routledge, 1998); Robert Jervis, *System Effects: Complexity in Political and Social Life* (Princeton: Princeton University Press, 1997); Raymond A. Eve, Sara Horsfall and Mary E. Lee (eds), *Chaos, Complexity, and Sociology: Myths, Models and Theories* (London: Sage, 1997); and Samir Rihani, *Complex Systems Theory and Development Practice: Understanding Non-linear Realities* (London: Zed Books, 2002).

11 Davi Depew and Bruce Weber, *Darwinism Evolving: Systems Dynamics and the Genealogy of Natural Selection* (Cambridge, Mass.: MIT Press, 1995), p. 437.

12 Terry Eagleton, *The Illusions of Postmodernism* (Oxford: Blackwell, 1996). Note the carefully argued exclusion of chaos theory from the argument of Paul Cilliers, *Complexity and Postmodernism* (London: Routledge, 1998), pp. viii–x.

13 Gang Hu, 'Transport and Land Use in Chinese Cities: International Comparisons', in Nicolas Low and Brendan Gleeson (eds), *Making Urban Transport Sustainable* (Basingstoke: Palgrave, 2003), p. 199.

14 Chris Bright, *Life Out of Bounds: Bio-Invasions in a Borderless World* (London: Earthscan, 1999).

15 Mike Moore, *A World Without Walls: Freedom, Development, Free Trade and Global Governance* (Cambridge: Cambridge University Press, 2003).

16 BBC News World Edition, ' SARS "could cost Asia $28bn"'. Online. Available HTTP: <http://news.bbc.co.uk/2/hi/business/3012821.stm> (accessed 9 May 2003).

17 James Lovelock, *Gaia: A New Look at Life on Earth* (Oxford: Oxford University Press, 1987).

18 Mark C. Taylor, *The Moment of Complexity: Emerging Network Culture* (Chicago: University of Chicago Press, 2001), p. 142.

19 Avner Arbel and Albert E. Kaff, *Crash: Ten Days in October: Will It Strike Again?* (London: Longman Financial Services Publishing, 1989) pp. 5; 116.

20 Geoffrey Vickers, op. cit., p. 17 (italics removed).

21 BBC News, 'Drug-resistant TB "threatens EU"'. Online. Available HTTP:
   <http://news.bbc.co.uk/1/hi/health/3513268.stm> (accessed 16 March 2004);
   Lee B. Reichman, with Janice Hopkins Tanne, *Timebomb: The Global Epidemic of
   Multi-Drug-Resistant Tuberculosis* (New York: McGraw-Hill, 2002).
22 See the special edition of *Emerging Infectious Diseases*, Vol. 4, No. 3. Online.
   Available HTTP: <http://www.cdc.gov/ncidod/eid/vol4no3/weinstein.htm>
   (accessed 12 July 2004).
23 *New Scientist*, 7 August 2004, special report, 'BSE Crisis 2004', p. 35.
24 Stephen Jay Gould, *Wonderful Life: the Burgess Shale and the Nature of History*
   (London: Hutchison, 1989).
25 These are well captured in the interviews contained in Waldrop, op. cit.
26 Paul Cilliers, op. cit., pp. 92–3 (italics original).
27 William Bechtel and Robert C. Richardson, *Discovering Complexity: Decomposition
   and Localization as Strategies in Scientific Research* (Princeton: Princeton University
   Press, 1993), p. 228. Robert Jervis makes the same point with specific reference
   to political and social systems: 'We cannot understand systems by summing up
   the characteristics of the parts of the bilateral relations between pairs of them.
   This is not to say that such operations are never legitimate, but only that when
   they are we are not dealing with a system.' Robert Jervis, *System Effects: Complexity*
   op. cit., p. 34 and Chapter 2 more generally.
28 Shoshana Zuboff, *In the Age of the Smart Machine: The Future of Work and Power*
   (London: Heinemann, 1988), p. 291.
29 See W. Brian Arthur, Steven N. Darlauf and David A. Lane (eds), *The Economy as
   an Evolving Complex System: Part 2* (Boulder: Perseus Publishing, 1999).
30 'Genetically Modified Piggies Go to Market in Quebec – Illegal release into
   animal feed second in two years', (18 February 2004). Online. Available HTTP:
   <http://www.greenpeace.org.au/truefood/news2.html?mode=intl&newsid=
   126> (accessed 20 February 2004).
31 Richard B. Norgaard, *Development Betrayed: The End of Progress and a Coevolutionary
   Revisioning of the Future* (London: Routledge, 1994), pp. 40–1.
32 Samuel Bowles, Jung-Kyoo Choi and Astrid Hopfensitz, 'The co-evolution of
   individual behaviours and social institutions', *Journal of Theoretical Biology*, 223
   (2003), pp. 135–47; Fikret Berkes and Carl Folke, 'A Systems Perspective on the
   Interrelationships between Natural, Man-Made and Cultural Capital', *Ecological
   Economics*, Vol. 5, No. 1 (1993), pp. 1–8.
33 Stuart Kauffman, op. cit., p. 299.
34 James N. Rosenau, *Distant Proximities: Dynamics Beyond Globalization* (Princeton:
   Princeton University Press, 2003), pp. 218–19.
35 See Jagdish Bhabwati, *In Defence of Globalization* (Oxford: Oxford University
   Press, 2004); also, Martin Wolf, *Why Globalization Works: The Case for the Global
   Market Economy* (New Haven: Yale University Press, 2004).
36 For a survey of natural systems, see W. G. Ernest (ed.), *Earth Systems: Processes and
   Issues* (Cambridge: Cambridge University Press, 2000).
37 C. S. Shapiro (ed.), *Atmospheric Nuclear Tests: Environmental and Human Consequences*
   (NATO ASI Series) (Berlin: Springer-Verlag, 1998).
38 Valerie Kuletz, *The Tainted Desert: Environmental Ruin in the American West*
   (London: Routledge, 1998).
39 W. Anderson and Liam D. Anderson, *Strategic Minerals: Resource Geopolitics and
   Global Geo-Economics* (Chichester: John Wiley & Sons, 1998).

40 See the chilling account of the ecological and eventual social and cultural disaster that befell the population of Easter Island in Ernest Zebrowski, Jr., *Perils of a Restless Planet: Scientific Perspectives on Natural Disasters* (Cambridge: Cambridge University Press, 1997), pp. 105–9; more recently, according to one report, 'The Indonesian pulp and paper industry is destroying rainforest at such an astonishing rate that it will run out of wood in five years . . . ' Paul Brown, 'Indonesian rainforests pulped to extinction', *The Guardian*, 11 February 2002, p. 14.

41 Zebrowski, op. cit.

42 James Lovelock, *Gaia: A New Look at Life on Earth* (Oxford: Oxford University Press, 1995).

43 A. J. McMichael, A. Haines, R. Slooff and S. Kovats (eds), *Climate Change and Human Health, An assessment prepared by a task group on behalf of the World Health Organization, The World Meteorological Organization and the United Nations Environment Programme* (Geneva: WHO, 1996).

44 See Presentation of Robert W. Watson, Chair, Intergovernmental Panel on Climate Change at the Sixth Conference of Parties to the United Nations Framework Convention on Climate Change (13 November 2000).

45 Bill Gates, *The Road Ahead* (London: Viking/Penguin, 1995), pp. 157–8.

46 'Wired for Mayhem', *New Scientist*, 4 July 1998, p. 7. For the full study summarised there, see Jeffrey O. Kephart, James E. Hanson and Jakka Sairamesh, 'Price-War Dynamics in a Free Market Economy of Software Agents,' in Christoper Adami, *et al.* (eds), *Artificial Life VI: Proceedings of the Sixth International Conference on Artificial Life* (Cambridge: MIT Press, 1998), pp. 53–62. A considerable literature has since developed on electronic 'intelligent agents'. The Massively Distributed Systems group at IBM's Thomas J. Watson Research Center runs a worthwhile gateway site. Online. Available HTTP: <http://www.research.ibm.com/massive> (accessed 7 January 2003).

47 Charles Perrow, *Normal Accidents: Living With High-Risk Technologies* (New York: Basic Books, 1984), p. 83.

48 David Quammen, *The Song of the Dodo: Island Biogeography in an Age of Extinctions* (London: Pimlico, 1997).

49 Philip A. Stephens and William J. Sutherland, 'Consequences of the Allee effect for behaviour, ecology and conservation', *Trends in Ecology and Evolution*, Vol. 14, No. 10 (10 October 1999), pp. 401–5.

50 Jonathan M. Mann and Daniel J. M. Tarantola (eds), *AIDS in The World II* (Oxford: Oxford University Press, 1996); see also Bernard Roizman (ed.), *Infectious Diseases in an Age of Change: The Impact of Human Ecology and Behaviour on Disease Transmission* (Washington, DC: National Academy Press, 1995).

51 G. Gardner and P. Sampat, 'Forging a Sustainable Materials Economy', in Lester Brown and Christopher Flavin (eds), *State of the World 1999* (London: Earthscan, 1999); Jennifer D. Mitchell, 'Nowhere to Hide: The Global Spread of High-Risk Synthetic Chemicals', *WorldWatch*, March/April 1997, pp. 26–36.

52 John Wargo, *Our Children's Toxic Legacy: How Science and Law Fail to Protect Us from Pesticides* (Yale: Yale University Press, 1996).

53 Lee B. Reichman, with Janice Hopkins Tanne, op. cit.

54 Chris Bright, op. cit.; see also John Cairns, Jr. and Joseph R. Bidwell, 'The Modification of Human Society by Natural Systems: Discontinuities Caused by the Exploitation of Endemic Species and the Introduction of Exotics', *Environmental Health Perspectives*, Vol. 104, No. 11, pp. 1142–5.

55 Federal Emergency Management Agency, 'World Disasters Report Predicts a Decade of Super-Disasters'. Online. Available HTTP: <http://www.fema.gov/nwz99/irc624.htm> (accessed 17 December 2002).

56 Charles Perrow, op. cit., p. 255; Bill Richardson, 'Why We Probably Will Not Save Mankind: A "Natural" Configuration of Accident-Proneness', *Disaster Prevention and Management*, Vol. 2, No. 4 (1993), pp. 32–59. For an overview of the risks and uncertainties of biotechnology, see Jeremy Rifkin, *The Biotech Century* (London: Victior Gollancz, 1998); for a wide-ranging conference discussion of biotechnology issues, see Ismail Serageldin and Wanda Collins (eds), *Biotechnology and Biosafety* (Washington, DC: The World Bank, 1999).

57 Francis Fukayama and Caroline S. Wagner, 'Information and Biological Revolutions: Global Governance Challenges – Summary of a Study Group'. Online. Available HTTP: <http://www.rand.org/publications/MR/MR1139/> (accessed 18 November 2002).

58 James N. Rosenau, 'Governance in the Twenty-First Century', *Global Governance* 1 (1995), p. 15.

59 Jim Whitman, 'Global Governance as the Friendly Face of Unaccountable Power', *Security Dialogue*, Vol. 33(1), pp. 45–57.

60 C. Kerr, J. T. Dunlop, F. Harbison and C. A. Meyers, *Industrialism and Industrial Man* (Oxford: Oxford University Press, 1960).

61 Jeremy Rifkin, *The Biotech Century*, op. cit., p. xv.

62 Marshall A. Martin, 'Agricultural Biotechnology: What's all the fuss about?' *Purdue Agricultural Economics Report* (March 2000), p. 5.

63 Online, available HTTP: <http://www.lostpacket.net/>.

64 A useful overview is Tony McMichael, *Human Frontiers, Environments and Disease: Past Patterns, Uncertain Futures* (Cambridge: Cambridge University Press, 2001).

65 For a full listing of the relevant regulatory bodies and instruments, see The Genomics Gateway maintained at the Department of Peace Studies, Bradford University. Online. Available HTTP: <http://www.bradford.ac.uk/acad/sbtwc/gateway/> (accessed 19 January 2004).

66 Safety Advisory Services, Leeds University, News Item 40. Online. Available HTTP: <http://www.leeds.ac.uk/rps/news/newsindex.htm?40.htm> (accessed 7 May 2004).

67 *European Union Agricultural News Digest*, No. 52 (18 July 2003). Online. Available HTTP: <http://europa.eu.int/comm/agriculture/newsdigest/2003/52.htm#book2> (accessed 1 June 2004).

68 Antony Barnett, 'GM genes "jump species barrier"', *The Observer*, 28 May 2000. Online. Available HTTP: <http://observer.guardian.co.uk/uk_news/story/0,,319418,00.html> (accessed 30 May 2000); Paul Brown, 'Scientists shocked at GM gene transfer', *The Guardian*, 15 August 2002. Online. Available HTTP: <http://www.guardian.co. uk/uk_news/story/0,,774788,00.html> (accessed 15 August 2002).

69 Clive James, Chair, International Service for the Acquisition of Agri-Biotech Applications, 'Global Review of Commercialized Transgenic Crops, 2002'. Online. Available HTTP: <http://www.isaaa.org/Press_release/Briefs29-2003/Briefs29-2003%20ESummary.pdf> (accessed 2 August 2004).

70 William McNeil, *Plagues and Peoples* (Oxford: Blackwell, 1976); see also his *The Human Condition: An Ecological and Historical View* (Princeton: Princeton University Press, 1980).

71 Mike Davis, *Late Victorian Holocausts: El Niño, Famines and the Making of the Third World* (London: Verso, 2001).

72 Geoffrey Vickers, *Freedom in a Rocking Boat: Changing Values in an Unstable Society* (London: Penguin Press, 1970), pp. 124–5.

5 Global governance: conceptual challenges

1 See Paul Kennedy, Dirk Messner and Franz Nuscheler (eds), *Global Trends and Global Governance* (London: Pluto Press, 2002).

2 Frank Benjamin Golley, *A History of the Development of the Ecosystem Concept in Ecology: More Than the Sum of the Parts* (Yale: Yale University Press, 1993), p. 189. For a contemporary example, see John Cairns and Eric P. Smith, 'Uncertainties Associated with Extrapolating from Toxicologic Responses in Laboratory Systems to the Responses of Natural Systems', in John Lemons (ed.), *Scientific Uncertainty and Environmental Problem Solving* (Abingdon: Blackwell Science, 1996), pp. 188–205.

3 Edward O. Wilson, *The Diversity of Life* (London: Penguin, 1992), pp. 142–3.

4 This story is recounted in Stephen S. Hall, *Mapping the Millennium: How Computer-Driven Cartography is Revolutionizing the Face of Science* (New York: Vintage Books, 1993), pp. 127–38.

5 W. Edward Stead and Jean Garner Stead, *Management for a Small Planet* (London: Sage, 1996).

6 Michael Perelman, *The Natural Instability of Markets: Expectations, Increasing Returns, and the Collapse of Capitalism* (Basingstoke: Macmillan, 1999), p. xi.

7 Frank G. Zarb, Chairman and CEO, National Association of Securities Dealers, 'The Coming Global Digital Stock Market.' Online. Available HTTP: <http://nasdaqnews.com/views/speech/digmarkets.html> (accessed 12 November 2002). The case favouring further government deregulation is made by US Secretary of Energy Spencer Abraham, 'Deregulation is Working', *Washington Post*, 14 January 2002, p. A17; for a critical examination of the role of deregulation in the collapse of Enron, see Public Citizen, 'Blind Faith: How Deregulation and Enron's Influence Over Government Looted Billions from Americans', www.citizen.org (December 2001).

8 BBC News Online Network, 'Greenspan defends hedge-fund buy-out'. Online. Available HTTP: http://news.bbc.uk/hi/english/business/the_economy/newsid_184000/184505. stm> (accessed 2 October, 1998).

9 Report of the President's Working Group on Financial Markets, 'Hedge Funds, Leverage, and the Lessons of Long-Term Capital Management', Washington, April, 1999.

10 CNN Financial Network, 'Omega: LTCM was unique'. Online. Available HTTP: <http://www.cnnfn.com/markets/9810/01/cooperman_intv/> (accessed 3 February 2003).

11 Geoffrey Vickers, 'Problems of Distribution', in C. West Churchman and Richard O. Mason (eds), *World Modeling: A Dialogue* (American Elsevier, 1976), p. 49. Vickers' three points follow in italics.

12 Sharon Bender, 'Insurers sweat over global warming', *Engineers Australia* (August 2001), p. 41; see also the US Environmental Protection Agency's global warming site. The section on the insurance industry is www.epa.gov/global warming/actions/industry/insurance.html.

13 A thematic illustration of which is the presence of hormones and drugs (in addition to pesticides) in drinking water. See 'Something in the water', *New Scientist*, 6 March 1999; Dana W. Koplin, Edward T. Furlong, Michael T. Meyer, E. Michael Thurman, Steven D. Zaugg, Larry B. Barber and Herbert T. Buxton, 'Pharmaceuticals, Hormones and Other Organic Wastewater Contaminants in US Streams, 1999–2000: A National Reconnaissance', *Environmental Science and Technology*. Online. Available HTTP: <http://pubs.acs.org/hotacl/est/es11055j_rev_html> (accessed 18 August 2002). For a broader consideration of the temporal dimensions of environmental risk/damage, see Barbara Adam, *Timescapes of Modernity: The Environment and Invisible Hazards* (London: Routledge, 1998).

14 James Rosenau, *Along the Domestic-Foreign Frontier: Exploring Governance in a Turbulent World* (Cambridge: Cambridge University Press, 1997), p. 173.

15 Ernst-Otto Czempiel, 'Governance and Democratization', in James N. Rosenau and Ernst-Otto Czempiel (eds), *Governance Without Government: Order and Change in World Politics* (Cambridge: Cambridge University Press, 1992), p. 250.

16 James Rosenau, 'Governance, Order, and Change in World Politics', ibid., pp. 13–14.

17 See Poul Harremoës, David Gee, Malcolm McGarvin, Andy Sterling, Jane Keys, Brian Wynne and Sofia Guedes Vaz (eds), *The Precautionary Principle in the 20th Century: Late Lessons from Early Warnings* (London: Earthscan, 2002).

18 'UNEP Warns Of Growth Of Ocean "Dead Zones"', *UN Wire*. Online. Available HTTP: <http://www.unwire.org/UNWire/20040329/449_22264.asp> (accessed 29 March 2004).

19 See the Intergovernmental Panel on Climate Change, 'Who Should Pay for the Response? Mitigation by Countries and Sectors: Equity and Cost-effectiveness Considerations.' Online. Available HTTP: <http://www.grida.no/climate/ipcc_tar/wg3/445.htm> (accessed 19 June 2004).

20 Mark Townsend and Richard Sadler, 'North Sea birds dying as waters heat up: Scientists warn that warmer conditions could have a catastrophic effect on east coast ecosystem', *The Observer*, 20 June 2004; John Vidal, 'Exotic species are now catch of the day', *The Guardian* 23 August 2004.

21 James C. Scott, *Seeing Like a State: How Certain Schemes to Improve the Human Condition Have Failed* (New Haven: Yale University Press, 1998), p. 347.

22 Amitabh Avasthi, 'Bush-meat trade breeds new HIV', *New Scientist*, 7 August, 2004, p. 8.

23 John E. Fa, Dominic Currie and Jessica Meeuwig, 'Bushmeat and food security in the Congo Basin: linkages between wildlife and people's future', *Environmental Conservation*, Vol. 30, No. 1 (2003), pp. 71–8.

24 Amitabh Avasthi, op. cit.

25 C. S. Holling, Lance H. Gunderson and Donald Ludwig, 'In Quest of a Theory of Adaptive Change', in Lance H. Gunderson and C. S. Holling (eds), *Panarchy: Understanding Transformations in Human and Natural Systems* (Washington: Island Press, 2002), p. 9.

26 Janet Raloff, 'Must We Pull the Plug?' *Science News Online*. Online. Available HTTP: <http://www.sciencenews.org/pages/sn_arc97/10_25_97/bob1.htm> (accessed 25 October 1997).

27 Theo Colborn, Dianne Dumanoski and John Peterson Myers, *Our Stolen Future* (London: Abacus, 1996), p. 88; see also Deborah Cadbury, *The Feminization of Nature: Our Future at Risk* (London: Penguin, 1997).

28 'Toxicological Profile for Polychlorinated Biphenyls (PCBs)', Agency for Toxic Substances and Disease Registry (US Department of Health and Human Services), November 2000. Online. Available HTTP: <http://www.atsdr.cdc. gov/toxprofiles/tp17.html> (accessed 14 April 2004); for a recent review of the endocrine-disrupting effects of a wide range of chemicals in the animal kingdom, see Ethan D. Cloftfelter, Alison M. Bell and Kate R. Levering, 'The role of animal behaviour in the study of endocrine-disrupting chemicals', *Animal Behaviour*, 68 (2004), pp. 465–76.

29 Wendy A. Ockenden, Knut Brevik, Sandra N. Meijer, Eiliv Steinnes, Andrew J. Sweetman and Kevin C. Jones, 'The global re-cycling of persistent organic pollutants is strongly retarded by soils', *Environmental Pollution*, Vol. 121, Issue 1 (January 2003), pp. 75–85.

30 John McNeil, *Something New Under the Sun: An Environmental History of the Twentieth Century* (London: Penguin Press, 2000).

31 Online. Available HTTP: <http://www.chem.unep.ch/pops/> (accessed 15 May 2004).

32 *New Scientist*, 25 May 2002, page 25; see also Debora Mackenzie, 'Still at large: PCBs' dangerous cousins have slipped through the UN's net', *New Scientist*, 4 July 1998, p. 6.

33 Dr Abou-Donia (notes from CIIN MCS Conference Lecture 27 August 2001), 'Synergistic Effects of Chemicals in the Nervous System'. Online. Available HTTP: <http://www.mindfully.org/Pesticide/Donia-CIIN-MCS-27aug01.htm> (accessed 12 May 2004).

34 Richard Alexander, 'Chemically Induced Diseases: Synergistic Effects and Cumulative Injuries caused by Toxic Chemicals – Understanding the Gulf War Syndrome and Multiple Chemical Sensitivity [MCS]'. Online. Available HTTP: <http://consumerlawpage.com/article/gulfwar.shtml> (accessed 12 May 2004).

35 Online. Available HTTP: <http://www.cas.org/cgi-bin/regreport.pl> (accessed 14 May 2004).

36 Online. Available HTTP: <http://www.scitechresources.gov/Results/show_result. php?rec=1324> (accessed 14 May 2004).

37 Online. Available HTTP: <http://www.atsdr.cdc.gov/01list.html> (accessed 15 May 2004).

38 Barbara Adam, op. cit., p. 166.

39 F. A. Hayek, 'The Use of Knowledge in Society', *The American Economic Review*, Vol. XXXV, No. 4 (September, 1945), pp. 519–20.

40 W. B. Arthur and S. N. Durlauf, op. cit., p. 3.

41 Paul Harremoës, *et al.* (eds), op. cit.; see also the European Commission's 'Communication on the Precautionary Principle'. Online. Available HTTP: <http://europa.eu.int/eur-lex/en/com/cnc/2000/com2000_0001en01.pdf> (accessed 5 June 2004).

42 'Concerns Related to Scientific Uncertainty, Policy Context, Institutional Capacity, and Social Implications', in Committee on Defining Science-Based Concerns Associated with Products of Animal Biotechnology, *Animal Biotechnology: Science Based Concerns* (Washington, DC: National Academies Press, 2002), pp. 108–21.

43 See Steven Epstein, *Impure Science: AIDS, Activism and the Politics of Knowledge* (Berkeley: University of California Press, 1996).

44 James Wilson, 'Scientific Uncertainty, Complex Systems and the Design of Common-Pool Institutions,' in Elinor Ostrom, Thomas Dietz, Nives Dolsak,

Paul C. Stern, Susan Stonich and Elke U. Weber (eds), *The Drama of the Commons*, Committee on the Human Dimensions of Global Change (Washington, DC: National Academies Press, 2001), p. 334.

45 Kenneth R. Foster, David E. Bernstein and Peter W. Huber, *Phantom Risk: Scientific Inference and the Law* (Cambridge, Mass.: MIT Press, 1994).

46 *Animal Biotechnology: Science Based Concerns*, op. cit., pp. 108–21.

47 James Wilson, op. cit., p. 335.

48 Virginia M. Walsh, *Global Institutions and Social Knowledge: Generating Research at the Scripps Institution and the Inter-American Tropical Tuna Commission, 1900s–1990s* (Cambridge, Massachusetts: MIT Press, 2004).

49 Ulrich Beck, 'Risk Society and the Provident State', in Scott Lash, Bronislaw Szerszynski and Brian White, *Risk, Environment and Modernity: Towards a New Ecology* (London: Sage, 1996), p. 42.

50 Valerie L. Kuletz, *The Tainted Desert: Environmental and Social Ruin in the American West* (London: Routledge, 1998).

51 Kenneth R. Foster, David E. Bernstein and Peter W. Huber (eds), *Phantom Risk: Scientific Inference and the Law* (Cambridge, Mass.: MIT Press, 1994), pp. 1–2.

52 'The law of tort – the word derives from the French for "wrong" – is the law of civil liability for wrongfully inflicted injury', Mark Lunney and Ken Oliphant, *Tort Law: Cases and Materials* (Oxford: Oxford University Press, 2000), p. 1.

53 Nan Goodman, *Shifting the Blame: Literature, Law, and the Theory of Accidents in Nineteenth-Century America* (Princeton: Princeton University Press, 1998), p. 6.

54 Ibid., pp. 6–7; Oliver Wendell Holmes Jr., 'The Theory of Torts,' *American Law Review* 660 (1873), pp. 652–63.

55 Emmanuel Agius and Salvino Busuttil (with Tae-Chang Kim and Katsuhiko Yazaki), *Future Generations and International Law* (London: Earthscan, 1998).

56 Lawrence E. Johnson, 'A Morally Deep World: An Essay on Moral Significance and Environmental Ethics' (Cambridge: Cambridge University Press, 1991).

57 Mark Lunney and Ken Oliphant, op. cit., p. 17.

58 A. P. Herbert, 'On the Reasonable Man', from *Misleading Cases in the Common Law* (London: Methuen and Company, 1927) and reprinted in Ephraim London (ed.), *The World of Law, Volume II: The Law as Literature* (New York: Simon and Schuster, 1960), pp. 557–8.

59 See Appendix II, 'The Precautionary Principle in International Law', in the European Commission's 'Communication on the Precautionary Principle', op. cit.

60 'Introduction', in Poul Harremoës, *et al.* (eds), op. cit., p. 4.

61 B. Weintraub, 'Science, international environmental regulation, and the precautionary principle: setting standards and defining terms', *New York University Environmental Law Journal* (1992), quoted in Julian Morris, 'Defining the precautionary principle', in Julian Morris (ed.), *Rethinking the Precautionary Principle* (Oxford: Butterworth, 2000), p. 9.

62 Ibid.

63 For the examples that follow here, I am indebted to ibid.

64 Jeremy Leggett (ed.), *Global Warming: The Greenpeace Report* (Oxford: Oxford University Press, 1990), cited in ibid., p. 4.

65 Ibid., p. 10.

66 For a view of the Kyoto Protocol from the perspective of Public Choice economics, see Bruce Yandle, 'The precautionary principle as a force for global political centralization: a case-study of the Kyoto Protocol', in ibid., pp. 167–88.

67 For example of this kind of argument, see Indur M. Goklany, 'Applying the precautionary principle in a broader context', in ibid., pp. 189–228.

68 United Nations Framework Convention on Climate Change (1992). Online. Available HTTP: <http://unfccc.int/resource/docs/convkp/conveng.pdf> (accessed 17 February 2004).

69 Mark Townsend, 'Now the Pentagon tells Bush: climate change will destroy us', *The Observer*, 22 February, 2004.

70 Communication on the Precautionary Principle, op. cit., p. 3 (italics original).

71 John M. Mendeloff, *The Dilemma of Toxic Substance Regulation: How Overregulation Causes Underregulation at OSHA* (Cambridge, Massachusetts: MIT Press, 1998).

72 The Science and Environmental Health Network is a useful source. Online. Available HTTP: <http://www.sehn.org/precaution.html>.

73 Desmond King and Amrita Narlikar, 'The New Risk Regulators? International Organisations and Globalisation', *The Political Quarterly*, 2003, p. 343.

6 Authority and accountability in a global arena

1 James N. Rosenau, 'Change, Complexity and Governance in a Globalizing Space,' in Jon Pierre (ed.), *Debating Governance* (Oxford: Oxford University Press, 2000), p. 193.

2 Lawrence S. Finklestein, 'What is Global Governance?' *Global Governance* 1 (1995), p. 369.

3 Ernst-Otto Czempiel, 'Governance and Democratization', in James N. Rosenau and Ernst-Otto Czempiel, *Governance Without Government: Order and Change in World Politics* (Cambridge: Cambridge University Press, 1992), p. 250.

4 James N. Rosenau, 'Governance in the Twenty-First Century', *Global Governance* 1 (1995), p. 15.

5 James N. Rosenau, *Along the Domestic-Foreign Frontier: Exploring Governance in a Turbulent World* (Cambridge: Cambridge University Press, 1997), p. 406.

6 Jan Aart Scholte, 'Civil Society and Democracy in Global Governance', paper presented to the British International Studies Association, December, 2000.

7 For example, see Ian Shapiro and Casiano Hacker-Cordón (eds), *Democracy's Edges* (Cambridge: Cambridge University Press, 1999).

8 Noam Chomsky, *Deterring Democracy* (London: Verso, 1991).

9 Rosenau, *Along the Domestic-Foreign Frontier*, op. cit, p. 410.

10 Thomas Risse, Stephen C. Ropp and Kathryn Sikkink (eds), *The Power of Human Rights: International Norms and Domestic Change* (Cambridge: Cambridge University Press, 1999).

11 'Governance is the sum of the many ways individuals and institutions, public and private, manage their common affairs. . . . At the global level, governance has been viewed primarily as intergovernmental relationships, but it must now be understood as also involving non-governmental organizations, citizens' movements, multinational corporations, and the global capital market.' *Our Global Neighbourhood* (Oxford: Oxford University Press, 1995), pp. 2–3.

12 Paul Hirst, 'Democracy and Governance,' in Jon Pierre (ed.), op. cit, pp. 21–22.

13 Ernst-Otto Czempiel, op. cit.

14 Rosenau, 1997, p. 174.

15 See David C. Korten, *When Corporations Rule the World* (London: Earthscan, 1995).

16 R. A. W. Rhodes, *Understanding Governance: Policy Networks, Governance, Reflexivity and Accountability* (Buckingham: Open University Press, 1997).

17 See Jennifer Clapp, 'The Privatization of Global Environmental Governance: ISO14000 and the Developing World', *Global Governance*, Vol. 4, No. 3 (1998), pp. 295–316.

18 Fred Pearce, 'Sold to the highest bidder', *New Scientist*, 16 December 2000, pp. 16–17; for the background and implications of the movement towards control of the knowledge economy, see Peter Drahos and John Braithwaite, *Information Feudalism: Who Owns the Knowledge Economy?* (London: Earthscan, 2000).

19 Granville Williams, 'Bestriding the World'. Online. Available HTTP: <http://www.mediachannel.org/ownership/granville.shtml> (accessed 2 August 2004).

20 European Commission, 'Green Paper on the Convergence of the Telecommunications, Media and Information Technology Sectors, and the Implications for Regulation (Brussels, 3 December 1997). Online. Available HTTP: <http://en.infosoc.gr/content/downloads/97623en.pdf > (accessed 29 July 2004).

21 A particularly useful source is the 'Who Owns What' section of the *Columbia Journalism Review*. Online. Available HTTP: <http://www.cjr.org/tools/owners> (accessed 30 July 2004).

22 Jounalism.org, *The State of the News Media 2004: An Annual Report on American Journalism*. Online. Available HTTP: <http://www.stateofthenewsmedia.org/narrative_overview_eight.asp?media=1> (accessed 30 July 2004).

23 Sarah Anderson and John Cavanagh, 'Top 22: The Rise of Global Corporate Power', (Washington: Institute for Policy Studies), Summary findings. Online. Available HTTP: <http://www.corpwatch.org/trac/corner/glob/ips/top200. html> (accessed 28 October 2002).

24 See Edward Alden, 'Washington may act on "shell banks"', *Financial Times*, 7 March 2001; subsequently, Jane Martinson and Charlotte Denny, 'Bush to scuttle OECD tax plan', *The Guardian*, 10 May 2001.

25 Report of the President's Working Group on Financial Markets, 'Hedge Funds, Leverage, and the Lessons of Long-Term Capital Management', Washington, April, 1999.

26 Charlotte Denny, 'Hedge fund vultures find rich pickings among poor', *The Guardian*, 19 October, 2000.

27 For a helpful introductory discussion of the concept, see Inge Kaul, Isabelle Grunberg and Marc A. Stern, 'Defining Global Public Goods', in Inge Kaul, Isabelle Grunberg and Marc A. Stern (eds), *Global Public Goods: International Cooperation in the 21st Century* (Oxford: Oxford University Press, 1999), pp. 2–19.

28 Richard Falk, 'Humane Governance and the Environment: Overcoming Neo-Liberalism', in Brendan Gleeson and Nicholas Low (eds), *Governing for the Environment: Global Problems, Ethics and Democracy* (Basingstoke: Palgrave, 2001), p. 224 (italics original).

29 Ibid., p. 223.

30 Claude Ake, 'Globalization, Multilateralism and the Shrinking Democratic Space', in Michael G. Schechter (ed.), *Future Multilateralism: the Political and Social Framework* (Basingstoke: Macmillam, 1999), p. 187.

31 See R. B. J. Walker, *Inside/Outside: International Relations as Political Theory* (Cambridge: Cambridge University Press, 1992).

32 The history of the development of the intellectual property rights regime is

instructive on this point. See Peter Drahos and John Braithwaite, *Information Feudalism: Who owns the Knowledge Economy?* (London: Earthscan, 2002).

33 Quoted in Richard B. Norgaard, *Development Betrayed: the end of progress and a coevolutionary revisioning of the future* (London: Routledge, 1994), p. 18.

34 Susan Strange, 'An International Economy Perspective', in John H. Dunning, *Governments, Globalization, and International Business* (Oxford: Oxford University Press, 1997), pp. 132–45.

35 Ibid., p. 136.

36 Jerry Mander and Edward Goldsmith (eds), *The Case Against the Global Economy* (San Francisco: Sierra Club Books, 1996).

37 Rodney Bruce Hall and Thomas J. Biersteker, *The Emergence of Private Authority in Global Governance* (Cambridge: Cambridge University Press, 2002).

38 See Ulrich Beck, *World Risk Society*, op. cit., Chapter 5.

39 Rodney Bruce Hall and Thomas J. Biersteker, *The Emergence of Private Authority in Global Governance* (Cambridge: Cambridge University Press, 2002).

40 James Rosenau, *Along the Domestic-Foreign Frontier*, op. cit., pp. 38–9.

7 Case study: disseminative systems and global governance

1 Oliver Burkeman, 'Take two PhDs, a library card and some notebooks and leave for two years . . .' *The Guardian*, 24 June 2003.

2 Judith Miller, Stephen Engelberg and William Broad, *Germs: Biological Weapons and America's Secret War* (New York: Simon and Schuster, 2001), pp. 297–8.

3 Rachel Nowak, 'Disaster in the making: an engineered mouse virus leaves us one step away from the ultimate bioweapon', *New Scientist*, 13 January 2001, pp. 4–5. Subsequently, a more deadly form of mousepox has been genetically engineered, opening an array of possible security and ecological dangers. See Debora Mackenzie, 'US develops lethal new viruses', *New Scientist*, 1 November 2003, pp. 6–7.

4 Ibid.

5 See Inge Kaul, Isabelle Grunberg and Marc Stern (eds), *Global Public Goods: International Cooperation in the 21st Century* (Oxford: Oxford University Press, 1999).

6 For a discussion of which, see Jim Whitman, 'Global Dynamics and Global Governance', *Global Society*, Vol. 17, No. 3 (July 2003), pp. 253–72.

7 Geoffrey Vickers, *Human Systems Are Different* (London: Harper & Row, 1983), p. 18.

8 John Wargo, *Our Children's Toxic Legacy: How Science and Law Fail to Protect Us from Pesticides* (Yale: Yale University Press, 1996).

9 Chris Bright, *Life Out of Bounds: Bio-Invasions in a Borderless World* (London: Earthscan, 1999).

10 In 1998, this stood at $1.5 trillion per day. 'Now more is traded in six hours on the world currency markets than the World Bank has lent in its entire history.' Cited in Jan Aart Scholte, *Globalization: An Introduction* (Basingstoke: Palgrave, 2000), p. 79.

11 *Terrorist Financing*, Report of an Independent Task Force sponsored by the Council on Foreign Relations, Maurice R. Greenberg, Chair (New York: Council on Foreign Relations, 2002), pp. 7–8; Stephen Braun and Judy Paternak, 'Long Before Sept. 11, Bin Laden Aircraft Flew Under the Radar', *Los Angeles Times*, www.latimes.com/news/nationworld/nation/la-111801osamair.story.

12 Mohammed El-Quorchi, 'Hawala', *Finance and Development, a Quarterly Magazine of the IMF*, Vol. 39, No. 4. Online. Available HTTP: <www.imf.org/external/pubs/ft/fandd/2002/12/elqorchi.htm> (accessed 20 January 2003); Patrick M. Jost and Harjit Singh Sandhu, 'The hawala alternative remittance system and its role in money laundering', Interpol General Secretariat, Lyon, January 2000. Online. Available HTTP: <http://www.interpol.int/Public/Financial Crime/Money> (accessed 21 January 2003); Laundering/hawala/default.asp; Gary Duncan, 'Efforts to halt al-Qaeda cash flow "doomed"', *The Times*, 13 January 2003; Meenakshi Ganguly, 'A Banking System Built for Terrorism', *Time*, 5 October 2001.

13 Julia Tricarichi, 'Hackers Defeat DVD Encryption and Post De-Encryption Software on the Web', *The Internet Law Journal*, 25 February 1999. Online. Available HTTP: <http://www.tilj.com/content/ipheadline02290001.htm> (accessed 24 November 2002).

14 Duncan Graham-Rowe, 'Antivirus strategies in crisis', *New Scientist*, 6 September 2003, pp. 6–7.

15 See Charles Perrow, *Normal Accidents: Living with High-Risk Technologies* (New York: Basic Books, 1984).

16 Gene I. Rochlin, *Trapped in the Net: The Unanticipated Consequences of Computerization* (Princeton: Princeton University Press, 1997). Online. Available HTTP: <http://pup.princeton.edu/books/rochlin/chapter_12.html#p21> (accessed 2 November 2003).

17 See Henryk Handszuh and Sommerset R. Waters, 'Travel and Tourism Patterns', in Herbert L. DuPont and Robert Steffen (eds), *Textbook of Travel Medicine and Health* (Hamilton, Ontario: B. C. Decker, Inc., 1997), pp. 20–6.

18 James Glanz, 'When the grid bites back: more are relying on an unreliable system', *International Herald Tribune*, 18 August 2003.

19 This has begun to change. See Robert Jervis, *System Effects: Complexity in Political and Social Life* (Princeton: Princeton University Press, 1997); and John Urry, *Global Complexity* (Cambridge: Polity Press, 2003).

20 Keith Devlin, 'Flying blind', *The Guardian*, 17 October 2002.

21 Stafford Beer, 'Managing Modern Complexity', presentation to the Committee on Science and Astronautics of the House of Representatives, Washington, DC, 27 January 1970, in *Platform for Change* (Chichester: John Wiley & Sons, 1975), p. 221.

22 See Ulrich Beck, 'Industrial Fatalism: Organised Irresponsibility', in *Ecological Politics in an Age of Risk* (Cambridge: Polity Press, 1995), p. 67.

23 Fred Pearce, 'We can save the Amazon, but not the South Pacific', *New Scientist*, 30 October 1999, p. 5.

24 Jenny Hogan, 'Global warming: the new battle', *New Scientist*, 13 September 2003, p. 6 (italics added).

25 Alfred Chandler, *The Visible Hand* (Cambridge: Harvard University Press, 1977), p. 414, cited in Shoshana Zuboff, *In the Age of the Smart Machine: The Future of Work and Power* (London: Heinemann, 1989), p. 77.

26 Susan Strange, *Retreat of the State: The Diffusion of Power in the World Political Economy* (Cambridge: Cambridge University Press, 1996).

27 United Nations Office for Drug Control and Crime Prevention, Global Report on Crime and Justice. Online. Available HTTP: <http://www.uncjin.org/Special/GlobalReport.html> (accessed 23 November 2003).

28 Carolyn Nordstrom, 'Shadows and Sovereigns', *Theory, Culture and Society*, Vol. 17, No. 4 (2000), pp. 35–54. The introduction of the Euro was thought likely to benefit sales of upmarket consumer goods because ' . . . the need to swap existing national currencies for the new supranational money will force Europeans to bring back into the legitimate economy up to $100 billion in black market cash. They won't want to exchange large wads of cash at the bank and raise suspicions of money laundering. So they'll probably channel a chunk of it into consumer durables – particularly luxury items with investment cachet.' 'Where the Euro is a "Buy" Signal', *Business Week Online*, 10 September 2001. Online. Available HTTP: <http://www.businessweek.com:/print/magazine/content/01_37/b37 48123.htm ?mz.> (accessed 6 November 2003).

29 Lawrence S. Finklestein, 'What is Global Governance?' *Global Governance* 1 (1995), p. 369.

30 Ernst-Otto Czempiel, 'Governance and Democratization', in James N. Rosenau and Ernst-Otto Czempiel, *Governance Without Government: Order and Change in World Politics* (Cambridge: Cambridge University Press, 1992), p. 250.

31 As defined by the Commission on Global Governance: 'Governance is the sum of the many ways individuals and institutions, public and private, manage their common affairs. . . . At the global level, governance has been viewed primarily as intergovernmental relationships, but it must now be understood as also involving non-governmental organizations, citizens' movements, multinational corporations, and the global capital market.' *Our Global Neighbourhood* (Oxford: Oxford University Press, 1995), pp. 2–3.

32 Jim Whitman, 'Global Governance as the Friendly Face of Unaccountable Power', *Security Dialogue*, Vol. 33, No. 1 (March, 2002), pp. 45–57.

33 James N. Rosenau and Ernst-Otto Czempiel, op. cit.

34 See James Muldoon, *The Architecture of Global Governance: An Introduction to the Study of International Organizations* (Boulder: Westview Press, 2002); Deepak Nayyar, 'The Existing System and the Missing Institutions', in Deepak Nayyar, *Governing Globalization: Issues and Institutions* (Oxford: Oxford University Press, 2002), pp. 356–84.

35 Rorden Wilkinson and Steve Hughes, *Global Governance: Critical Perspectives* (London: Routledge, 2002).

36 John Braithwaite and Peter Drahos, *Global Business Regulation* (Cambridge: Cambridge University Press, 2000), Chapter 19, 'Air Transport', pp. 454–71.

37 US Bureau of Transportation Statistics, 'Home Shopping Increases Neighborhood Parcel Deliveries', Vol. 3, Issue 2. Online. Available HTTP: <http://www.bts. gov/products/omnistats/volume_03_issue_02/html/entire. html> (accessed 9 November 2003).

38 'Knives, guns and explosives carried by federal undercover inspectors were missed by Los Angeles International airport screeners at checkpoints an astonishing 41 per cent of the time in an airport security test.' BBC News, 'Attack Shows Limits to Airport Security', 5 July 2002. Online. Available HTTP: <http:// news.bbc. co.uk/1/hi/world/americas/2096081.stm> (accessed 10 November 2003).

39 Francis Fukuyama and Caroline Wagner, 'Information and Biological Revolutions: Global Governance Challenges – Summary of a Study Group', p. 11. Online. Available HTTP: <http://www.rand.org/publications/MR/MR1139> (accessed 12 September 2003).

40 Marlies Glasius, Mary Kaldor and Helmut Anheier (eds), *Global Civil Society 2002* (Oxford: Oxford University Press, 2002).

41 In a list compiled by Paz Estrella Tolentino, the approach adopted in the main international intergovernmental instruments concerning transnational corporations from 1948 to 1998 was 'facilitation' in more than half of the cases. See 'Transnational Rules for Transnational Corporations: What Next?' in Jonathan Michie and John Grieve Smith (eds), *Global Instability: The Political Economy of World Economic Governance* (London: Routledge, 1999), pp. 171–97.

42 Committee on Science and Technology for Countering Terrorism, Division on Engineering and Physical Sciences, National Research Council, *Making the Nation Safer: The Role of Science and Technology in Countering Terrorism* (Washington, DC: National Academy Press, 2002), pp. 25–6. Note too that the National Security Strategy for the United States (the Bush Doctrine) contains the following: 'The gravest danger our Nation faces lies at the crossroads of radicalism and technology.' *The National Security Strategy of the United States of America*, September 2002, Introduction.

43 'The President had announced his intention to create an advisory group on bioethics eighteen months before, on the day that he received the disturbing report of the cavalier way in which ionizing radiation had been administered experimentally to unsuspecting subjects.' Richard Lewontin, 'The Confusion Over Cloning'. in *It Ain't Necessarily So* (London: Granta Books, 2001), pp. 283–4.

44 James N. Rosenau, *Along the Domestic-Foreign Frontier: Exploring Governance in a Turbulent World* (Cambridge: Cambridge University Press, 1997).

45 Geoffrey Vickers, op. cit, p. 49.

46 American Association for the Advancement of Science, 'Science and National Security in the post-9/11 Environment'. Online. Available HTTP: <http://www.aaas.org/spp/post911/sbu/> (accessed 22 September 2003).

47 Amnesty International, 'People's Republic of China: State Control of the Internet in China', 26 November 2002. Online. Available HTTP: <http://web.amnesty.org/library/print/ENGASA170072002> (accessed 4 December 2003).

48 Jonathan Watts, 'China tightens net around online dissenters', *The Guardian*, 7 February 2004.

49 At a 'Creating Digital Dividends' conference in 2000, Microsoft Chairman Bill Gates rounded on several speakers who argued for the benefits of computer technology for the world's poor, arguing, '[Poor mothers] are not going to sit there and, like, browse eBay or something. What they want is for their children to live. They don't want their children's growth to be stunted. Do you really have to put in computers to figure that out?' Sam Howe Verhovek, 'Gates Nettles the Digital World With a Message About the Poor', *International Herald Tribune*, November 4–5, 2000.

8 The limits of global governance

1 Lester Salamon 'The Global Association Revolution: The Rise of the Third Sector on the World Scene', *Foreign Affairs* (July/August 1994).

2 James N. Rosenau, *Distant Proximities: Dynamics Beyond Globalization* (Princeton: Princeton University Press, 2003), p. 393.

3 Charles Lindblom, 'Still Muddling, Not Yet Through', *Public Administration Review*, 1979, pp. 252–3.

4 Rorden Wilkinson and Steve Hughes (eds), *Global Governance: Critical Perspectives* (London: Routledge, 2002).

5 Eşref Aksu and Joseph A. Camilleri (eds), *Democratizing Global Governance* (Basingstoke: Palgrave, 2002).

6 Ian Bache and Matthew Flinders (eds), *Multi-level Governance* (Oxford: Oxford University Press, 2004); Robert O'Brien, Anne Marie Goetz, Jan Aart Scholte and Marc Williamms, *Contesting Global Governance: Multilateral Institutions and Global Social Movements* (Cambridge: Cambridge University Press, 2000), especially Chapter 6, pp. 206–34.

7 Report of the Commission on Global Governance, *Our Global Neighbourhood* (Oxford: Oxford University Press, 1995).

8 Fred Pearce, 'Altered trees hide out with the local poplars', *New Scientist* (18 September 2004), p. 7. ' . . . Wang Huoran, who represents the Chinese Academy of Sciences at the UN's Food and Agriculture Organization . . . is reported to have told an FAO panel that GM poplar trees "are so widely planted in northern China that pollen and seed dispersal cannot be prevented"'.

9 The Royal Society (Royal Academy of Engineering), 'Nanocience and nanotechnologies: opportunities and uncertainties', RS Policy document 19/04 (London: The Royal Society, 2004), p. 56. The quoted passage from Joy is Bill Joy, 'Why the future doesn't need us', *Wired* 8.04 (April 2000). Online. Available HTTP: <http://www.wirednews.com/wired/archive/8.04/joy_pr.html> (accessed 15 June 2003).

10 Although as Francis Fukuyama points out, 'Embryo research is only the beginning of a series of new developments created by technology for which societies have to decide on rules and regulatory institutions.' He lists preimplantation diagnosis and screening; germ-line engineering; the creation of chimeras using human genes; and new psychotropic drugs. Francis Fukuyama, *Our Posthuman Future: Consequences of the Biotechnology Revolution* (London: Profile Books, 2002), pp. 206–7.

11 David Forrest, 'Regulating Nanotechnology Development', (rev. 1.1, 23 March 1989), Foresight Institute. Online. Available HTTP: <http://www.foresight.org/NanoRev/Forrest1989.html> (Accessed 19 August 2004). The author then adopts the classic Realist 'security dilemma' position: 'If we tried to block or slow the development of nanotechnology in the United States, or in other democracies, we would increase the chances that nanotechnology is first developed in a country without a free press. In which case we could not be certain that that country would not use nanotechnology to oppress its neighbours or the rest of the world. So efforts to slow progress only serve to threaten our freedom.'

12 Charles E. Lindblom, 'The Science of "Muddling Through"', *Public Administration Review*, 19 (2), (1959), p. 84.

13 Ibid., p. 86. Italics original.

14 Geoffrey Vickers, *Value Systems and Social Processes* (London: Tavistock, 1968), pp. 170–1.

15 Caroline Thomas, 'Global governance and human security', in Rorden Wilkinson and Steve Hughes, op. cit., p. 129.

16 Geoffrey Vickers, *Human Systems Are Different* (London: Harper & Row, 1983), p. xxvii.

17 Yehuda Elkana, 'Rethinking – Not Unthinking – The Enlightenment', in Wilhelm Krull (ed.), *Debates on Our Common Future*, Volkswagen Foundation Symposium (Velbrück Wissenschaft, 2000), pp. 284–5.

18 For example, Hans Küng, *A Global Ethic for Global Politics and Economics* (Oxford: Oxford University Press, 1998).

19 For example, see the International Forum on Globalization. Online. Available HTTP: <http://www.ifg.org/about.htm>.

20 Report of the Commission on Human Security, *Human Security Now* (New York, 2003). Online. Available HTTP: <http://www.humansecurity-chs.org/final report/index.html> (accessed 2 June 2003).

21 Notable works of this kind include: Independent Commission on Disarmament and Security, *Common Security: Blueprint for Survival* (New York: Simon and Schuster, 1982); The World Commission on Environment and Development, *Our Common Future* (Oxford: Oxford University Press, 1987); *North-South: A Program for Survival* (The Brandt Report) (Boston: MIT Press, 1990); The Commission on Global Governance, *Our Global Neighborhood*, op. cit.; Report of the Independent Commission on International Humanitarian Issues, *Winning the Human Race?* (London: Zed Books, 1998). See also the 1994 *Human Development Report* (New York: UNDP, 1994) and in subsequent years.

22 Jonathan A. Fox and L. David Brown (eds), *The Struggle for Accountability: The World Bank, NGOs and Grassroots Movements* (Cambridge, Massachusetts: MIT Press, 1998).

23 Dennis L. Meadows, 'It is too Late to Achieve Sustainable development: Now let Us Strive for Survivable Development', in ibid., pp. 107–27.

24 Geoffrey Vickers, *Value Systems and Social Processes*, op. cit., p. 67.

25 Henry Morgenthau, 'Bretton Woods and International Cooperation', *Foreign Affairs*, Vol. 23, No. 2 (January 1945) p. 193.

26 Note that in his *Foreign Affairs* article (note 25, above), which was in part a plea for Senate ratification of the Bretton Woods Agreements, Morgenthau argued, 'We must always keep in mind that other nations are anxiously asking whether the United States has the desire and ability to co-operate effectively in establishing world peace. If we fail to ratify the Bretton Woods Agreements . . . they would have little alternative but to seek a solution for their pressing political and economic problems on the old, familiar lines, lines which will inexorably involve playing the old game of power politics with even greater intensity than before because the problems with which they will be confronted will be so much more acute. And power politics will be as disastrous to prosperity as to peace.' Morgenthau, ibid., p. 184.

27 Dennis Leech and Robert Leech, 'Weighted Voting Doesn't Work for the World Bank and the IMF: Some Important Results from the Voting Power Approach'. Online. Available HTTP: <http://www.pubchoicesoc.org/papers/leech.pdf> (accessed 30 July 2004).

28 Robert O. Keohane, 'Governance in a Partially Globalized World', in *Power and Governance in a Partially Globalized World* (London: Routledge, 2002), p. 265.

29 Fred Pearce, 'Sowing the seeds of starvation: Rapid urbanization is destroying China's agriculture and its ability to feed one-fifth of the world's people', *New Scientist*, 18 September 2004, pp. 6–7; Lester Brown, *Who Will Feed China? Wake-up Call for a Small Planet* (London: Earthscan, 1995).

30 Geoffrey Vickers, *Value Systems and Social Processes*, op. cit., pp. 75–6.

31 The Commission's report is 'Dams and Development: A New Framework for Decision-making'. Online. Available HTTP: <http://www.dams.org/report/over views.htm> (accessed 3 May 2004).

32 Wallace Broecker, 'Unpleasant Surprises in the Greenhouse?' *Nature*, Vol. 328, No. 6126 (9 July 1987), pp. 123–6. See also James Gleick, 'Instability of Climate Defies Computer Analysis', *New York Times*, March 20, 1988, p. 30. 'William Clark has made a similar point about interlinked physical, ecological, and social systems: "Typically in such systems, slow variation in one property can continue for long periods without noticeable impact on the rest of the system. Eventually, however, the system reaches a state in which its buffering capacity or resilience has been so reduced that additional small changes in the same property, or otherwise insignificant external shocks, push the system across a threshold and precipitate a rapid transition to a new system state or equilibrium."' See William Clark, *On the Practical Implications of the Carbon Dioxide Question* (Laxenburg, Austria: International Institute of Applied Systems Analysis, 1985), p. 41. This note and the quoted passage in the text are taken from Thomas F. Homer-Dixon, 'On The Threshold: Environmental Changes as Causes of Acute Conflict', *International Security*, Vol. 16, No. 2 (Fall 1991), pp. 76–116, f.n. 25.

33 Inge Kaul, Isabelle Grunberg and Marc A Stern, 'Introduction,' in Inge Kaul, Isabelle Grunberg and Marc A Stern (eds), *Global Public Goods: International Cooperation in the 21st Century* (Oxford: Oxford University Press, 1999), p. xxvii.

34 Bruce Stokes, 'Here's Food for Thought: Fears of famine have faded, but we're never more than one or two bad harvests away from crisis', *The National Journal* (Section: Economics), Vol. 31, No. 37, p. 2570 (11 September 1999).

35 'According to estimates by the UN Food and Agriculture Organization, the number of chronically hungry people increased by nearly 60 million in 26 countries in the last decade.' WFP Press release, 'WFP Chief in Brazil for talks with President Lula on rising global hunger', 20 May 2004.

36 Online. Available HTTP: <http://www.jubileedebtcampaign.org.uk/default. asp?action=article&id=423> (accessed 1 August 2004).

37 Jan Aart Scholte, 'Civil society and governance in the global polity,' in Martin Ougaard and Richard Higgott (eds), *Towards a Global Polity* (London: Routledge, 2002), p. 152 (italics original).

38 Sidney Tarrow, '"Global" Movements, Complex Internationalism and North-South Inequality', Paper prepared for the workshop on contentious politics, Columbia University, 27 October 2003. Online, Available HTTP: <http://www. ksg. harvard.edu/inequality/Seminar/Papers/Tarrow.pdf> (accessed 12 August 2004).

39 See Richard Falk, *Humane Governance: Towards a new Global Politics* (Cambridge: Polity Press, 1995).

40 A continuous update can be found at http://costofwar.com/.

41 A.W. DePorte, *Europe Between the Superpowers: The Enduring Balance* (New Haven: Yale University Press, 1986), p. xv.

42 Geoffrey Vickers, *Freedom in a Rocking Boat: Changing Values in an Unstable Society* (London: The Penguin Press, 1970), pp. 126–7.

43 The Report of the Bruntland Commission, *Our Common Future* (Oxford: Oxford University Press, 1987).

44 Simon Dresner, *The Principles of Sustainable Development* (London: Earthscan, 2003), especially Chapter 5, pp. 63–74; Ian Drummond and Terry Marsden, *The Condition of Sustainability* (London: Routledge, 1999), Chapters 1–4, pp. 7–64.

45 James N. Rosenau and Mary Durfee, *Thinking Theory Thoroughly: Coherent Approaches to an Incoherent World* (Boulder: Westview Press, 1997), p. 1.

46 A deeper, less immediately functionalist and less benign view is Gregory Bateson, 'Pathologies of Epistemology', in *Steps to an Ecology of Mind* (Northvale, New Jersey: Jason Aronson, Inc., 1987), pp. 486–95.

47 Hence James Rosenau's identification of 'the limits of contemporary concepts and methods' which 'justify jailbreaks', Chapter 2 of *Turbulence in World Politics: A Theory of Change and Continuity* (London: Harvester Wheatsheaf, 1990).

48 John Volger, 'Introduction: The Environment in International Relations: Legacies and Contentions', in John Volger and Mark F. Imber, *The Environment and International Relations* (London: Routledge, 1996), pp. 6–7.

49 John Urry, *Global Complexity* (Cambridge: Polity Press, 2003), pp. 17–18 (italics original).

50 Instructive in this regard is the scope of Ian Douglas, Richard Huggett and Mike Robinson (eds), *Companion Encyclopedia of Geography: The Environment and Humankind* (London: Routledge, 1996).

51 Thomas Risse, Stephen C. Ropp and Kethryn Sikkink, *The Power of Human Rights: International Norms and Domestic Change* (Cambridge: Cambridge University Press, 1999).

52 Geoffrey Vickers, *Value Systems and Social Processes*, op. cit., p. 83.

Index